D1481902

Reason vs. Racism

Reason vs. Racism

A Newspaper Family, Race, and Justice

Jack Lessenberry

BCI
PRESS

The Publishing Unit
of Block Communications, Inc.
405 Madison Avenue, Suite 2100
Toledo, Ohio 43604

All rights reserved. Published in the United States by BCI Press

Library of Congress Cataloging-in-Publication Data
Names: Lessenberry, Jack, author|
Title: Reason vs. Racism: A Newspaper Family, Race, and Justice
Description: First edition|Detroit, Michigan 2020|Includes bibliographical references and index|
ISBN: 978-1-7357067-0-2 (Paperback)
ISBN: 978-1-7357067-1-9 (Hardcover)
Subjects: Education|American History|Journalism|Biography|Business|General|

Book and cover design by Anne Zimanski
Typography text font: Garamond, Adobe Garamond Pro

Manufactured in the United States of America
by Sheridan Press, Grand Rapids, Michigan

First United States Edition

To Allan and John Block and the legacy of their family, which has continued to support and produce quality newspapers and journalism for more than a century.

And to Elizabeth, my love and partner in life, a skilled archivist who made this book, as she makes me, much better than either would be otherwise.

-Jack Lessenberry, August 2020

Contents

Introduction

Reason, Racism, and the Record

Most newspapers these days are no longer owned by the families that started them. Those that remain are usually owned by chains and, all too often, the legacies of the founders – the Chandlers in Los Angeles. say, or the Binghams of Louisville – have been reduced to little more than names on the masthead – if that.

But Block Communications, Inc. (BCI), which still operates old and famous newspapers in Toledo and Pittsburgh, is an exception. Paul Block, the founder of what today is a multi-media national communications company, did not start these papers,[1] but his family has now owned both for nearly a century.

Throughout their history, Paul Block (1875-1941), his sons Paul Jr. (1911-87) and William (1915-2005) and now his grandsons Allan and John Robinson Block, have taken courageous stands on many issues – including race. Paul Block was essentially run out of the newspaper business in Memphis for championing a Black man who saved the lives of many people, all of them white, in 1925.

Later he pushed his papers to expose a U.S. Supreme Court justice's ties to the Ku Klux Klan, a story for which the *Pittsburgh Post-Gazette* won the 1938 Pulitzer Prize. His sons continued that tradition.

Both the *Toledo Blade* and the *Post-Gazette* hired Black reporters and editors years before most newspapers did. The *Blade* assigned its first Black reporter, William Brower, to travel around the nation to investigate racial conditions in 1951, years before the first sit-in or even before the U.S. Supreme Court's decision in *Brown v. Board of Education* outlawing segregation in the

---

1. The weekly *Toledo Blade* was one of Abraham Lincoln's favorite newspapers; he often read David Ross Locke's satirical Nasby letters to cabinet meetings or political gatherings. See Louis Morris Starr, *Bohemian Brigade: Civil War Newsmen in Action,* New York: Alfred A. Knopf, 1954.

public schools.

A legendary *Post-Gazette* investigative reporter lived for a month as a Black man in the Deep South in 1948, more than a decade before John Howard Griffin's famous book *Black Like Me*.[2] That early venture into American apartheid, itself later published as a book called *In the Land of Jim Crow*,[3] was a story that richly deserved another Pulitzer, but was sabotaged by a respected southern editor who first led a disinformation campaign against it and then sat on the Pulitzer jury.

In modern times both papers were among the first nationally to champion the presidential campaign of Barack Obama, beginning at a point when his main rival, Hillary Clinton, was still expected to be the 2008 Democratic nominee.

None of that was remembered, however, when the papers were attacked for an editorial called "Reason as Racism," which argued that the term "racist" was being abused, and suggesting that legitimately wanting to limit immigration, or believing that some nations are hellholes,[4] didn't make someone a racist.

The editorial was bitterly attacked as insensitive at best and racist at worst, mostly by people who had no idea of the heritage of this newspaper family.

Regardless of how one feels about that editorial their story, and the story of their newspapers, deserves to be known.

I want to add a personal note – I was a reporter and editor for the *Toledo Blade* in the 1970s and early 1980s and then worked for other newspapers, including the *Detroit News* and the *Memphis Commercial Appeal*.

Later I taught journalism and journalism history for many years and also served as a non-employee ombudsman for the *Toledo Blade*. The first Paul Block died before I was born but I knew both his sons and his grandsons.

Allan Block, today the chair of BCI, asked me to author this book; he put no restrictions on what I could write, only asking me to research the history of his family's newspapers as completely as possible. To that end I have looked, with the aid of my archivist partner in life, Elizabeth, at microfilm copies of newspapers present and past in cities from Brooklyn to Los Angeles, Toledo to Pittsburgh, and Memphis to Milwaukee, and many other cities in-between.

What I found and the conclusions I have come to are my own and no one else's – as are any errors I may have inadvertently made.

I would also like to add in the interests of full disclosure, since a political

---

2. John Howard Griffin, *Black Like Me,* New York: Houghton Mifflin, 1960.
3. Ray Sprigle, *In the Land of Jim Crow,* New York: Simon & Schuster, 1949.
4. Or, as President Trump is supposed to have said, "Shithole countries."

controversy over "Reason as Racism" was the stimulus for this book, that I do not support the immigration policies of President Trump. But I also do not believe that the "Reason as Racism" editorial was meant as racist, though one may disagree profoundly with its conclusions, take issue with some passages, or criticize the tone as insensitive. I also think there are arguments in it, especially its point about the dangers of calling those we don't like "racists," that are not only accurate, but a message that many of us need to hear.

– Jack Lessenberry

1

Against All Odds

You cannot understand any business, particularly a family-owned business, without knowing something about the founder. That may be especially true when it comes to the newspaper business – especially, perhaps, Block Communications, Inc.

Imagine a disheveled, probably dirty, nine-year-old immigrant child landing at Castle Garden in New York City's lower East Side on September 7, 1885, following a difficult and cramped passage across the ocean. He barely speaks more than a few sentences of English.

Within days, little Paul and his family move to the small town of Elmira, halfway across the state, near the Pennsylvania border. His father has next to no money, a flock of children, and becomes a rag picker, about the only job he could find.

Not only are the Blocks (originally Bloch) poor, they are Jewish, which in that era meant that they faced considerably more discrimination than African-Americans face today.

But within months, maybe weeks, Paul is a messenger boy for the local newspaper, the *Elmira Telegram*, which has a huge regional circulation. Soon, he loses every trace of a German or Yiddish accent, and gradually comes to work for the paper in virtually every capacity, from reporting to public relations to advertising sales.

Within a few years, he goes on to play a key role in the invention of modern national newspaper advertising. He becomes a multi-millionaire publisher in his own right and the close friend and confidant of mayors, governors, and even a president or two, plus international newspaper tycoons like Fleet Street's Lord Beaverbrook.

The boy who had arrived in America in the cargo hold of a steamship became a frequent visitor to the White House, especially when President Calvin Coolidge, who regarded him as a trusted friend, came to live there. The immigrant publisher once took a poor black man from Memphis, Tennessee, to meet the president – something that met with eye-rolling and hostility from some who read and advertised in his paper in that city.

Later Paul Block would successfully push his top investigative reporter to turn up stories that would conclusively prove that U.S. Supreme Court Justice Hugo Black was a life member of the Ku Klux Klan, stories that would win a Pulitzer Prize.

He even played a key role in the success of the most important political figure of the century, a man he would later turn against – Franklin D. Roosevelt.

Paul Block revitalized newspapers from Brooklyn to Los Angeles, was a force in early twentieth-century journalism, and succeeded fairly, honestly, and mostly on his own terms. And, considering where he started, against tremendous odds.

Paul Block's life was in many ways a stunning and quintessentially American success story – one too little known, despite the publication of a belated and largely academic biography, *The Publisher: Paul Block: A Life of Friendship, Power and Politics* (University Press of America, Inc., 2001) by Frank Brady, which appeared sixty years after his death.

Block being largely forgotten today is probably due in part to his having been overshadowed by his older friend, sometime business partner, and occasional competitor, William Randolph Hearst, who was far wealthier and owned many more papers.

Hearst was also widely despised and reviled by many writers and critics of the press, and Block was often seen as his puppet or stooge, or at best as sort of a little imitator. The younger man was unfairly lampooned by the courageous but often one-sided media critic George Seldes, who, in his 1938 book *Lords of the Press*, contemptuously labeled him "Little Lord Northcliffe," called him a "little man with a big complex," and quoted the *New York Post* as saying Block was a Hearst stooge.[1]

That was unfair.

Block and Hearst were indeed friends, and friendship and loyalty were enormously important to Paul Block; it was no accident that he named both his Connecticut estate and his private railroad car "Friendship."

Like Harry Truman, an honest man who, as vice president, insisted on attending the funeral of Tom Pendergast, the corrupt political boss who gave him his start, Block stood by his friends, even when they were caught up in hardships and scandals.

That was true when it came to William Randolph Hearst, or New York's flamboyant mayor, Jimmy Walker, and several others.

But Hearst and Block were very different, and in many ways Paul Block's story was far more remarkable. Hearst was born to money; his father was a millionaire mining engineer who owned the *San Francisco Examiner*. Paul Block was entirely self-made, a brilliant advertising entrepreneur and publisher who was superb at cultivating relationships.

That was how he pulled himself out of poverty; that's why those who worked for him tended to be extremely loyal to him. Hearst, in fact, made a major effort to woo Grove Patterson, the legendary editor of the *Toledo Blade*, away from Block.

Patterson, who was a national newspaper figure, turned him down, even though Hearst offered to more than double his salary. He also turned down, at various times, Frank Gannett, Scripps-Howard, and E.D. Stair, the then-owner of the *Detroit Free Press*.

"I have never had cause to regret that decision," Patterson wrote in his autobiography many years later, saying that while Paul Block could be critical and exacting, "he was a man with an infinite capacity for kindness... his graciousness to those he liked, and his generosity, outweighed all else." [2]

Toledo's African-American community shared in that opinion, more than once. In February 1930, with the Great Depression deepening across the nation, Paul Block gave $25,000 to help the YMCA, which was then building the first-ever branch on Indiana Avenue for what were then called "colored" people.

That was equivalent to $386,399 in 2020 dollars – an enormous sum.

Block came from New York for a dinner celebrating the success of the building fund, which came during what was then called "Race-Relations

---

1. George Seldes, *Lords of the Press,* New York: Blue Ribbon Books, 1938, 65-71.
2. Grove Patterson, *I Like People,* New York: Random House, 1954, 125-36.

week," and heard an eloquent black preacher, Dr. Channing Tobias, speak about how great the need was, in that rigidly segregated area, for more facilities and opportunities for colored youth.

Paul Block then sent a note to Grove Patterson:

"After I have left the room, please say that I will give another $5,000 ($77,280 in 2020) in tribute to the great speech this man has just made."

It is important not to overstate Paul Block's commitment to equality. He was not a fearless crusader for civil rights in the modern sense – he couldn't have been and survived as a publisher in his era.

That's not to imply he shrunk from a fight. To be fair, there is no indication that he – or almost any other publisher at the time – thought in those terms. Indeed, the very words "civil rights" were not in common use in his lifetime.

Nor did Block apparently give a lot of thought to fighting racism, though he always stood for decency and fair treatment of Blacks and other minorities on those rare occasions when the subject came up, and he always opposed the Ku Klux Klan.

He was far-seeing in many ways and a genius in some, but he also was very much a man of his time – and a man who had to be conscious that as an immigrant of Jewish origins, that he had come to this country as a stranger in a strange land.

"He clearly had a basic sense of fairness that was passed on to my father," Allan Block, the current chairman of Block Communications Inc. (BCI) and the grandson of the founder. "Of course, he wasn't – he couldn't – risk his business on any issue."

"He was entirely a self-made man. You have to consider his time and context – he would not want to be wiped out."

Time and context are, indeed, critically important.

Historians know that while there are such things as right and wrong, you cannot judge someone who lived in the past exclusively by the standards of today. Anyone who did might look at what Abraham Lincoln said and wrote in his time and judge him to be more racist than any politician in either major party in modern America.

Paul Block was a man of his time – but an exceptional one.

While newspaper historians have often lumped him in with Hearst, he was in fact uncannily far more like another immigrant who had an enormous impact on broadcast media: David Sarnoff, the founder of NBC, RCA, and of commercial radio and TV broadcasting.[3]

Sarnoff, who was fifteen years younger than Paul Block, also arrived in New York City when he was nine years old, with his family, who seem to have been even poorer and more wretched than the Blocks.

The main difference may be that Paul's family moved to Elmira, where he almost immediately got a job with the local newspaper. Sarnoff's family stayed in New York City, where he got a job as a messenger boy for the Marconi wireless company, where the great inventor himself soon took a shine to him and helped start his career.

Ironically, Sarnoff had originally hoped to get a job on a newspaper, and Paul Block loved new advances in technology all his life. It would be easy to imagine that their professional roles might have been reversed.

Though they were contemporaries, and both spent a great deal of time in New York, it isn't clear if they ever met. They were alike in another way as well; not only were they both Jewish, they were essentially Eastern European Jews. Sarnoff came from a shtetl in Minsk. Though the Blocks emigrated from East Prussia, his family had fled an area that is now Lithuania a few years before largely to escape Czarist-era pogroms.

That mattered because Eastern European Jews were looked down on even within the Jewish community, where those with the highest status were those of German origin.

These men who grew up to be media powerhouses, Block and Sarnoff, were both outsiders – minorities even within their own minority community.

They knew antisemitic discrimination of a kind almost unimaginable today. Though his career had already begun to take off, David Sarnoff was denied a commission as an officer during World War I. (Block was too old for the military when the war began.)

Despite that, both men were extremely proud Americans. By the time they were adults, both had lost any trace of any foreign accent. Block, in fact, loved the United States so much he pretended that he had been born in Elmira.[4]

Not till after his death did his descendants learn where he was actually born. He was not, of course, the only immigrant who wanted people to think

---

3. While there are numerous works on Sarnoff and his importance, one of the best and most readable is Tom Lewis' *Empire of the Air: The Men Who Made Radio,* New York: Harper Collins, 1991. The story was later made into a documentary of the same name by Ken Burns.

4. Frank Brady, *The Publisher. Paul Block: A Life of Friendship, Power & Politics,* Lanham, MD: University Press of America, Inc., 2001, xiii.

he was a native.

While we cannot know for sure, it is possible that Block concealed his origins, at least in part, because he was just beginning to rise to prominence when America entered World War I in 1917. There was tremendous anti-German feeling and having been born in Germany – on top of being Jewish – would have been bad for business.

There were, however, two other major differences between the media giants. David Sarnoff was essentially a workaholic, who once sweated his way through four crisply laundered white shirts in an afternoon while pushing his engineers to work harder on perfecting the inventions that eventually made television feasible.

Paul Block worked hard all his life – but was also a very social being who enjoyed nightlife, especially in New York, and who was a devoted and attentive father to his two sons, Paul Jr. and William, who followed him into the newspaper business.

Both men had brains, personality, and considerable drive for success. But they were different in that Sarnoff was utterly ruthless. "I don't get ulcers, I give them," he liked to say. Many of the inventions that made commercial radio successful, including FM, were discovered and refined by his longtime friend Edwin Howard Armstrong, who for years would stop by the Sarnoff home for coffee in the morning.

But when the men became embroiled in a patent fight over FM, Sarnoff used the power of his corporation to ruin Armstrong, driving him to despair and suicide.

Nobody could even have imagined such behavior on the part of Paul Block. The most he ever seems to have done when he found people treacherous or impossible to work with was to get out of business or social relationships with them.

While being social was essential for his success, especially in advertising, he was genuinely warm. His best-known editor, Grove Patterson, wrote an autobiography called *I Like People*. That title could have served equally well for Block, had he had a chance to author his story before his untimely death from fast-moving cancer on June 22, 1941.

He died, ironically, the day Nazi Germany invaded the Soviet Union, and nearly six months before the United States was drawn into the war.

Nobody can say with any certainty how he would have felt had he survived the war and lived to see Harry Truman desegregate the armed forces in 1948, or lived into his eighties, long enough to see *Brown v. Board of Education* and the beginnings of the modern civil rights movement. But it seems likely he would have been supportive.

Paul Block was a strong supporter of female suffrage, and made that clear as early as 1913, when allowing women to vote was still highly controversial. While cautious, he spoke up for decent treatment of African-Americans whenever he could easily do so.

Editorially, his newspapers usually showed considerable sympathy for those who were oppressed, and he strongly, even viciously, denounced the Ku Klux Klan in 1937 in a series of signed editorials when Franklin D. Roosevelt appointed a U.S. Supreme Court justice who had been a longtime secret member of the so-called Invisible Empire.

To be fair, his zeal may have been partly out of satisfaction that this embarrassed FDR, whose New Deal policies Block loathed.

But it seems clear that Paul Block was essentially a good and decent man whose sons, Paul Jr. and William, revered their father, with whom they were very close.

When it came to racial fairness, and justice, they went much further than he could have. They were, in many respects, pioneers in their field.

And it is clear that Paul Block did much to shape their values.

2

Race, Newspapers, and America

"It is my purpose to publish a newspaper which will be fair, just and independent in all its relations to public questions and to the people, no matter what may be their political beliefs, their race or their religion."
– Paul Block, February 12, 1931

Paul Block made that statement to the press when he bought his last newspaper, the *Los Angeles Express*. While he was certainly sincere, the nation was an entirely different place in the years during which he owned and ran newspapers.

Different from today, certainly, in terms of the press, which was as rigidly segregated as was baseball, and most of society itself. Only Black-owned newspapers covered the Black community. While no one referred to the *Detroit Free Press,* the *Chicago Tribune* or any of the newspapers Block owned as "white newspapers," that's what they were. They essentially ignored African-Americans – unless there was a race riot, or they were accused of committing of a crime against a white person.

While most people know that segregation in the South was enforced by a series of now-unconstitutional "Jim Crow" laws, many don't understand that in many ways, the North wasn't greatly different – and that as far as the media was concerned, Black people were very much like the title of Ralph

Ellison's novel, *Invisible Man.*

Want proof? On Labor Day, 1931, William Powell, a remarkable African-American pilot and veteran of World War I, organized a first-ever air show with all-Black pilots at the Los Angeles airport. Powell had been turned down by the U.S. Army Air Corps, which told him they "wouldn't accept colored men in the air corps."

The air show was designed to show them how wrong they were. Three Black pilots, members of the Bessie Coleman Aero Club, performed all sorts of stunts in honor of Coleman, a pioneering Black woman aviator who was thrown from her plane and died in 1926. Two others performed parachute jumps. The nation was aviation-mad in those days, and the Black press reported that 15,000 spectators turned out for the show.

Three months later, on December 6, 1931, William Powell put on an even bigger show, the first-ever "Colored Air Circus," featuring a group of Black pilots known as the Five Blackbirds, at that time the largest number of African-Americans ever to take to the air at once. This time, according to Powell, 40,000 spectators showed up.[1]

William Randolph Hearst's Los Angeles *Evening Herald* didn't devote a word to either air show – although the death of a white pilot who crashed his plane in Detroit was a page one story in Los Angeles the week the Colored Air Circus was going on.

Neither did Paul Block's *Los Angeles Express,* which within days would be sold to Hearst and merged with the *Evening Herald.* Nor did either paper devote a word to either event in the days leading up to them. They left any coverage of anything in the Black community to the *California Eagle,* the Black paper in town.

That may sound incredible, but America was indeed two nations in those days – separate, and very much unequal, in every sense of the term.

Incidentally, the terms "Black" and "African-American" were not in common use until the 1970s; "Negro" tended to be the preferred and respectful term, although some members of the race used "colored." Martin Luther King, Jr., who died in 1968, virtually always referred to himself as a Negro. What we today call the "n-word" was just as insulting then as now, though many whites didn't fully understand that – or care.

African-Americans who made efforts to improve the lot of all Blacks, or who took courageous stands against discrimination and lynching were

---

1. Phil Scott, "Blackbirds and the Colored Air Circus of 1931," *Air Facts Journal* (June 1, 2012).

spoken of, admirably, as "race men," men who stood up for their race.

In the newspaper world, possibly the most flamboyant of these was Robert S. Abbott, the publisher of the *Chicago Defender*, which for many years was the largest and most influential African-American newspaper in the nation, until it was overtaken by the *Pittsburgh Courier* and its politically astute publisher, Robert Vann, in the 1930s.

Abbott loudly called for an end to segregation in hiring in both the public and private sector, denounced Jim Crow laws, and constantly pushed for Blacks to move north.

He raged against lynching, and published sensational headlines urging resistance, saying things like, "when the white fiends come to the door, shoot them down… take at least one with you." He would run annual lynching statistics, noting in 1915 that in addition to forty-nine Black victims, five white people had been lynched the year before.

"Five white people lynched!" Abbott wrote, in a front-page article dripping with sarcasm. "Maybe the fun wasn't coming fast and furious enough and so they threw in a few of their own number for good measure." The editorial went on to acidly note that while colored people had been led to believe lynching was a form of punishment "especially prepared for us, it seems we can have nothing exclusive."

Lynchings were indeed terrible – a form of sadistic murder that commonly involved not only hanging, but castration, torture, and burning the victims alive, often before large jeering and cheering crowds.

But lynchings were, in fact, on the decline even before Robert Abbott assembled the first edition of his *Defender* on his landlady's table in 1905. The worst year on record was in 1892, when 230 people were lynched nationwide – 161 of them black.

After that, the unspeakable practice began to decline. The last year that there were more than one hundred lynchings was in 1901, according to the Tuskegee Institute's archives; the number then gradually dwindled to three in 1964, the year the three civil rights workers were killed in Mississippi. There were likely a number of reasons for this:

Frank Ahlgren, the legendary editor of the *Memphis Commercial Appeal*, told me in 1990 that while the ruling class, the "Brahmins," of the South weren't especially interested in equal justice, they came to oppose lynching and take steps to curb it because it was lawlessness, and they didn't want mob rule and anarchy.

However, the National Association for the Advancement of Colored People (NAACP), which was founded in 1909, also devoted much of its energy to fighting lynching prior to World War II. Ironically, while segregation was far more common in almost every other walk of life, the NAACP leadership was far more integrated in Paul Block's time.

Walter White, the group's field secretary who investigated the many of the lynchings, was indeed Black. But the founding president of the NAACP, who held that post until this death in 1929, was Moorfield Storey, a white lawyer from an upper-class Boston family who could trace their ancestry to the seventeenth century-Puritans.

Jewish Americans were also heavily involved in the NAACP and were prominent on its board; for some years, in fact, the only black member was W.E.B. DuBois.

But while the NAACP slowly won a series of groundbreaking court decisions that gradually eroded the foundations of legal segregation, they did it mostly below the radar.

Disgraceful as it may seem today, most mainstream newspapers paid little attention to anything involving "Negroes," which was seldom capitalized.

With one great exception – that of a heroic Black man in Memphis, a case we will later examine in detail – Paul Block's papers were not much different from any others when it came to race issues during the years he owned and ran them.

That's not to say he was opposed to using his newspapers, on occasion, to crusade for what he believed was right. He did so often, in fact, sometimes in signed, front-page editorials that called for better streets or schools or election reform.

However, the various reforms he called for did not include trying to win more opportunities for African-Americans. (It is worth noting that, with the exception of Memphis, Black populations in virtually all the cities where he owned papers were miniscule – often no more than one or two percent.)

Paul Block's newspapers never, so far as I could determine, hired an African-American reporter or editor during his lifetime. But neither did other major papers.

Professor Dave Davies, the interim chair of Mass Communication and Journalism at the University of Southern Mississippi, has spent years studying and writing about race and the press in America. "I don't know a case of anyone hiring Black reporters prior to World War II. It was rare enough after World War II that it was mentioned in trade journals when it happened," he said.[2]

---

2. Dave Davies, interview by the author, August 29, 2019.

Paul Block's sons would eventually hire Black reporters in Toledo and Pittsburgh more than a decade before the first black reporter succeeded at the *New York Times.*

Today, we would find the neglect of African-Americans in news coverage and their absence in major newsrooms utterly indefensible – and in a very real sense it was – especially for a paper like the *New York Times,* which thought of itself as the nation's newspaper of record, publishing, as its motto says, "All the News That's Fit to Print."

But it has to be remembered that this was thought of as just the way things naturally were by not only white publishers, but by some in the Black press.

The newspaper world in the America of Paul Block's day closely mirrored major league baseball. Blacks were not welcome in the National and American Leagues, thanks in large part to the policy of Commissioner Kenesaw Mountain Landis, a former federal judge from Georgia who ruled the sport with an iron hand and flatly opposed integration.

As a result, parallel Black major leagues formed. The same was true with the press. The best Black reporters in the 1930s and '40s commonly aspired to work, not for the major white newspapers, but for the best papers in the Black press, especially the *Chicago Defender* and the *Pittsburgh Courier,* both of which had national circulations.

Those who worked for and read those papers took huge pride in them and what they represented. The Black press was far more extensive than today, and historians have judged that they were vastly important in those communities.

"We didn't exist in the other papers. We were neither born, we didn't get married, we didn't die, we didn't fight in any wars, we never participated in anything of a scientific achievement. We were truly invisible unless we committed a crime," Vernon Jarrett, a star reporter who got his start at the *Chicago Defender,* said in Stanley Nelson's award-winning 1999 documentary *Soldiers Without Swords*[3].

"(But) in the Black Press, the Negro press, we did get married. They showed us our babies when born. They showed us graduating. They showed our PhDs," added Jarrett, who became a columnist for the *Chicago Tribune* after the color bar was broken.

The University of Southern Mississippi's Davies thought that white editors at newspapers like those in Los Angeles may well have justified not

---

3. Stanley Nelson, dir., *Soldiers Without Swords* (1999; Half Nelson Productions).

covering events like those huge air shows. "They may have thought, that's something the black papers will catch," he said.

Indeed, Black papers often did cover many events the mainstream media missed or ignored. But the Black press, like Black baseball teams, had one major handicap – lack of money. Papers operated on such a shoestring budget that the legendary *Pittsburgh Courier* photographer Charles "Teenie" Harris was known as "one-shot," there was so little money for flash bulbs he had to make every picture count.

However, this didn't mean that Black journalists were fighting to get hired by the mainstream newspapers. Nor were Black publishers fighting in the 1920s and '30s to get the *New York Times* or the *Philadelphia Inquirer* to hire Black reporters.

They may have shrewdly realized that they had a vested interest in <u>not</u> doing so. A few mainstream newspapers, including the *Toledo Blade* and *Pittsburgh Post-Gazette,* began hiring a few Black reporters in the early 1950s.

That trickle increased considerably after the civil rights movement, and then civil unrest, became huge national stories in the 1960s.

Some Black reporters who were hired by major newspapers and broadcast outlets would later say, sardonically, that they could trace their being hired to a particular riot; white editors, most of whom clearly hadn't seen unrest in the Black community coming, finally decided they needed Black reporters if they wanted to find out what was going on.

Reporters for African-American newspapers usually jumped at the chance to work for major newspapers or broadcast outlets for a variety of reasons. Gaining a wider reputation was one, and many were proud to help break down one more barrier.

But the biggest reason for many was that mainstream papers paid far higher salaries. And once many of the stars of the Black press began jumping to larger papers, and those papers began not only hiring Black reporters but covering Black communities, the same thing happened to Black newspapers as happened to the Negro baseball leagues after Jackie Robinson joined the Brooklyn Dodgers and paved the way for integration – they withered and mostly died.

The Negro National and American baseball leagues died in the 1950s. Though there are still Black papers, including the *Chicago Defender* and a new incarnation of the *Pittsburgh Courier,* which originally ceased publication in 1966, they are mostly tiny, almost vestigial, with few subscribers even among African-Americans.

Yet all this was too far in the future to be imagined when Paul Block was pouring his energies into the newspaper business nearly a century ago. How those papers covered race is well worth examining, keeping in mind the standard of that day.

3

The Early Years: Detroit and Newark

In politics, Paul Block was mostly Republican. He had close Democratic friends, including New York Mayor Jimmy Walker. But he usually endorsed Republicans, and always endorsed their presidential nominees. The GOP was the party of the rich and successful, and that's what he, from boyhood, aspired to become. They were also, he believed, less prone to corruption than the Democrats.

The Republican Party was also, we sometimes now forget, the party supported by the overwhelming majority of African-Americans until the Great Depression and the New Deal. Democrats, whose strongest base back then was in the Deep South, were seen even by many northern liberals as the party of segregation.

Even Franklin D. Roosevelt, whose economic policies did move a lot of minorities, including Blacks, into the Democratic Party, refused to support a federal law outlawing lynching, out of the fear that if he did, southern Democrats would "block every bill I ask Congress to pass to keep America from collapsing."[1]

---

1. Paul Sparrow, "Eleanor Roosevelt's Battle to End Lynching," Franklin D. Roosevelt Library and Museum website: https://fdr.blogs.archives.gov/2016/02/12/eleanor-roosevelts-battle-to-end-lynching/ (accessed September 20, 2019).

Republicans in his era may not have done a lot for African-Americans, but they at least opposed lynching, did not oppose allowing Blacks to vote, and were proud that they were the party of Abraham Lincoln and the party that ended slavery.

Blacks knew that while not all Democrats were members of the Ku Klux Klan, it could be assumed that all Klan members saw themselves as Democrats. Accordingly, when African-Americans could vote, they overwhelmingly voted Republican.

That is, until 1932, when Robert Lee Vann, the publisher of the *Pittsburgh Courier,* advised Blacks to "turn Lincoln's picture to the wall," and vote for FDR. The *Courier* had a nationwide circulation by then; and Vann was rewarded by being appointed the first Black assistant U.S. attorney general when Roosevelt won.

But Paul Block did know and like some Democrats, famously including his close friend, New York Mayor Jimmy Walker – and New York Governor Al Smith, who in 1928 became the first Roman Catholic nominee for president. Block couldn't quite bring himself to endorse Smith, a man who, like himself, came from extremely humble origins.

He liked Smith, but not his party. Both men had a number of things in common: they were almost the same age, were highly intelligent and largely self-educated, and were members of religious minorities who knew discrimination.

In fact, Paul Block was so fond of Smith that he deposited more than $2,000 in his thirteen-year-old son Billy's bank account, and had him present it to the chairman of the finance committee for Smith for president in 1928.[2] The gift, equivalent to about $30,000 in 2020 dollars, had no effect on the election. Smith was swamped, even losing his native New York. But Smith and Block remained friends. Both strongly opposed Prohibition, and later in the 1930s, they also became political allies when Smith turned sharply against FDR and the New Deal and began endorsing Republican candidates for president.

Al Smith had a gravelly voice and a blunt, no-nonsense way of talking that his friends loved. His favorite phrase, especially when he was explaining some hidden truth, was "Now, let's look at the record."

That's a good motto for not only politics, but history and journalism as well.

Paul Block owned, at various times, papers in a number of cities in many

---

2. Frank Brady, *The Publisher: Paul Block: A Life of Friendship, Power & Politics,* Lanham, MD: University Press of America, Inc., 2001, 375-76.

regions of the country, from New York to Los Angeles with Memphis and Milwaukee thrown in.

When it comes to assessing how he and his papers treated racial questions, there is no better way than taking Al Smith's advice: Look at the record.

So I have looked carefully at virtually every paper that Paul Block ever owned, and/or played a significant role in running.[3] In a few cases early in his career, especially in New York and Detroit, it is not always clear how much Block, who was first and foremost an advertising man, was actually involved in editorial policy.

He was also not always a sole owner of his newspapers, and, in a few cases, it isn't clear whether he really did own papers he published. That matters little, for the purposes of this book, if he was actually running and controlling them.

But most of the time I've found that Paul Block set his own distinctive, energetic editorial stamp on every newspaper with which he was associated.

What I wanted to do primarily was establish how these papers, both in a news and editorial sense, covered issues having to do with race. Again, it is necessary to keep two things in mind: Racial issues were not covered as news in the same way as they are now.

Also, again, most of the cities where Paul Block owned newspapers had miniscule Black populations; nearly 90 percent of African-Americans lived in the South when he began buying newspapers; more than three-quarters still did when he died.

Not until the "Great Migration" which began in the early twentieth century peaked with Blacks arriving to work in the factories during World War II and the years after did most northern cities have substantial African-American populations.

Race has always, however, been a significant story in America.

How these papers covered any aspect of it is significant in itself.

---

3. This research did not examine *Pictorial Review*, which Block joined as director of advertising in 1907, and which he then built into one of the most successful women's magazines in the country, with a circulation of two million. Though Block gradually acquired a significant degree of editorial control, he was never the sole owner, and the publication was largely concerned with clothing, fashion and publishing high-quality fiction – though it eventually did, apparently at Paul Block's urging, take on controversial women's issues including sex education and birth control. It also urged its readers to work to pass the nineteenth amendment that gave women the right to vote. Block left the publication after a disagreement with the founder in 1931, and it swiftly declined, finally closing in 1939.

Newark Star-Eagle, 1916-1939

Paul Block probably had dreamed of being a publisher and owning his own newspapers from the time he first went into business for himself in 1900, if not before.

He finally succeeded in January 1916, when he and two partners managed to buy the *Newark Star,* and combine it with another afternoon paper to form the *Newark Star-Eagle.* Though he was not a sole owner at first (he eventually bought out his partners) he was clearly the dominant one, and he almost immediately became publisher and threw himself into every aspect of the business – including the news and editorial departments.

Ironically, though the *Star-Eagle* was the first paper he really owned, it was not the first time he had been a publisher. He had been a vice-president and held stock in a small New York City paper called the *Evening Mail,* starting before World War I.

He apparently had no involvement with the editorial content – which turned out to be a good thing. The paper was later purchased in 1915 by a shadowy figure named Dr. Edward Rumely, a pro-German sympathizer who got into major trouble and was later sent to prison for having secretly taken money from the German government, which became the enemy when the United States entered the war in April 1917.

Paul Block assumed the role of publisher, first without and then later with the title, after Rumely's demise. His longtime friend and associate Henry Stoddard was responsible for the editorial content, but the *Evening Mail* was not in a good position to be competitive in the crowded New York market, and Block left it in early 1921.

Though his biographer, Frank Brady, believes Paul Block's dream was to own a major paper in Manhattan, he enthusiastically threw himself into building up the paper in Newark, which was, it should be noted, a mere eight miles across the river.

The city the *Newark Star-Eagle* covered a century ago was a vastly different place than it is today. Today's Newark, which has about 280,000 people, is poor, somewhat rundown, and ethnically very diverse. African-Americans made up 53 percent of the population in 2010; those identifying as white 27 percent; and the rest a wide variety of races, with slightly more than a third of the population Hispanic.

The Newark Paul Block knew was an entirely different place, bustling, growing, and on its way to the peak population of 442,437 it reached in 1930.

It was also overwhelmingly white. The Black population was less than 4 percent of the population when he bought the paper, but had begun rapidly growing around 1915, as southern Blacks began migrating north for better paying jobs.

By the time economic pressure forced Block to finally close the paper in November 1939, it had reached 10 percent; a few months later, the census would count 45,760 African-Americans in Newark, most living in inner-city neighborhoods.

That was a distinct community – and one that was largely uncovered by *any* newspaper, at least until the late 1930s, when an African-American paper called the *New Jersey Herald News* (later the *Newark Herald News*) finally began publishing. The much better known *New Jersey Afro-American* wasn't founded until after the *Star-Eagle* died.

***

Paul Block's *Newark Star-Eagle,* it must be said, paid little attention to the city's growing Black community. Sadly, white publishers didn't put much thought into covering communities of color, even many years later.

"Look at the minutes of ASNE (American Society of Newspaper Editors) meeting in the 1950s." Professor Dave Davies said. "They defended not covering Black communities by saying, they aren't our readers; they don't pay our bills."[4]

That, however, was when the civil rights movement and pressure to integrate was beginning. Prior to that, few editors saw any reason to think about covering Black communities at all.

What Paul Block did think about was improving his newspaper and making it as competitive as possible. More than most publishers, he had a talent for improving circulation, and he threw himself in improving the editorial product.

Looking at microfilmed copies of newspapers across the nation, it is striking that whenever Block took command of a paper, the energy level almost instantly, and visibly, seemed to increase. When he and his two partners bought the *Star-Eagle,* its circulation was less than 50,000. By the mid-1920s, it had reached 85,000.

But its main competitor, the *Newark Evening News*, reached 100,000. This was in a day when most readers preferred afternoon papers to morning ones; they tended to work early shifts, and afternoon papers would contain

---

4. Dave Davies, interview by the author, August 29, 2019.

some news from the same day.

Block threw himself into the fray, adding features and staff, calling it "New Jersey's Most Interesting Newspaper," and starting a weekly magazine section, serialized novels, and even a style column. Some of his innovations were decades ahead of their time. *The Detroit Free Press*, for example, won a lot of attention in the 1960s with its "Action Line," which promised to try to solve readers' problems. Paul Block was more than forty years ahead of them; by 1919, he had started a "*Star-Eagle* Free Information Bureau," located in the Washington office, which promised to try to tell anyone, "without charge, 'Whatever You Want to Know,'" as long as that reader included a two-cent stamp for a reply. (The paper did say that "certain classes of medical and legal questions cannot in their nature be answered by the bureau.")

Even from century-old microfilm it is easy to see the paper quickly crackling with new-found energy. Two of the partners were part owners of the *Toledo Blade*, and in a move that would be hard to imagine today, they managed to persuade Grove Patterson, the then-famous editor of the *Blade*, to shuttle between Ohio and New Jersey to also serve as editor of the *Star-Eagle*.

Unfortunately, the local Black community does seem to have been largely ignored, based on my reading of scores of issues over the nearly quarter-century Paul Block owned the newspaper. The *Star-Eagle* did run wire stories covering national news involving race, which was mainly outbreaks of violence against African-Americans.

They seldom, if ever, sent reporters to cover out-of-town news; their resources were limited, very few newspapers did that then, and they were embroiled in a spirited and competitive newspaper war.

We can, however, glean some indication of the editors' attitudes – which were more than likely Paul Block's attitudes – from the wire stories and editorials they ran.

The *Star-Eagle* did not like violence and lawlessness, including any against minorities. The nation was swept by vicious outbreaks of racial violence during what came to be called the "Red Summer" of 1919, in which hundreds of people, the vast majority of them Black, were killed. The violence did not extend to New Jersey, and the *Star-Eagle* did not take note of every riot; some, in fact, were poorly reported at the time.

But the newspaper did pay a fair amount of attention to the worst urban riot of that year, which took place in Chicago and began when a young Black man on a raft in Lake Michigan drifted into an area commonly used by whites, and was murdered.

When police refused to take action, Blacks and whites battled each other in the streets for almost two weeks, with at least thirty-eight killed and many buildings and a thousand homes, almost all of them the homes of Black families, destroyed.

Many newspapers ran lurid stories blaming Blacks, or "negroes,"[5] for the violence. But the *Star-Eagle's* coverage was generally nuanced. It is impossible today to know who edited the wire stories, but the accounts of the riot were even-handed, and in some cases showed some sympathy for the African-Americans.

For example, a story that ran on the front page on July 29, 1919, under the headline "More Die As Riots Spread Over Chicago," indicated that whites had renewed the violence by attacking Blacks: "Disorders spread to the north side of the city, where a number of negroes were chased and threatened. Very few negroes live in that side of the city," the story reported, noting also that an innocent Black porter had reportedly been dragged out of a restaurant and beaten senseless with a bottle.

The story went on to say that a mob had threatened to attack a white funeral home after the body of a Black man killed in the rioting had been taken there, and "thereafter dead negroes would not be accepted at white mortuaries."

The *Star-Eagle* apparently did not editorialize on the Chicago riot. Nor were there any stories on how Newark's Black community felt about what was happening in Chicago and elsewhere that year. Though that would be almost an automatic story today, that wasn't something newspapers did back then, outside of the African-American press.

Newark itself remained largely free of large-scale racial violence until its epic riot in July 1967, long after both the *Star-Eagle* and Paul Block had passed into history.

The *Star-Eagle* did report from time-to-time, often on the front page, about incidents of out-of-town, unprovoked violence against African-Americans, or about Klan activity, as in this story from August 27, 1923.

---

5. Newspapers commonly did not capitalize "Negro" or "Negroes," the preferred term for the race, until the 1940s or later.

WHITES ATTACK NEGRO'S COLONY

Men in Autos Fire Into Houses in Savannah, Killing One.

SAVANNAH, Ga., Aug. 27 (AP).—A number of white men in three automobiles drove through East Savannah, a negro settlement, firing into houses, early today. One negro is reported dead, one seriously wounded and several slightly injured.

More than one hundred shots were fired from three automobiles into the homes of the negroes. County policemen, who were rushed to East Savannah, have been able to learn only that the men in the cars were white men.

In an odd editorial four days earlier, "Throw-Backs to Barbarism," the paper denounced "flogging parties" in "certain circles of the states of Georgia, Texas and Oklahoma," incidents where "groups of strong-biceped men go out at night and whip into ribbons the backs of people who, at least at the time, cannot fight back."

The editorial went on at some length to denounce those who "have a taste for cruelty for its own sake," and noted that "the southern floggers probably derive more satisfaction in giving pain than in serving a warning."

What seems strange about all this is the editorial never mentions that most of these floggings were motivated by race. Instead, it notes that the reason "is said to be popular indignation over violations of the moral code. It may be or again it may not be."

It is difficult to believe that the writer of the editorial didn't know that race was the main motivating factor in these incidents, or that "violations of the moral code" usually meant romantic or sexual involvement between people of different races.

Whether or not that editorial deliberately sought to mask the truth, it is clear that when it came to race, the *Star-Eagle*, and almost certainly its owner, were still in many respects naïve. For example, that same year of 1923, a summer in which Paul Block and the nation were stunned by the sudden death of President Warren Harding, the *Star-Eagle* took note of the Great Migration that had begun about the time World War I began.

Millions of African-Americans would eventually migrate from the cotton fields of the South to better opportunities in the North. They had begun to arrive in Newark in some numbers. The newspaper noted that in an editorial "The Flight Out of the South" on June 9, and also noted – correctly – that economic reasons were a major motivating factor. "They are here because there is money to be earned faster than at home."

But the *Star-Eagle* editorial erred badly in its main premise, which was that money was the *only* reason Blacks were migrating north. "An attempt has been made to show that the northern migration of negroes is a quest for relief from oppressive social conditions, a flight from hatred and prejudice, and burning desire to exercise constitutional rights denied at home [the South]."

The editorial said there was no truth to that – though it correctly noted that, "no race has been exploited politically more than the negroes." Unfortunately, it then added, incredibly, that most Black people had no interest in voting. "The average negro sees little of benefit for himself on exercising the franchise, and long ago in the South he gleaned from it all its possibilities of interest and excitement."

What the second part of that sentence meant wasn't clear. Did the editorial writer not know that after Reconstruction ended most Blacks were no longer allowed to vote – and that trying to do so could mean a midnight visit from the Ku Klux Klan, or worse?

The editorial also forecast – incorrectly – that after the Blacks who had migrated north made some money, most of them would go home. "A colored worker was heard to say 'I'm goin' to work here until I gets $3,000 and then I'm goin' back to Mobile and never work again,'" That statement, the paper thought "probably reveals fairly accurately the ideas of thousands of the migrants. The ties with the South are not broken."

One wonders if the writer really personally knew any "negroes."

The late U.S. Sen. Daniel Patrick Moynihan, one of the last great public intellectuals, once wrote to President Richard Nixon that "the issue of race could benefit from a period of benign neglect" – a statement he later regretted making.

Most of the time, the *Star-Eagle's* coverage of race could be described as naïve or ignorant neglect, even though the publisher's motives seem to have been totally benign, to the degree he thought about race at all.

Unfortunately, that sometimes led to the perpetuation of stereotypes that were unconsciously and unthinkingly accepted by the editors. Fontaine Fox (1884-1964) was one of the most popular syndicated cartoonists in the 1920s and '30s; his syndicated "Toonerville Folks" cartoon ran in between 250 and 300 newspapers in its heyday.

However, the Kentucky-born Fox was also known for his racist gags. Note this cartoon, which appeared in the *Newark Star-Eagle* on Election Day, Nov. 3, 1936:

America, and its newspapers, had a long way to go.

Detroit Journal, 1917-1922

Paul Block's second experience in owning a newspaper came in Detroit, when he and his business partners from the *Star-Eagle* bought the *Detroit Journal* in February 1917, just a year after he had purchased the Newark paper.

This must have been an exciting venture. For years, the nation has thought of Detroit as a synonym for urban failure; a mostly Black, mostly poor city that has been losing population since the early 1950s, and which collapsed into bankruptcy in 2013.

The city is now showing some signs of improvement. But the Detroit in which Paul Block owned a newspaper was a city vastly different from today. For one thing, it was booming, thanks to Henry Ford and the automobile revolution.

The population soared from approximately 800,000 to 1,100,000 in the five short years Block was involved with the afternoon *Journal,* then the newspaper of the conservative business elite. During those years, his energetic marketing techniques increased the circulation of the paper by almost 50 percent, taking it to 146,000.

He also helped make the newspaper extremely profitable. While it never caught up to the competing *Detroit News* in circulation, it ended up getting more advertising, and much more automobile advertising, which was growing more lucrative by the day. [6]

Perhaps unfortunately for Detroit journalism, Block, according to his biographer Frank Brady, came to realize that he neither liked nor trusted his business partners, and they ended up selling the paper to the *Detroit News* in July 1922, which added its mailing lists, advertising contracts, and other assets to its own – and closed the paper.

How much did Paul Block have to do with the editorial content? That's hard to say, looked at from across a century. He was known to have intervened at least once to see that a picture of a starlet he admired (Marion Davies) was run in the paper.

But he and his partners did perform the rather amazing feat of persuading Grove Patterson, who at the time was editor of both the *Newark Star-Eagle* and the *Toledo Blade*, which Block did not yet own, to also become the editor

---

6. Brady, *The Publisher,* 176-72.

of the *Detroit Journal*.

Patterson managed to straddle three cities for a couple of years but then sent Willard Bowman, the capable managing owner of the *Journal*, to Newark, after which, he noted in his autobiography *I Like People*, he seldom went to New Jersey.

Toledo, he felt, was more or less a well-oiled machine, the *Journal*, however, needed a lot of attention, and as Patterson told it, he appointed a deputy to act as managing editor in Toledo, made himself managing editor of the *Journal*, "moved into Detroit and for the next three years I gave the *Blade* one or two days a week."[7]

Most of that time, he says, he got up before daylight and "never left the journal office until after seven in the evening." Paul Block noticed, and a close relationship grew between the men that lasted the rest of their lifetimes.

We cannot know how much they discussed editorial content, though it is likely that whenever Block had an editorial idea, his editor did his best to make it happen.

It is equally likely that Patterson came to understand his boss's way of looking at the world and saw that his newspapers reflected that.

So how did the *Journal* do when it came to covering issues involving race? Perhaps the most startling difference in the Detroit of 1917 is that its Black population was still very small, just starting to boom as a result of the Great Migration.

There were few Blacks at all in the city – barely one percent – as late as 1910. But two months after Paul Block and his partners bought the *Detroit Journal*, the United States entered World War I, and factory workers were desperately needed, both to cope with needed war production and to replace men who had entered military service.

Still, the Black population was still only 4.1 percent in 1920, most of them laborers, assembly line workers, and an assortment of artisans and domestic servants.

Few of them would have read the *Journal*, which performed roughly the function the *Wall Street Journal* does today for Detroit in that era. Yet, while I found no instances of the newspaper covering the Black community in those days, when race was mentioned, the tone was surprisingly liberal – somewhat more so than the *Star-Eagle*.

Much of this may have been due to Grove Patterson, who was characteristically sympathetic to Blacks. The *Detroit Journal* covered the

---

7. Patterson, *I Like People*, 108-18.

atrocities of the Red Summer in considerably more volume than the *Star-Eagle*, perhaps in part because many of the hardest-hit areas, especially Chicago, are far closer to Detroit than to Newark.

The paper also gave a fair amount of coverage to other riots that year, including a rural massacre of Blacks in Arkansas that September in which as many as 237 Black people were killed, evidently because they tried to organize a sharecroppers' union.

After a mob in Omaha dragged Will Brown, a Black man accused of rape, from the county courthouse, lynched him, burned his body, and posed for pictures with it, the *Journal's* editorial page acidly noted that "following the Omaha affair, the Hun may wonder why the people of this nation made so much fuss about his depredations in Belgium," a reference to supposed atrocities committed by the German army when they invaded and occupied that country during the First World War.

However, there was an ethnic group Paul Block's newspapers seemed to loathe. It was not Blacks… but Germans. Both the *Detroit Journal* and the *Newark Star-Eagle* had no sympathy for the "Huns" in the months after the November 1918 armistice that ended World War I, nor while the Treaty of Versailles was being negotiated.

For example, on May 14, 1919, the *Journal* ran an unusual – and very long – editorial at the top of the front page under the headline "Let the Hun Pay for His War."

Dripping with venom, it reminded readers that a year earlier, there were "thousands of brave young Americans going to their death," and added "knowing these things, remembering these things, it is almost inconceivable that anywhere in America a voice should be lifted in defense of the Hun or in criticism of a peace which strips him of his power for evil and demands that he pay a price all too small for his crimes."

"America won the war. And she intends to keep it won."

Those sentiments were shared by millions – though it is fair to wonder whether Paul Block heaped it on in part because he hadn't revealed that he was born in Germany and wanted to emphasize his American loyalties. Then, too, it is possible that he was worried lest his connection with Edward Rumely, the disloyal pro-German publisher of the *New York Evening Mail*, become widely known.

Ironically, when the real German monster appeared on the scene, Paul Block, like the great satiric columnist H.L. Mencken and many other wise men, discounted his potential to do harm. In 1934, more than a year after Adolf Hitler took power, Block took a tour of Europe, including stopovers in Germany, Austria, and France.

Soon after Block returned, he told a reporter for the Associated Press that Hitler was just "a male Aimee Semple McPherson who won't last," referring to a show-biz style preacher and faith healer who was then a nationwide sensation.

Many others made the same mistake.

Paul Block was consistently against disorder and violence, and found it hard to understand why anyone would tolerate it. When the Chicago riot was winding down, the *Journal* denounced rioting in an editorial, "Preventing a Race War."

It took the step, rare at that time, of capitalizing the name of the race. It noted that there were "undeniable facts concerning the cancellation of the Negroes' constitutional rights," but indicated that this was not the time and place to do anything about it.

"These are matters which only time, education, a growing sense of decency, and honest and not a make-believe democracy can cure," the paper said.

It also curiously said there was far more murderous hatred among whites for Blacks in the North than the South. It urged the public and police to unite in efforts to suppress rioting, adding "let it be made clear that any riot leader or any mob member, be he white or colored, will be knocked down where he stands or runs, and possibly shot."

The editorial went on to say that "not one lynching in a thousand was ever conducted by men who were determined to go through with their crime despite of determined police opposition. Lynching persists only where the lynchers are certain in their minds there will be no retribution."[8]

Two years later, Paul would buy a newspaper in a community that had been traumatized by the lynching of three Black men just months before.

But it wasn't in Alabama, Mississippi, or even Tennessee.

It was in Minnesota.

---

8. "Preventing a Race War," *Detroit Journal* editorial, July 30, 1919.

4

Duluth: The Shadow of a Lynching

By late 1920 Paul Block was in his mid-forties. He had become a successful publisher in Newark, was nationally recognized as one of masters of the newspaper advertising business, and was in a position to acquire more newspapers.

He was only a few months from withdrawing as publisher of the *New York Evening Mail,* a paper he ran but didn't own – and which would not long survive without his leadership. He was also barely a year and a half from selling the *Detroit Journal,* primarily because he wasn't happy with his business partners.[1]

But in the first two months of 1921, he began expanding his empire geographically, first acquiring the *Duluth Herald,* then the largest newspaper in what was a gritty but bustling, medium-sized Minnesota city on Lake Superior.

Though today's Duluth is a beautiful, white-collar town whose economy is largely dependent on banking and tourism, the city then was a thriving, but mostly blue-collar place dedicated largely to shipping countless tons of iron ore pellets to factories in the Midwest, including those that were beginning to

---

1. The best source for detailed information on Paul Block is Brady's *The Publisher,* though Grove Patterson's *I Like People,* while not a comprehensive study, provides a portrait of his personality as a human being.

mass-produce cars and trucks.

Duluth, with a population that hovered around 100,000 when Block bought the paper, had a large population of immigrants, especially from Finland, a fair number of them left-wing radicals who were members of the "wobblies" – the near-anarchist Industrial Workers of the World. One worker, a man named Olli Kinkonnen, had, in fact, been lynched by an angry mob in 1918, apparently because he wanted to return to his native Finland instead of fighting in World War I.

But Duluth is not a place where anyone would have expected violence against Blacks – largely because there were very few, considerably less than one percent of the population. The city seems to have been peaceful through the "Red Summer" of 1919, when major and murderous race riots occurred in cities from Chicago to Omaha.

But Duluth's reputation took a major and shocking blow in June 1920, just seven months before Paul Block bought the *Herald*. The John Robinson Circus came to town, and two local teenagers, Jimmy Sullivan and Irene Tusken, claimed they had been assaulted and robbed by six Black circus workers after the performance was over.

The police arrested the workers as suspects, and locked them up in the city jail. But an ugly mob stormed the jail, pulled Elias Clayton, Elmer Jackson, and Isaac McGhie from their cells, and lynched them on a downtown street corner.

To add to the disgrace and horror, postcards of the event were later sold. Irene Tusken's personal physician later examined her and said he found no evidence she had been raped or assaulted.

The lynchings seem to have been instantly seen as a black mark against the city, and the Duluth newspapers, after covering them thoroughly at the time, seem to have soon decided to have a case of "collective amnesia" about the embarrassment.[2]

The authorities swiftly convened a grand jury to look into the rioting, and twenty-five white men were indicted for rioting and twelve for the murder of the three men.

But in the end, nobody was prosecuted for the murders; three white men were convicted on rioting charges, none of whom served more than fifteen months in prison.

Despite the lack of any evidence, one of the surviving Black circus

---

2. Minnesota Historical Society, "Duluth Lynchings: Background and historical documents related to the tragic events of June 15, 1920," https://www.mnhs.org (accessed July 28, 2019).

workers, Max Mason, a twenty-one-year-old from Alabama, was convicted of rape, served four years in a state prison, and was released on the condition he leave the state immediately.

These events are worth recounting in some detail, because it is necessary to understand the atmosphere in Duluth when Paul Block bought the *Herald*.

The entire city – and perhaps most of Minnesota – seems to have been traumatized by the lynchings; these were the only Black men ever lynched in that northern state, before or since.[3] To its credit, the Minnesota legislature swiftly passed an anti-lynching bill in April 1921… and then Duluth did its best to forget.

That form of voluntary "collective amnesia" was clearly registered in the *Duluth Herald*. There was no mention of the shocking events of June 15, 1920, on the first anniversary of the lynchings, as there certainly would be in any paper today.

---

3. They were not, however, the only lynchings in Minnesota. Twenty other people, mainly whites and Native Americans, had been lynched in the state in earlier years, though apparently none since.

Nor were they mentioned on the fifth or tenth anniversary… or in any other issue of the paper I read on microfilm in the Duluth Public Library; nor could I find any mention of them in the clipping files the librarians had diligently maintained.

People only began to remember the lynchings in 1965, thanks to the son of a man who was nine years old in 1920 and lived two blocks from the scene of the crime.

That boy's name was Abram Zimmerman. His son is better known as Bob Dylan, and he mentioned the murders in the first lines of his song *Desolation Row:*

> *They're selling postcards of the hanging, they're painting the passports brown*
> *The beauty parlor is filled with sailors, the circus is in town*
> *Here comes the blind commissioner, they've got him in a trance …*
> *And the riot squad they're restless, they need somewhere to go*
> *As Lady and I look out tonight, from Desolation Row*[4]

Interpreting Dylan's lyrics was a national pastime in the 1960s, and people in Duluth began asking questions about a crime of which many of them had never known.

In subsequent years, the city took pains to come to terms with its past. The unmarked graves of the victims were given tombstones and in 2003 a plaza and statues of the martyrs was erected across the street from where they were hanged.

Speaking at the dedication, the great-grandson of one of the riot leaders called it "a long-held family secret," and spoke of its "deeply buried shame."

How many of these sentiments Paul Block shared is not known, but it seems likely that he – like Duluth's leaders—would have wanted to forget the embarrassment as thoroughly as possible. Duluth was the epitome of a boom town in 1921 – its population, slightly larger than now, had nearly doubled in the twenty years since he bought the *Herald.*[5]

Paul Block was always an avid booster of business; on the very day he and his partner, Michael Hanson, took over the paper, one of the *Herald's*

---

4. *Desolation Row* lyrics © Songtrust Ave, Audiam, Inc.

5. It has often been said that Duluth was the model for "Zenith" the complacent, boring, and unintellectual location of Sinclair Lewis' famous 1922 novel *Babbitt.* In fact, most literary scholars believe it almost certainly was not. Zenith was a composite, and was likely based more on Cincinnati than anywhere else.

editorials was headlined, "Think Prosperity and Work For It."

Interestingly, while Block, according to his biographer, put up most of the $500,000 or so ($6.8 million in 2019 dollars) to buy the *Herald,* they announced the sale in a way that made it appear that Hanson, who came from the *Philadelphia Record,* was the principal partner; he took the title of both president and publisher and moved with his family to Duluth; Paul Block remained based in New York, but was a frequent visitor.

That poses the question of how much Block knew about the paper's daily editorial operations – and how much, if anything, he had to do with the coverage, or rather non-coverage, of issues pertaining to race. However, we do know that Block kept an eye on virtually all aspects of all his papers and was known to constantly shower his editors with lists of commands, suggestions, and complaints.

Nor is there any evidence that he and Hanson ever failed to see eye-to-eye on any major issue. The partnership, indeed, lasted fifteen years until 1936, when they sold the *Herald* and the morning *Duluth News-Tribune,* which they added to their holdings just weeks after the stock market crash in 1929.

As was commonly the case in that era, neither Duluth paper paid much attention to the local African-American community, but there wasn't much of one to cover – only 495 Black people lived in the city, and after the lynchings in 1920, that small community got even smaller. While Duluth kept growing, its Black population fell by 16 percent over the next decade.[6]

Paul Block's paper did cover national violence against Blacks more than many papers of the time. When a major race riot broke out in Tulsa, Oklahoma, at the end of May 1921, the *Duluth Herald* titled the large, seven-column headline "Seventy-five Are Killed In Race Outbreak," and covered the story extensively for the next few days.

The newspaper didn't send any reporters of its own to the riot; regional newspapers of the day felt that was the responsibility of the Associated Press.

But the stories that ran were much closer to the truth than what Tulsa officials claimed, both in terms of the number of casualties (the city tried to suppress how many people actually died) and the nature of the riot itself, which occurred when a mob of thousands of whites rampaged through the Black community, murdering more than one hundred people and burning thirty-five square blocks of what was then the wealthiest African-American community in the United States. Tulsa itself decided to have its own form of collective amnesia about the rioting, and did not honestly admit what had

---

6. Minnesota Historical Society, "Duluth Lynchings."

happened until 1996.

Ironically, while the *Duluth Herald* was covering the events in Tulsa, one of the very few local stories about race in that era also made the paper.

This was less than a year after the infamous lynching and tensions were clearly still high between Black and white residents. While Tulsa was still a front-page story, a fascinating short story appeared on page 2. The *Herald* reported that one Harry Willson, "the only negro policeman on the Duluth force," had gotten in trouble while off-duty one afternoon. According to the paper, he was stuck with some of his friends one Saturday night in a traffic jam near Third Avenue, and someone shouted, "Drive on, niggers."

Willson, described as a "temporary policeman," waded into the crowd and arrested a sailor whom he accused of making the remark, took him to the station, booked him for disorderly conduct, and then allegedly struck the sailor's "chum" for giving him an "ugly look." Charges were soon dismissed against the sailor, and the paper reported that the police chief and the safety commissioner would decide that day whether Willson would be "exonerated, reprimanded, or recommended for dismissal."

The story itself seemed free of bias or bigotry and is mainly interesting as an indication of the state of relations between the races at the time.

Unfortunately, the paper evidently never reported what happened to the Black policeman, who thereafter seems to have disappeared from history.

Even had Paul Block been inclined to investigate racial conditions in Duluth in a way that might have upset the city leadership, he might have had another potential handicap. Minnesota passed an infamous "gag law" in 1925 that permitted any judge to shut down any newspaper that was "malicious, scandalous, and defamatory."

The law was actually directed against a racist publication called the *Saturday Press,* but had a chilling effect throughout the state until it was struck down as violating the First Amendment by the U.S. Supreme Court in 1931.

There was no indication it affected the Block newspapers' coverage of race. But to the *Duluth Herald's* great credit, it took on the Ku Klux Klan (KKK) in no uncertain terms, lashing out at it and attacking the racism it stood for in a long 1922 editorial that was as or more powerful than any seen in almost any newspaper at the time.[7]

Under the headline: "The Ku Klux Klan: A Snake to Be Stamped Upon," the paper attacked the Klan as "a skulking, cowardly, infamous organization that was created to spread the poison of religious and racial hate," and "a

---

7. "The Ku Klux Klan: A Snake to Be Stamped Upon," *Duluth Herald,* July 2, 1922.

thing that can appeal only to half-fledged moron minds."

Lest anyone think the Klan, which many still associated with slavery and the South, was a safe target in far-off Minnesota – think again. The Ku Klux Klan was rapidly growing in the North in the early 1920s – including Minnesota.[8]

It would eventually attract perhaps five million members, mostly in the north before a series of scandals virtually destroyed the KKK by the end of the decade. But it was still growing rapidly in 1922, including in Duluth, where the *Herald* reported it had as many as 1,500 members,[9] and the paper was alarmed.

"One had hoped that Duluth was one community, anyway, that couldn't be drawn into such a preposterous and shameful movement," the paper said, expressing regret that, alas, the Klan had found a foothold there. The *Herald* urged any citizens who had been duped into joining to "get out of it, and warn others to stay out of it."

The editorial concluded with remarks about race that based on other things he has known to have said, seem to directly express Paul Block's personal creed:

> *There could be no pettier, nastier, meaner spirit than that of the 'anti' who is against anybody because of his race, religion or birthplace... Black man, Jew, Catholic, "foreigner," Protestant, Ku Kluxer – they are all folks – just folks. Their curse and doom is disunity, and their only hope is in unity. They may differ in color, in creed, in race, in birthplace, but they are the same stuff underneath, and the stuff in which they are alike is the real thing, and the things that distinguish them but that should not make them enemies are largely of the surface.*

Despite the Klan's evident growing popularity, the *Duluth Herald*, and the morning *News-Tribune* after Block acquired it in 1929, frequently ran stories about violent Ku Klux Klan activities, especially in the region.

One evidently staff-written story in the *Herald* on September 13, 1924, featured an interview with the wife of one L.E. McKenzie from the nearby Wisconsin town of Bayfield, who feared her missing husband had been kidnapped by the Ku Klux Klan; a disoriented man branded with the initials KKK had been found in Illinois.

---

8. Elizabeth Dorsey Hatley, *The Ku Klux Klan in Minnesota*, Mount Pleasant, SC: The History Press, 2013.

9. "Ku Klux Klan in Duluth," *Duluth Herald,* July 1, 1922, 1.

Mrs. McKenzie (in a telling indication of that unconsciously sexist era, her first name is never mentioned) reported that her husband had reason to fear the Klan, as he had run a KKK organizer out of Bayfield. What actually happened to her husband was not, so far as I could tell, reported, though a few issues of the paper have been lost.

Incidentally, while the Duluth papers did not crusade for racial equality, they acknowledged it – at least in theory – and did not hesitate to attack bigotry in any form. The *Duluth Herald*, more than once, attacked Henry Ford's notorious antisemitism.

When it was reported that Mendel Beilis, who had been falsely accused of the ritual murder of a Christian child in Kiev in a case that caused an international sensation, was moving to the United States, a sardonic 1921 *Herald* editorial noted "and now he is coming to America, where Mr. Ford's queer campaign against the Jews, when he hears of it, will surely bring up grim recollections of life in Russia."[10]

Fifteen years later, just as the papers were both being sold, a *News-Tribune* cartoon depicted Michigan's famous bigoted and demagogic radio priest, Charles Coughlin, chasing a third-party bid and promoting "government by radio."[11]

While those sentiments were sincere, cultural sensitivities were much different in the 1920s and '30s than they are now. One wouldn't have to be especially politically correct by today's standards to cringe at the main page of the local morning *Duluth News-Tribune* on March 13, 1931, a little more than a year after Paul Block had bought it with the idea of dominating both the city's morning and evening newspaper markets.

Two stories dominated the middle of the page. On the right is a short, but well-executed story, "Robeson Sees Similarity in Russian, Negro Music," from an interview a reporter had conducted with the great baritone in the Hotel Duluth the night before.

Robeson, the story notes, was in town to give a concert that evening. The story, which does not have a byline, shows no hint of racism, is intellectually respectful, and capitalizes the term Negro, something that would not have been done a decade before.

Interestingly, it also notes that Robeson was staying in a suite at the Hotel Duluth, then the city's best hotel, and the one where Paul Block stayed when

---

10. "A Celebrated Case," *Duluth Herald*, n.d, 1921.
11. *Duluth News-Tribune,* June 29, 1936.

in town.[12] The story even quoted playwright Eugene O'Neill as having praised the young Robeson as "a Negro with great ability," and having encouraged him to keep at it.

That was remarkably progressive for that day. However, placed next to the Robeson story was another, best described by its headline:

'Y' MINSTREL SHOW TONIGHT

Vaudeville Acts Will Follow 'Black Face' Presentation.

This seems profoundly insensitive, in an era in which a Democratic governor of Virginia and a liberal prime minister of Canada had their careers seriously threatened after charges surfaced that they had dressed up in "blackface" in their youth.

Were any newspaper to juxtapose two stories like this today, it would be easy to believe that there was a deliberate racist agenda at work. But 1931 was a very different era, something that is critically important to remember whenever the present attempts to assess the past. Minstrel shows certainly promoted racist stereotypes – but they also sometimes lampooned whites and

---

12. An amusing anecdote unrelated to the main theme of this book is that early in the morning of August 18, 1929, a hungry black bear smashed though the plate glass of the hotel coffee shop, marauded around, and started up the stairs before a policeman shot and killed it. Paul Block and his wife Dina were sleeping in the hotel at the time, according to Block family legend. But oddly, neither Block-owned paper mentioned it the next day. Only the competing *Duluth News-Tribune* had the story, and it did not mention Paul Block.

were not universally condemned by the Black community; they sometimes provided Black performers with high-paying jobs.

It's worth noting too, that the most popular radio show then – and for many years thereafter – in both the Black and white communities was Amos 'n Andy.

Beyond the headline, the story isn't really even a story, but mainly a laundry list of the vaudeville act and the names of high-schoolers who were to take part.

The Duluth newspapers were, possibly, as racially progressive as times would allow. When four white children under the age of seven pushed a Negro child off a pier to his apparent drowning death in 1934, they noted the race of the children, but didn't ask whether race might have been why they thought that it was all right to do such a thing.

The Great Depression profoundly affected all newspapers in the 1930s, and Paul Block, while continuing to be solvent, increasingly found himself spread too thin. Finally, in June 1936, he sold both Duluth papers to the Ridder brothers, who would eventually form half of the famous Knight Ridder newspaper chain.

Even viewed across nearly a century, it is clear that Paul Block made them vibrant – better and more energetic newspapers in virtually every way, and while he may not have crusaded for racial justice in what was virtually an all-white town, he did firmly oppose the Klan in an era when it was the height of its popularity and power.[13]

---

13. To the extent that Paul Block's newspapers had a serious journalistic flaw, it didn't have to do with race, but with his coverage of Franklin D. Roosevelt, who he had initially liked but developed an intense distaste for after he saw the full extent of his New Deal policies. This caused the coverage in all his newspapers of FDR's presidential election campaigns to be extremely slanted; any reader dependent on them for news would have concluded that Alf Landon was headed for a landslide victory in 1936, when in fact FDR won the greatest electoral college landslide since James Monroe. Block had also convinced himself every time that Roosevelt was certain to lose; perhaps the only time he ever looked ridiculous was in his front-page editorial in all his papers the day after the 1936 election, which FDR won by an electoral vote of 523 to 8: "We cannot believe that the result of yesterday's election is to be construed as an endorsement of the New Deal in its entirety," he wrote. A more ringing endorsement would be hard to imagine.

5

Memphis: Recognizing a Black Hero

When a negro lies bleeding to death, there is no other call than that of humanity.

— Memphis News-Scimitar, July 1925

Paul Block bought the *Memphis News-Scimitar* in February 1921, just weeks after he bought the *Duluth Herald;* he was reportedly able to do so because of the money he got from liquidating his interest in the *New York Evening Mail.*[1]

On paper, buying the Memphis newspaper made a lot of sense. The city was prosperous and growing fast – it had increased in population from barely 100,000 at the turn of the century to 162,351 by 1920, and would be more than a quarter-million by the end of the decade.[2] The newspaper was one he knew well; he had been its advertising representative and a major stockholder since before World War I.

In fact, the newspaper's previous publisher, Bernard Cohn, reportedly said that the *News-Scimitar,* a paper founded in the 1880s, would have gone

---

1. Brady, *The Publisher,* 172.
2. Campbell Gibson and Kay Jung, *Historical Census Statistics on Population Totals By Race, 1790 to 1990,* U.S. Census Bureau, February 2005.

out of business if it hadn't been for Block securing big national advertisers including Ford, Chevrolet, and Coca-Cola, to buy ad space.[3]

Though the *News-Scimitar* was in intense competition with the older *Commercial Appeal* and a weaker Scripps-Howard paper, the *Press,* it was highly respected, had a healthy circulation of 42,000, and was well-positioned to grow.

Block, as usual, threw himself into building the paper and increasing circulation by doing everything from sponsoring contests and tennis tournaments to flying the newspaper daily into Helena, Arkansas, fifty-five miles away. This was seen as revolutionary at the time. Aviation was still in its near-infancy; it was five years before Charles Lindbergh managed to cross the Atlantic.

But as Paul Block correctly predicted, air delivery would soon become commonplace. Fast regional delivery was especially important in Memphis, the unofficial capital of the "Mid-South" and a city that bordered on both Arkansas and Mississippi.

For many years, in fact, Memphis was also seen by many as "the most important city in Mississippi," and after the *News-Scimitar's* demise, the rival *Commercial Appeal* would, for decades, be the largest circulating paper in Mississippi as well as in Tennessee.

Tennessee was attractive to northern businessmen like Paul Block for another reason: it was seen as one of the states of the more progressive "Upper South," which was ripe to move away from cotton and the legacy of the Civil War to a more progressive, modern business outlook. For years, ever since the last union soldiers left in 1877, the "Solid South," still resenting Reconstruction, had voted solidly Democratic.

But by 1921, some saw signs that things might be changing. Slowly and quietly, the Republican Party was gaining a toehold among business classes in larger southern cities. Tennessee itself had broken from tradition by voting Republican for president in the Harding landside the year before, and Block had to be hopeful that would continue.

It's important to remember again, that a century ago the Republican Party was seen by a few farsighted business leaders in the South as the party of progress, the party in favor of moving the region beyond its traditional cotton economy.

Republicans, including Paul Block, also tended to be in favor of better and more decent treatment for African-Americans. That didn't mean they

---

3. Brady, *The Publisher,* 172.

thought that they were ready for anything like fully equal status. Block's own sentiments may have been best expressed in an editorial in his *Duluth Herald* that attempted to explain the Klan.

"The original Ku Klux Klan, though lawless and an outlaw, had some excuse for being. Government had failed through a combination of politician carpetbaggers and negroes, just out of slavery, given power too soon."[4]

That was historically too simplistic. But though it may not be politically correct to say so, it seems likely that many people newly out of bondage, held until 1865 in a situation where learning how to read and write was illegal, may have needed a learning curve before they were fully ready to enact legislation or administer governments. When he arrived in Tennessee, Block seems to have thought he could persuade Memphians to help African-Americans improve their lives and become more fully capable citizens.

But what he didn't realize is that there are three "states of Tennessee," as the state flag with its three stars makes clear. East Tennessee is more like Appalachia, much of it is in the Eastern Time Zone, and its largely hardscrabble farmers were basically unionist and Republican. Middle Tennessee, a region of rolling hills which revolves around Nashville as its center, is today the country music capital of the world. In Paul Block's time it was the seat of government and the state's major universities. But Western Tennessee, where Memphis is the capital, was really part of the cotton south, the home of Nathan Bedford Forrest, early Klan leader and virulent white supremacist. The "War Between the States," as Southerners preferred to call it, had started only sixty years before Paul Block bought the *News-Scimitar.*

Reconstruction had ended barely forty years before Block arrived. The South was not ready in the 1920s to embrace tolerance and more opportunities for Blacks. Tennessee itself recorded more lynchings after Reconstruction – 251 victims, 204 of them Black – than South Carolina, and the three states where the *News-Scimitar* circulated – Arkansas, Mississippi and Tennessee – had well over a thousand lynchings.[5]

Memphis also had a fair percentage of African-Americans in its population – then about 38 percent – than did any other city where Block ever owned a newspaper.

Most of them lived in fairly wretched conditions. Paul Block wrote occasional editorials pleading for Memphians – and the entire Republican Party – to do more to help their Black citizens. But these seem to have been

4. "The Ku Klux Klan: A Snake To Be Stamped Upon," *Duluth Herald,* July 2, 1922.
5. Tuskegee Institute Archives.

ignored – or met with reaction from resentment to open hostility – including among some in the *News-Scimitar* newsroom. [6]

But then a Memphis story came along that captured the nation's attention – and which one might have thought offered a chance to change local attitudes about race.

On May 8, 1925, members of the Mid-South Society of Civil Engineers, in town for a big annual meeting, had piled into two excursion boats for an outing that was supposed to be part work and part pleasure; they were going to view a major engineering project underway down the river. They never made it. One of the ships, the *Norman*, had been overloaded and soon capsized, throwing scores of people into the water.

Tom Lee, a thirty-nine-year-old Black laborer from Memphis, was the only possible help in sight; he was coming up the river in a twenty-eight-foot wooden skiff, returning to Memphis after dropping his boss off at a job in Helena, Arkansas. Though he could not swim, he gallantly went to work saving the lives of those who had been thrown into the water.

He managed to haul thirty-two people, many of them half-drowned, aboard his battled old boat, which was named the *Zev*. He ferried them to the riverbank, going back repeatedly until there were no more to be saved.

Twenty-three people drowned, some trapped in the overloaded boat when it capsized. A few others managed to swim to shore or were rescued by other small boats.

But the real hero was plainly the modest, soft-spoken Tom Lee.[7]

This was a good news story if there ever was one, and instantly, both the city's major newspapers, the *Commercial Appeal* and the *News-Scimitar*, jumped on the story. For a few days, it was all Tom Lee, all the time – and Paul Block's newspaper was not about to be outdone by the competition.

Two days later, the *News-Scimitar* ran an editorial praising Tom's heroism, though in somewhat patronizing tones: "Tom probably wouldn't care for a medal, nor would the adoption of resolutions commending his heroism interest him in the least."

Instead, the newspaper advised that, "we don't know what the rule of the government is about giving pensions to civilians, but if there is no rule against it, Tom ought to be made comfortable for life – and if there is a precedent against it, this is a favorable time to break it," the editorial concluded.

Later, a columnist for the paper argued that Tom should be given the

---

6. Brady, *The Publisher,* 179.
7. For a good modern account of Tom Lee's heroism and its aftermath, see Michael Finger, "Tom Lee: A Hero's Tale," *Memphis Magazine,* May 1, 2014.

Carnegie Medal for Heroism. Despite the editorial acclaim, the coverage in the news columns was marked by racial stereotypes and condescension unimaginable today.

"Tom is only a black, kinky-haired negro," a front-page story in the *News-Scimitar* said two days after the tragedy. "But he proved he had red blood in his veins."

"I didn't do no more than any other 'nigger' would have done," the hero was quoted as saying, adding. "I'm goin' to church Sunday mornin' and evenin'. I always prays Sunday for forgiveness of my sins foh de past week," he supposedly added.

Indeed, whenever Tom Lee was quoted in the *News-Scimitar,* his speech was rendered as something straight out of an Uncle Remus tale.

Additionally, whenever Lee or any other Black citizen was referred to in the paper, only his first name would be used on second reference, as if he were a small child.

What Paul Block thought of this is unknown, though it is known that he increasingly didn't see eye-to-eye with his Memphis editors on many things, including racial issues, and his call to treat African-Americans with more dignity was meeting with increasingly stony hostility. Undaunted, he arranged to take Tom Lee to Washington to meet President Calvin Coolidge, who was a close friend.

The *News-Scimitar,* naturally, reported on this in detail, complete with a front-page picture on May 31, 1925, of a somewhat uneasy looking Tom Lee shaking hands with President Coolidge while a beaming Paul Block and George Morris, editor of the newspaper, looked on.

Later, when the hero got back to Memphis, the *News-Scimitar* reported that he had been "sho tickled" to get back home. He reportedly said that the president "done shuck ma han', treated me jes lak white folks." Lee did say he had been horrified by a suggestion that he go on-stage to talk about his heroic deed.

"Ah done say, 'Gemin, Ah's jes' a cawn field, river-running nigger from Memphis!' Ah shore ain't gwine to appear on no stage."

After that, Tom Lee passed fairly quickly from history. He never got a Carnegie Medal, but the Engineers' Club of Memphis, some of whose members he had saved from drowning, led a successful campaign to raise money to buy Tom a house.[8]

The city didn't settle a pension on him immediately, as the *News-Scimitar*

---

8. Finger, "A Hero's Tale," *Memphis Magazine.*

suggested, but did give him the best job it had available for a Black laborer: they made him a 20-cent per hour garbage man, a job he held until he retired in 1948, at which point he was granted a larger pension than usual.

Bizarrely, years later, the city named a Black-only swimming pool after Tom Lee, a man who couldn't swim and was famous for an accident in which people drowned. After Lee died in 1952 the city erected an obelisk commemorating his good deed and calling him "A Very Worthy Negro." It was destroyed by a freak windstorm in 2003. (A more tasteful modern sculpture showing Tom in his boat replaced it.)

Paul Block, however, faced a storm of criticism and hate mail for his celebration of Tom Lee. Even though the Black hero had been made to seem and sound like a real-life Stepin Fetchit in the news columns of the *News-Scimitar*, many Memphians, including leaders of the Ku Klux Klan, were angry that he had been so lionized.

They hated that Block had taken him to the White House, and they sent the publisher a huge volume of hate mail. Nor did race relations seem to be getting better in Memphis, despite editorials continually urging more tolerance.

Two months after Tom Lee's heroism was touted, Andrew Jordan, a Black switchman on a Memphis railroad, was badly injured in an accident, losing an arm and a leg and bleeding to death. Two ambulances were called and arrived but refused to take Jordan to the hospital because he was Black, and they were white-only rescue vehicles.

By the time an ambulance arrived that would accept African-Americans it was too late. The *News-Scimitar* covered this outrage in a series of front-page stories in July 1925 that indicated how deep the city's racism went.

"I'm not promising I would carry negro emergency cases," J.J. Collins, the proprietor of one funeral home and ambulance service said. "It all depends… what's all this rumpus about, anyway?"[9] Frazier Hinton, the owner of another ambulance service, said, "My men would render first aid to a dying dog, in order to save the animal's life. But consideration must be given to established precedent," which evidently meant dogs, yes; Black people, no. The previous day, another front-page story had quoted many Memphis physicians as denouncing the callousness of the ambulance drivers.

"Refusing help to that man was one of the most inhuman things I ever heard of, coming as it did right after Tom Lee's heroism," another doctor said. Other physicians agreed – but evidently none were willing to be identified by

---

9. "Ambulances Are to Aid All," *Memphis News-Scimitar*, July 22, 1925, 1.

name.

Paul Block's *News-Scimitar* then ran one of its most courageous editorials on race. Noting that Memphis's acting mayor had said that the city couldn't compel white firms to convey Black people in their ambulances, the editorial said, "he may be right, but he is only half right." The newspaper then suggested the city tell the ambulance firms, "We are going to take away all your privileges unless you agree to give aid to any emergency case, regardless of religion, race or color."

If Memphis did that, the editorial suggested, "the ambulance firms would be ready to get in line pretty quickly." If that weren't enough, the paper suggested that the real factor motivating the ambulance drivers was not race, but greed.

Ambulances in Memphis at that time were all owned by funeral homes. They made no money doing emergency runs, but if the patients were to die afterwards the ambulance firm that tried to save them would presumably be hired for the funeral.

"We might as well be frank about this ambulance business... White firms do not bury negroes. Therefore, there is no chance for profit in hauling an accident victim who happens to be a negro. When a negro lies bleeding to death, there is no other call than that of humanity," the editorial went on, asking plaintively, "How long will the citizens of this community tolerate such a state of affairs?"

Sadly, the answer took longer than Paul Block was prepared to wait. On top of his failure to improve race relations, he was also facing increasing hostility for his attempts to win support for the Republican Party. Tennessee had swung back to the Democrats the year before, despite a national landslide for his friend President Coolidge.

Additionally, despite the *News-Scimitar*'s opposition, a corrupt Democratic machine led by "Boss" E.H. Crump was in firm control of Memphis and would remain so for well over a decade after Paul Block's death.[10] Disillusioned, Block sold the *News-Scimitar* to the Scripps-Howard newspaper group in 1926. They promptly combined it with their *Memphis Press*, to form the *Memphis Press-Scimitar*.

That was to be Paul Block's last foray into owning a newspaper below

---

10. Oddly, unlike most southern politicians in his era, "Boss" Crump was not against Blacks voting, and handed out just enough patronage to make sure they voted for him. Tom Lee, however, said after he met President Coolidge that he would happily vote for Paul Block if he could.

the Mason-Dixon line. "My grandfather advised my father never to have a business in the South," Allan Block, chairman of the board of Block Communications, told this writer in 2019.

"Racial attitudes were, I am sure, the main reason."[11]

What is clear is that while he did own a newspaper in Memphis, Block not only tried to make it the best modern paper he could, he did attempt to improve racial attitudes and conditions for Black residents in the five years he was there – even though that likely wasn't good for business. He may not have succeeded.

But he tried, and that was far more than most publishers in his time.

---

11. The world has changed greatly since 1926 and Paul Block's heirs have returned to the South, though they have never had another newspaper there. Their MaxxSouth broadband subsidiary now includes two cable television systems in Mississippi, one of which is in an area where the *News-Scimitar* once circulated.

6

From Lancaster to Los Angeles

The nation's economy was booming by early 1923; the painful recession that followed World War I had ended, and Paul Block was forty-seven years old [1] and at the peak of his powers. By then he owned papers in Newark, Duluth, and Memphis – all acquired in the previous seven years – and was heavily involved with all of them.

Given his hands-on involvement, and the national newspaper advertising business he also ran, one might suppose that he would have more than had his hands full. But when the opportunity to buy the *New Era* in Lancaster, Pennsylvania, arose he jumped at the chance, and plunged into a vigorous, small-town newspaper war.

Lancaster, in the heart of Pennsylvania Dutch country, has almost exactly as many people – 59,322 in 2010 – as it did in the five years that he owned what was then the city's largest paper. But it is now a very different place today.

Downtown Lancaster is gentrified, somewhat hip, and extremely diverse; one-sixth Black and nearly a third Puerto Rican. During the 1920s, the

---

1. He was thought to be forty-five. Though during his lifetime he claimed to have been born in 1877, it was later established that he had been born in what was then Konigsberg, East Prussia, in 1875.

Black population trickled up only from 1.7 to 2.1 percent. While the Great Migration from the cotton fields of the South to the factories of the North was in full swing, Lancaster did not have the sort of large and well-paying manufacturing operations that tended to attract migrants.

But the city was historically significant in terms of race. It had been the home of James Buchanan, the president who refused to take any action in 1860 and 1861 when he was still in office and the southern states began to secede. Lancaster, coincidentally, had also been the home of Buchanan's contemporary and enemy, Thaddeus Stevens, the abolitionist firebrand who scandalized 1860s Washington by living with a Black woman.

Both are buried in Lancaster and had been long dead by the time Paul Block came to town. But the Ku Klux Klan was very much alive in Pennsylvania, and in Lancaster. In fact, the Klan operated so openly in the city that it had its own downtown offices in 1924, and eventually split into two major factions, the traditional and the "reformed" Klan.[2] The *New Era* covered the Klan fairly thoroughly – but did not often denounce it on the editorial pages, though I haven't been able to locate every issue.

There may have been a number of reasons for this. While Paul Block was heavily involved in trying to improve the newspaper, he seldom spent much time in Lancaster and seems to have directed most of his advice on editorial direction toward adding more light features and a color comics section – rare at the time.[3]

He seems to have left most of the specific decisions about editorial coverage to his editor, Oliver Keller, who seems to have been highly respected though only in his mid-twenties. The *New Era* was in an intense battle for circulation, and for advertising revenue as well.[4]

Could either Keller or Block or both have been less than aggressive in denouncing the Klan because they feared alienating, and losing, subscribers? That may be impossible to determine. The newspaper did not shrink from covering the Klan, however.

The story about the local Ku Klux Klan breaking into factions was very long, especially for a small newspaper in that era. It began on the front page and included a great deal of detail, including the precise address of the Klan's downtown office.

---

2. *Lancaster New Era,* June 18, 1924, 1.

3. Brady, *The Publisher,* 213.

4. The newspaper frequently and proudly ran what are known as "house ads" touting their audited circulation, which it reported as 22,886 on April 14, 1924, "nearly as much circulation as the other two Lancaster newspapers combined."

The story ("Ku Klux Klan Splits In Two Factions Here") was locally written but lacked a byline. That was not uncommon in many newspapers at that time, though it is possible that a byline was withheld for a reporter's protection. The Klan office had been disguised as a publishing company, and it's hard to imagine that the KKK was happy that the *New Era* revealed that or the real name (Sam Rich) of their "King Kleagle."

Readers were also told that the new "reformed Klan" had abolished the mask and hood (except for special initiation purposes) and would be an entirely democratic organization, no longer taking justice into its own hands but would instead only work through "the properly constituted authorities."

Whether the "reformed" and supposedly law-abiding Klan ever amounted to much in Pennsylvania, or elsewhere, is extremely doubtful. The Klan was a significant presence in the Keystone State and throughout much of the North until 1925, when David Stephenson, the leader of the Klan in Indiana, was convicted of the brutal rape and murder of a young woman,[5] something that shocked the nation.

But if the *New Era* didn't win any awards for denouncing the Klan (ironically, the *Memphis Commercial Appeal* had won a public service Pulitzer in 1923 for its coverage of the Klan), it did not shrink from covering it, or other racial outrages.

Barely two months after Block bought the paper it ran a front-page story,[6] evidently from an unattributed wire service, reporting that the Florida House of Representatives had passed a bill outlawing the bullwhipping of convicts on work gangs in that state; such convicts, as the story hinted, were usually "negroes."

The article mentioned that those opposed to ending the practice feared the "inability to control negro convicts without the use of the lash."

Whether the article caused indignation among Lancaster readers at so barbaric a practice taking place in the faraway South is hard to say. The story also mentioned, almost in passing, that the death by whipping of a North Dakota man named Martin Tabert had sparked calls for investigating alleged brutality in the work camps, which often involved convicts leased by private industry to the state.

Ironically, the death of Tabert, a twenty-one-year-old vagrant who was white, would become a huge story that would win the *New York World* the 1924 Pulitzer Prize for public service, lead to a famous poem by Marjory

---

5. Joshua Rothman, "When Bigotry Paraded Through the Streets," *Atlantic Monthly*, December 4, 2016.

6. *Lancaster New Era,* April 19, 1923.

Stoneman Douglas, and end the practice of leased convict labor in Florida. (Given the standards of the day, it seems unlikely that the case would have attracted attention if Tabert had *not* been white.)

Pennsylvania, for all its heroism and sacrifices in the Civil War (think Gettysburg) may not have been in the practice of whipping Black convicts to death, but it was scarcely a trendsetter in what would later be called civil rights. The very next day after the Florida whipping story the *New Era* noted on its front page that an "equal rights" bill, introduced in the state legislature by a Representative Asbury of Philadelphia, "has been indefinitely postponed by the House Judiciary Committee."

Readers were told that Asbury was a "negro," but it didn't bother to mention his first name. (It was John, and he was a Republican, as were nearly all Blacks in that day.) The bill, an evident forerunner of the Civil Rights Act of 1964, would have, it noted, assured "equal rights to persons of all races and religions in all places of amusement, hotels and similar establishments."

Asbury, the story noted, introduced a similar bill in 1921, which passed the House but died in the state senate. Perhaps trying again was seen as an exercise in futility.

As the decade wore on, the *Lancaster New Era* did not shrink from covering Klan violence. In one especially shocking story, the paper published a photo at the top of the front page of July 16, 1924, showing the naked back of a white minister from Michigan who had been mysteriously kidnapped, tortured, and branded with a large "KKK."[7]

The newspaper, especially in 1924, prominently covered Klan activities, from a major clash between Klansmen and locals in April that left two dead in Lilly, a mining town near Johnstown, to a strange incident in Lancaster on July 26, when a large group of Klansmen showed up in front of Lancaster's convention hall and simply stood there, eyeballing and perhaps trying to intimidate anyone who considered entering. [8]

In another odd incident two weeks before, on Sunday, July 13, a group of more than a hundred Klansmen showed up at Lancaster's Laurel Street Mission, where The Rev. J.B. Bowermaster was holding religious services, evidently on the theme of patriotism.

The Klansmen, dressed in full regalia, filed in docilely, filling the hall, leaving other Klansmen who couldn't fit in outside. They sang the *Star-*

---

7. The case of the Rev. Orrin Van Loon drew nationwide attention and led to considerable controversy over whether the Klan had actually done it; the consensus is that it had.

8. *Lancaster New Era*, July 28, 1924.

ROBED KNIGHTS GUARD LOCAL HALL

Spangled Banner and *America* with the congregation (one presumes it must have been all white) and then each Klansman tossed a dollar in the collection plate.[9]

Was this a strategy to make the Klan seem like good, patriotic folks? The newspaper didn't offer an opinion.

The *New Era* also covered an outbreak of Klan violence in the mining town of Lilly, near Johnstown, that April, where two local men were killed reportedly when the local townspeople attacked a group of Klansmen.

Reporting on the trial, however, while sporadic, made it seem as if the local people were more to blame than the Klan.[10] It is possible, again, that the decision to handle the Klan gingerly was made by local editors.

Paul Block clearly had given his managers instructions to do everything they could to increase circulation and advertising and beat the competition – two other newspapers owned by the long-established Steinman family.

---

9. *Lancaster New Era.* July 14, 1924, 1.
10. *Lancaster New Era,* April 7 and June 17, 1924, 1.

Again, it seems possible, even likely, that his executives wanted to do nothing to alienate what may have been a significant pro-Klan readership. It is also uncertain to what extent Block paid attention to how the *New Era* handled Klan stories. He was running three larger papers and a national advertising business at the same time, and as we will later see he clearly hated the Klan – and demonstrated that in a huge story that would later win the Pulitzer Prize.

Paul Block's *New Era* made virtually no attempt to report on Lancaster's miniscule Black community. But to its credit it did fairly frequently report stories about racial violence, Klan-generated and otherwise. Soon after he bought the paper, Block ran an editorial that defended the ability of Blacks to hold executive positions and attacked those who would keep them down.

The editorial, "Tuskegee Terrorism,"[11] criticized the South for its attempts to keep African-Americans from becoming more than common laborers: "It resents and tries to block his efforts to improve himself."

What sparked the editorial was the decision of the federal veterans' bureau – a forerunner of today's Department of Veterans' Affairs, or VA – to open a new hospital for Black veterans at the Tuskegee Institute, the famous Black institute of higher learning, and to put Black physicians in charge of it.

This seemed completely sensible to the *New Era*, which evidently never dreamt of questioning segregation itself. "The hospital is entirely and exclusively for negroes; it is operated in conjunction with a negro school; there is no reason why competent negro physicians should not take charge of it."

Unfortunately, the editorial continued, "The Ku Klux Klan in Alabama does not like the idea of any colored people placed in positions of executive responsibility, and it has staged demonstrations and sent threats ...".

"Tuskegee Institute, founded by Booker T. Washington for the advancement of his race, has been doing a splendid work, but the South evidently can't reconcile itself to it," the editorial said, concluding acidly, "The South sometimes boasts that it knows how to treat the negroes whereas the North does not. Perhaps – but it is just such treatment as this that accounts for the rapid trek to the industrial centers of the North and West."

Whether Paul Block himself suggested this editorial or was directly involved in its writing is not known, but it seems perfectly plausible, based on sentiments expressed in many of his other papers. (Whether anyone in

---

11. *Lancaster New Era,* July 1923.

authority ever noticed the editorial is not known, but in the end, despite Black protests, the government put a white physician in charge of the Tuskegee veterans' hospital.)

Two years later in Memphis, as we have seen, the publisher got a sharp and painful lesson in just how much white southerners resented any attempt to make too much of even a Black hero like Tom Lee.

Five years after he came to Lancaster, Paul Block attempted to buy out the Steinman family so that there would be only one newspaper in what was a rather small city. They refused to sell, and instead made an offer to buy the *New Era*.[12]

Block thought it over and agreed, selling the paper in early 1928 for the equivalent of a little more than $14 million in 2019 dollars. He had recently bought out his partners to become sole owner of the *Newark Star-Eagle*, and had purchased both the much larger *Pittsburgh Post-Gazette* and *Toledo Blade*.

He likely needed the cash. There is no question that competition had made all three papers better, and the Steinmans, who had been his competitors, promptly hired him to be their special advertising representative.

By the time he said goodbye to Lancaster, however, the publisher had his hands full with newspapers in five much larger cities – with more to come.

Brooklyn

Paul Block never owned a newspaper in Manhattan, though he always dreamt of doing so, and it was clear that for him, as for so many others in his day, that New York City was the most important city in the world, and the place he always considered home.

He did, however, own the *Newark Star-Eagle* for more than two decades, and in August 1928, just months after selling the Lancaster paper, he managed to buy the *Brooklyn Standard-Union*, saying simply, "I wanted a newspaper nearer my home."[13]

Historically, it was a good fit in many ways.

New York City had been virulently anti-Republican, anti-Abraham Lincoln, and the scene of huge draft riots during the Civil War: and the *Standard-Union* was founded in 1863 by William Berri, a Lincoln supporter who wanted a paper for those who supported the union and the war.[14] His heirs owned it until they sold it to Paul Block.

12. Brady, *The Publisher,* 215.
13. Brady, *The Publisher,* 278.
14. Brady, *The Publisher,* 377.

Brooklyn was, in 1928, not only the most populous of New York's five bustling boroughs, but had only lost its status as a separate city thirty years before. Brooklyn then had more than 2.5 million people – almost as many as today – and three fiercely competitive newspapers, including the *Brooklyn Eagle* and *Brooklyn Daily Times,* both of which had more circulation than the *Standard-Union.*

Ethnically, Paul Block's Brooklyn was a very different place. Today, Brooklyn is perhaps the most diverse place in the nation. Contemporary estimates in 2019[15] are that Brooklyn's non-Hispanic white and Black populations are virtually equal, with about 36 percent each. Hispanics make up nearly 20 percent; Asians, 11 percent.

But Brooklyn in 1930 was more than 97 percent white. Blacks were less than three percent of the population, or only 68,921 people. They were largely laborers and domestic servants and would not become a major demographic presence until long after Block sold the paper to the rival *Brooklyn Times* in March 1932.

Paul Block was an ardent supporter of women's rights and women voting, and the *Standard-Union,* like his other papers, was soon adding more coverage of women as well as features for them.

However, coverage of African-Americans in all the Brooklyn papers was, as you might expect, sparse. Interestingly, it picked up during the campaign of 1928, one in which Paul Block, who was usually fiercely Republican in presidential contests, had perhaps more divided loyalties than in any other such campaign in his adult life.

He felt, as he always did, that the nation was better off when it was governed by Republicans, and he ultimately endorsed Herbert Hoover, who won in a landslide.

But he was also both an admirer and a personal friend of the Democratic nominee that year – Al Smith, the governor of New York, who was the first Roman Catholic nominated for president. (Block, like Smith and unlike Hoover, was a fierce opponent of Prohibition.) Anti-Catholicism played a big role in that campaign; many people actually believed that if Smith won, America would be governed by the Pope.

The *Standard-Union* repeatedly denounced religious bigotry in its editorials, and on Hallowe'en that year took a swipe at the Ku Klux Klan and the Anti-Saloon League at the same time, suggesting that the "most effective line of attack" would be to push a program of sound policies and ignore "the

---

15. *World Population Review,* 2019.

dry league, the bigots or the klansmen."[16]

Paul Block had also expressed the feeling in Memphis that the Republican Party hadn't been doing enough to help African-Americans, even though nearly all Blacks who could vote then registered their loyalty to the party of Lincoln, something that began to change only with the Great Depression and the New Deal.

And in an interesting news story five days before the election,[17] "Colored Voters Swing to Smith; Bishop Charges Race Mistreated by Republicans, at Rally," the paper reported that a group of 500 Black New Yorkers listened as The Rev. Reverdy Ransom told them they had been taken for granted by the Republican Party.

"We have kept the Republicans in power for the last sixty years, and now it is our right to vote as we think best so our entire population may benefit from it," he said. "If Al Smith wins, we'll have more recognition than we've had in the last five years."

On the other hand, the newspaper reported two days later that Norman Thomas, the perennial socialist candidate, spoke to an audience three times the size of the Black voters' meeting, and attacked the Democrats for racial bigotry after praising them for having the courage to nominate a Roman Catholic. When it came to race, he told them, "Here your party is the chief, though not the only sinner… ."

"I have seen paid advertisements in southern papers appealing to racial intolerance in such a way that you would not dare to let the Negroes of the north, whose votes you want, see or read them if you can possibly help it."

Thomas went on to urge the chairman of the Democratic National Committee to urge southern Democrats to "let people vote on the basis of personal qualification, not color." That would not happen for more than thirty years.

Al Smith did get considerably more Black votes than other Democrats had, though a number of imprecise surveys showed a large majority of African-Americans still voted Republican. Not until four years later, during the depths of the worst depression in history, would a majority of Black voters follow the advice of *Pittsburgh Courier* publisher Robert Vann and "turn Lincoln's picture to the wall."

Following the election, references to Black voters in the *Standard-Union* were few and far between. A story buried deep in the newspaper on Dec. 2,

---

16. *Brooklyn Standard-Union,* October 31, 1928, 5.
17. *Brooklyn Standard-Union,* November 1, 1928, 25.

1929,[18] is indicative of what attitudes were towards Brooklyn's Black citizens. The article tells the story of one Mrs. Ella Morris, who had fallen afoul of her local neighborhood association in what was then an exclusive and somewhat ritzy area. She had been taking in boarders in defiance of a local rule, and the Lefferts Manor Association sued her to make her stop.

In retaliation Morris nailed up a sign saying the property was for sale or rent "to colored people only," which was clearly done to horrify her antagonists.

Then she announced that a Black family, "a very large one, seven adults and five children," had taken an option on the property, and was about to move in, renting it with an option to buy. "Just what action the Lefferts Manor Association will take to put a stop to this invasion… remains a mystery," the newspaper said.

Alas, what finally happened is lost to history, though it isn't at all clear whether there was ever a mysteriously large and wealthy black family at all.

While the *Brooklyn Standard-Union* wasn't especially notable for its coverage of racial issues, it might have been able to provide the key to a historical mystery that became a political issue nearly a century later, when Donald Trump ran for president.

Might have, that is, if Paul Block had bought the paper more than a year before he actually did. While he owned the *Standard-Union,* Block pressed his reporters and editors to cover major news in Manhattan and the other boroughs as well – and he was usually very sensitive in all his cities to any local news regarding the Ku Klux Klan.

On May 30, 1927, an immense Memorial Day march of a thousand robed Klansmen took place in the adjacent borough of Queens – and soon turned into a vicious, all-out brawl. Seven men were arrested. The next day, six of them were charged with various offenses from disorderly conduct to felonious assault.

One, however, was released. He was twenty-five-year-old Fred Trump, father of the future president of the United States. He lived in the Jamaica neighborhood of Queens where the brawl had broken out… was he indeed a member of the Klan? Was he, instead, a local guy who was trying to stop the Klan or at least the violence? Or could he have been a bystander who just got swept up when the police moved in?

Nobody has been able to answer those questions. Fred Trump died in 1999. Donald Trump, who wasn't born until years later, has vehemently

---

18. "Negro Family Has Option on Morris House; Seven Adults, Five Children May Take Midwood Street Home," *Brooklyn Standard-Union,* December 2, 1929.

denied that his father had anything to do with the Klan, or that he was even there that day.

Despite that, it has been clearly established that the Fred Trump who was there and was arrested was indeed President Trump's father. Newspaper accounts at the time said that the Klansmen came to the march hooded and in full Klan regalia.

What we don't know was what Fred Trump was wearing. Had Paul Block owned the *Standard-Union,* might he have insisted on a more thorough reporting job?

We will never know. We do know, however, that Paul Block's editorials and assistance may have changed history in a way he probably later regretted:

Flash back to that 1928 campaign. Al Smith's campaign for president was doomed; he even narrowly lost his home state of New York, which had elected him governor five times. Since he couldn't run for re-election and run for president, he tapped a protégé to run instead: the forty-six-year-old Franklin D. Roosevelt.

As I have noted, Paul Block was clearly ambivalent about the presidential contest that year. But he had no doubt about the race for governor. For once in his life, he gushed over and idolized the Democrat – FDR. "The political magic that lies in his surname, the glamour that surrounds his personality, the forcefulness and sincerity that are his in public address… make him an ideal choice," the *Standard-Union's* editorial said on October 2. Nor was that all: more pro-Roosevelt editorials were forthcoming.

On October 30, exactly a week before the election, another editorial ran under the headline, "The Roosevelt Wave Grows." It said, in part, "so unusual is the opportunity presented by this man's candidacy that it would be a (negative) story about the people of this city," if FDR didn't win New York City by a handsome majority.

"To watch the spread of the Roosevelt plurality will be one of the pleasantest tasks of the aftermath of the election."

How invested was Paul Block in Franklin D. Roosevelt? So much so that he bought an expensive ad the day before the election in the *New York Times*, a paper whose circulation dwarfed that of the *Standard-Union*. In it, he proclaimed that FDR "possesses the honesty, the courage, the idealism, the ability and the leadership so necessary for the office to which we now have the courage to elect him."[19]

Election Day came. Smith, probably to Paul Block's surprise, lost in a

---

19. Brady, *The Publisher,* 282.

tremendous landslide, even losing his beloved New York State by more than 100,000 votes. Not until sometime the next day was it clear that FDR had squeaked through, with 2,130,193 votes to 2,104,129 for Republican Albert Ottinger.

That was, and remains, the closest gubernatorial election in New York history. Did Paul Block's intense support make the difference? That's hard to say.

But it is clear that had FDR not won that election, he never would have been elected president of the United States four years later, and American history would have been devastatingly different. Different, and likely worse, for many Blacks who would benefit from New Deal programs, even if treatment was by no means equal.

Ironically, in one of history's many ironies, Block and Roosevelt would end up bitter enemies, and remain so until the newspaperman died on June 22, 1941.

Milwaukee

There was a reason they called the decade the "Roaring Twenties" – it really did seem as if its booming prosperity would never end, and Paul Block was no exception to that.

On October 1, 1929, readers of the evening *Milwaukee Sentinel* were greeted by a front-page letter from their new publisher headlined "An Announcement."

It began: "With today's issue the *Milwaukee Sentinel* passes to my ownership ... .It is my purpose to publish a paper which will be fair, just and independent in all its relations to public questions and to the people, no matter what may be their political beliefs, their race or religion." It continued on to praise the staff and the historic legacy of the paper, and pledged to devote his "best efforts" to the publishing of it.

There was controversy then in publishing circles as to whether Block actually owned the *Sentinel,* or whether the real owner was William Randolph Hearst, who had owned it before and to whom Block eventually sold the paper in September 1937.

That has never been satisfactorily settled, though Frank Brady dealt with it in great detail in his biography of Paul Block.[20] However, the answer isn't really relevant in this case. Block clearly ran the paper, and made vast changes

---

20. Brady, *The Publisher,* 295-305.

in everything from how news was covered to its distribution. He improved and modernized the typeface and design to make the *Milwaukee Sentinel* resemble his other papers.

Most importantly, he set the tone for coverage and determined what positions the paper would take, and even often wrote – and signed – editorials, which often appeared on the front page. His pledge of ethnic fairness was undoubtedly sincere, but when it came to race, Milwaukee in 1929 had a Black population that was especially miniscule.

Milwaukee today – the city proper – has virtually the same population as it did in Paul Block's day; there were 578,249 residents in 1930, and 594,833 in 2010.

Yet the makeup of that population has drastically changed. The 2010 census found Milwaukee to be 40 percent Black; 37 percent non-Hispanic white, with Hispanics and a growing Asian population accounting for most of the rest.

However, six months after Paul Block assumed control of the *Sentinel*, the census would show a virtually all-white city – 98.6 percent, very few of them Hispanic. African-Americans were barely over one percent – 7,501 people. Asians and Native Americans combined amounted to fewer than 500 people.[21]

Most papers, as we have seen, systematically ignored even much larger Black communities, and the afternoon *Sentinel* wasn't much different. While the newspaper occasionally carried stories about efforts to pass anti-lynching legislation[22] and took a dim view of the Ku Klux Klan, stories involving race were few in number.

That may be because both Klan activity and membership had greatly diminished nationwide by 1929. The local Black population was virtually invisible to *Sentinel* readers. The only exception I could find was on the front page of the sports section on February 16, 1935, under the banner headline "Five Lincoln Cagers Ruled Ineligible." The paper ran individual photos of five high school basketball players who were disqualified because of a technicality as to where they had gone to school.

The top two were African-American, identified by the *Sentinel* as "Vernal

---

21. "Historical Census Statistics On Population Totals By Race, 1790 to 1990," and "By Hispanic Origin, 1970 to 1990, For Large Cities And Other Urban Places In The United States."

22. See, for example, the *Milwaukee Sentinel,* April 18, 1937, 2. The paper's denunciation of the Klan was most energetic in August 1937, when Hugo Black was nominated and speedily confirmed as an associate justice of the U.S. Supreme Court.

Britton, colored guard," and "Pat Goggana, colored forward." The story had nothing to do with race, and neither the student-athletes nor their coach were accused of wrongdoing.

Still, it is curious that the sportswriter felt the need to inform readers that two of the young men were "colored," especially since their photographs made that clear.

Apart from sports, when it came to the newspaper, Milwaukee's Blacks were indeed invisible. When Ethel Waters, even then a nationally famous jazz and blues singer, came to town to star in the play "Rhapsody in Black" on March 27, 1932, it was big news in Milwaukee's struggling Black weekly newspaper, the *Wisconsin Enterprise-Blade,* which also ran ads for the performance. But the *Sentinel* ignored it.[23]

Paul Block likely had little time to think about Milwaukee's small Black community; he was running six other papers when he bought the *Milwaukee Sentinel.* In addition, Hearst asked him to simultaneously run his Milwaukee paper, the *Wisconsin News,* in something that looked like one of the Joint Operating Agreements, or JOAs, that became common in the newspaper industry later.

As the Depression gradually deepened, Block was consumed with efforts to keep the papers profitable and arguing with Hearst over the best way to raise advertising revenue. By September 1937, the economic and personal stress had become too much.[24]

He sold the newspaper back to William Randolph Hearst, though he continued to handle national advertising for the newspaper.

However, there is clear evidence that while Paul Block may not have been focused on the plight of America's racial minorities, he was very much in favor of defending immigrants and their right to stay in this country.

Just as he was taking over the *Sentinel* in 1921, the story broke of two Finnish girls, evidently teenagers, who had immigrated to Canada with their father. After he died, they innocently crossed the border into Michigan, and later ended up in Milwaukee.

They evidently loved America and wanted to become citizens. But when they went to apply for naturalization papers, they discovered they hadn't

---

23. The *Wisconsin Enterprise-Blade,* which lasted until 1961, made a gallant effort to cover the state's small Black population, but during the Great Depression sometimes didn't even manage to appear weekly. "How the Negro press has advanced with such meager support from the real business firms of our group [Blacks] is a wonder," an editorial on January 16, 1932, lamented.

24. Brady, *The Publisher,* 304, notes that Block says the stress of the Milwaukee operation "was making him sick, that he was actually suffering from headaches."

entered the country legally, and immigration officials told them they'd had to be deported.

Paul Block instantly jumped on this. He whipped off a signed, front-page editorial proclaiming that "America is Their Home."[25]

"What a travesty… to send from the country two young women whose dilemma was revealed only by their earnest desire to prove themselves better Americans!" he wrote. "They should be allowed to remain, and if the present law prevents this, the law should be changed." This time, his editorial did have an effect.

Many readers wrote in to support the Finnish sisters; Paul Block appealed to President Herbert Hoover and his secretary of labor, and they were eventually allowed to stay. Some might wonder if that was a stunt designed to build circulation.

Block was, indeed, always looking for ways to boost readership, and he surely was aware that a story like that might well help. But it seems clear that he was completely sincere. Though he let people think he had been born in Elmira, N.Y., he had in fact been born in Konigsberg to parents who had themselves fled Lithuania.

He knew very well what it was like to be a small child coming to this country, and throughout his career he stood up for immigrants and their rights.

Shortly after buying the *Duluth Herald,* he had a lead editorial sarcastically skewering those who claimed to be "one hundred percent Americans," most of those who did, he noted, "sound more Prussian than American." As for those who were isolationist, and sneered at the thought of America helping war-torn Europe, they were people with ideals that "are not even one percent of what Americanism ought to be."[26]

On at least one other occasion, he expressed support for immigrants learning English as rapidly as possible, but cautioned that they should not be forced to do so.

Paul Block strived to better himself all his life, to achieve the American dream, and clearly admired others who tried, and hated bigots, most notably the Ku Klux Klan.

And as he was wrapping up his affairs in Milwaukee, his best reporter was working on a story that would take on both the Klan and the man who was becoming the politicians he most liked to hate, Franklin D. Roosevelt.

The result would embarrass FDR and the Klan – and win a Pulitzer

Prize.

Los Angeles Herald-Express

The last newspaper Paul Block ever bought was the *Los Angeles Herald-Express,* an evening paper which was the oldest daily published in the city. This was also the paper he owned for the shortest amount of time; he took control of it on Valentine's Day, 1931, and, as the Great Depression deepened and he felt his energies were needed elsewhere, sold it to William Randolph Hearst in early December of the same year.

Though there were always rumors that Block was a front man and that Hearst really owned the newspaper all along, Block certainly didn't act like that was the case. He threw his energies into the paper, adding new features, beefing up baseball coverage (always a Block trademark), crusading against gangsters and movies that glorified them, and raising circulation from 90,000 to 140,000.[27]

Adolph Ochs, the owner and publisher of the *New York Times,* said during a March vacation to Los Angeles that he admired what Paul Block had done with his papers elsewhere, and was happy for journalism that he owned the *Express.*

There was, however, essentially no coverage whatsoever of local or national African-American events in the *Express.*[28] That differed little from the other papers in town, except for the Black-oriented *California Eagle.*

That was likely due in part to Los Angeles' still-miniscule Black population, which was barely three percent of the total.[29] But there was possibly a feeling, there as elsewhere, that "we don't have to worry about covering events" like the "Colored Air Circus" that drew 40,000 spectators to Los Angeles, and an earlier African-American air show that attracted 15,000 to the city's airport, then called Mines Field, on Labor Day.

But there may also have been a feeling, according to newspaper historian Dave Davies, a professor at the University of Southern Mississippi, that "white editors may have justified non-coverage of events like that (the

---

27. Brady, *The Publisher,* 323.
28. About the only time Blacks were mentioned in the *Express* while Paul Block owned it was in police story descriptions, as in the front page story from November 14, 1931, "Officer Shoots Bandit Suspect."
29. The census counted 38,894 Blacks in Los Angeles in 1930 out of a total population of 1,236,048.

Colored Air Circus) by thinking, "oh, that's something black newspapers will catch."

Paul Block was pro-women's rights, as always. When some legislators suggested prohibiting the employment of married women by state or local governments, Paul Block denounced the idea on March 5, 1931, in a fiery, signed front-page editorial. "It would be a step backward from the progress the world has made in giving women equal rights with men."

"Thousands of women have prepared themselves by long years of study for teaching positions," he wrote. "There is no fairness and no sound economic excuse in depriving them of their jobs and the state of their training."

To be sure, the publisher likely gave little, if any, thought to the fast-growing city's small Black population. When he wasn't fighting crime and dirty movies, his signed editorials were largely designed to boost the city's economy ("Buy In Los Angeles") or aimed at better government.[30]

But there was never any hint of prejudice against minority groups or reaction against immigrants. On the contrary, a March 14 editorial, "Undesirable Aliens" – about a bill aimed at curbing the flood of illegal immigrants into California – showed marked skepticism that the bill would work – and no hostility at all towards the undocumented aliens, who it said found it easy to get past "the weak and in some cases indifferent guards of the immigration service." Calling out some for hypocrisy, it added:

"Until confronted by an unemployment problem, few paid attention to the influx of unqualified aliens. There was work aplenty, and the aliens, those that had come to seek only honest labor, demanded only low wages." That was not only a principled, but gutsy stand, given that this was the era when some cities in California erected billboards saying "Jobless Men Keep Going. We Can't Take Care of Our Own."

---

30. California – and Los Angeles – had grown at an almost unimaginable pace throughout the 1920s. The city more than doubled in size, and the state gained nine seats in Congress after the 1930 census.

7

Winning a Pulitzer, Exposing the Klan

Paul Block may not have spent a lot of time overtly campaigning on behalf of better conditions for African-Americans. But he hated their greatest enemy – the Ku Klux Klan, whose popularity had soared to alarming levels nationally in the 1920s.

Klan support, which had reached four to five million in the mid-1920s, had receded dramatically, thanks in part to a series of scandals, and by the summer of 1937 was probably less than 30,000[1] and was no longer a major factor in American life, outside of a few pockets in places like Birmingham, Alabama.

But in August 1937, President Franklin D. Roosevelt had nominated a U.S. Senator from Alabama, one Hugo Lafayette Black, to the U.S. Supreme Court. Today, it takes weeks, usually months, to confirm any nominee to the nation's highest court. But the political world was a very different place then.

Battles over court nominees were seldom ideological, and even if Republicans had been inclined to oppose Black, who had been a reliable supporter of FDR's New Deal, there was very little they could do about it. Thanks mostly to the enormous Roosevelt landslide the year before, the

---

1. "The Ku Klux Klan, a brief biography," from The African American Registry, https://aaregistry.org/ (accessed August 30, 2019).

GOP had been reduced to a mere sixteen Senate seats.

Additionally, while the U.S. Capitol was air-conditioned, most of official Washington wasn't, and most members wanted to adjourn and go home. FDR formally nominated Black on August 12, and he was confirmed on August 17, sixty-three to sixteen.[2]

For years, there had been rumors that Black had been a member of the Klan, rumors that the senator directly addressed, saying he had nothing to do with the Klan since he arrived in the Senate ten years earlier.

And his integrity was championed by a famous maverick conservative Republican, William Borah, the "Lion of Idaho," and the ranking member of his party on the Judiciary Committee. During what were very brief Judiciary Committee hearings, Borah roared, "There has never been at any time one iota of evidence that Senator Black was a member of the Klan. He has said in private conversation… that he was not a member of the Klan, and there is no evidence to the effect that he is. What is there to examine?"[3]

But Hugo Black, in fact, really *was* a secret life member of the Klan.

And two men were more willing to examine the evidence: Paul Block and the best reporter who ever worked for him, a character worthy of a Mark Twain novel, a corncob pipe-chewing 51-year-old chicken farmer named Ray Sprigle.[4]

Several days after Black was nominated, Block was on vacation in Saratoga Springs, N.Y., attending horse races, playing cards, and relaxing. He was playing bridge one night with Herbert Bayard Swope, the former editor of the *New York World*, when Swope asked a question that stunned Paul Block.

Did he know that Hugo Black was a member of the Ku Klux Klan?[5]

Block knew instantly that Swope had to know what he was talking about. Viewed by some as the greatest reporter of his time, Swope had won the first-ever Pulitzer for reporting in 1917, for a series called "Inside the German Empire." Four years later, he directed a team of *World* reporters in

---

2. A highly unusual seventeen members abstained, some because they were Roman Catholics and were concerned that Black might in fact share the Klan's bias against them; others, apparently, because they objected to Black's ardently pro-New Deal views.

3. Roger Newman, *Hugo Black: A Biography,* New York: Pantheon Books, 1994.

4. Sprigle was a fascinating man who, had he worked for a newspaper in New York or Washington, would likely have been nationally famous. Journalist Bill Steigerwald's excellent *30 Days a Black Man: The Forgotten Story That Exposed the Jim Crow South,* Guilford, CT: Lyons Press/Globe Pequot, 2017, is largely an account of an even more amazing Sprigle story (see Chapter 9) but also is the closest thing we have to a full biography of Sprigle.

5. Brady, *The Publisher*, 453-60.

an investigation of the Klan that had won a Pulitzer Prize.

Paul Block, as his biographer noted, knew a potential blockbuster story when he saw one. He left the game, returned to his room, and called the *Pittsburgh Post-Gazette*, a newspaper of which he had become publisher in 1927. He reached the night editor, told him to call Sprigle, and get him on the next plane to Alabama.

To be fair, Block likely had multiple motives for wanting to expose Hugo Black's membership in the Klan. He did loathe the Klan, to be sure. But he also had come to loathe Franklin D. Roosevelt, his New Deal, and all it stood for.

Though the men had once been good friends, and Block had been enthusiastically supportive of FDR throughout his first year in the White House, that quickly faded.

By 1935, he thought the New Deal was leading the nation to "socialism and even communism,"[6] and deeply regretted having helped elect FDR governor in 1928.[7]

So when the chance appeared to expose an ardent New Dealer as a Klansman, Paul Block had a variety of reasons to enthusiastically jump at the opportunity – although his son, Paul Block, Jr., later told a researcher, "Father just wanted to go after Black because of the Klan – he just abhorred it."[8]

There were plenty of other people who had suspicions about Black and the Klan, and a number of newspapers sent reporters to Alabama to see what they could find out.

None of them, however, had the tenacity of Sprigle. He managed to find out that a disbarred lawyer named James Esdale had been Grand Dragon of the Alabama Klan during the years in which Hugo Black had supposedly been an active member.

Within hours, he had craftily begun to win Esdale over. Paul Block had told Sprigle to spare no expense in getting the story, and that helped. He did

---

6. Coverage of a Paul Block speech to the Toledo Bar Association, *Toledo Blade*, December 3, 1935.

7. Block may also have helped make him president. Accounts vary, but it seems likely that during the Democratic National Convention of 1932 Block telephoned William Randolph Hearst and told him that Hearst's preferred candidate, John Nance Garner, couldn't be nominated, and that if Hearst didn't support FDR, the Democrats would again nominate Al Smith or Newton Baker, both of whom Hearst loathed. The lord of San Simeon then signaled to the California delegation to back Roosevelt. See Brady, *The Publisher*, 395-98.

8. Newman, *Hugo Black: A Biography*, 247.

his research and interviewed former Klansmen, as any good reporter would do.

But he went far beyond that. When he went to see Esdale at his office, it was full of other reporters, and the old Klan leader wasn't talking.

Sprigle left. But that night, he took a cab and went to Esdale's farm – after first securing a supply of the Alabamian's favorite chewing tobacco. Esdale let him in and agreed to talk to him – but only about chickens, unaware that, by an incredible coincidence, Sprigle was not only a reporter, but a chicken farmer. Esdale had a financially struggling son who he was thinking of setting up with a flock of Leghorns.

"I wouldn't do that, if I were you," Sprigle told him. Leghorns were good egg-layers, all right, but too skinny for good eating. Wyandottes were better birds. They were meaty and tasty, and prolific egg-layers as well. Esdale was evidently impressed.

But Sprigle knew a lot more than chickens. He had turned up that James Esdale lost his law license because he had set up a fake corporation to handle bail bonds for his own clients.[9] Slyly, he said it was a shame that somebody powerful hadn't put in a word to prevent the lawyer from being disbarred.

Someone, say… like Hugo Black. "After all, you are responsible for the election of Hugo Black to the U.S. Senate," the reporter said.

That was the right trigger to get the man talking.

For the next two and a half hours, Esdale poured out his resentments. Though Black had been the Klan's candidate when he was first elected to the U.S. Senate, once he got there he seemed to have forgotten where he came from.[10]

He failed to give any jobs to Klansmen, did nothing to help the secret society that had so helped his career, and, indeed, when Esdale had lost his license to practice law for illegally soliciting legal business earlier that year, Black had refused to help him.

In other words, the former Grand Dragon felt he owed his former friend – who by then had been confirmed as the U.S. Supreme Court's newest justice – nothing.

Esdale invited Sprigle to his office the next morning, opened a safe, and showed the reporter documentary proof that Black had been a life member of the Klan. In a cloak-and-dagger plot twist, Sprigle, evidently fearing that

---

9. Clarke M. Thomas, *Front-Page Pittsburgh: Two Hundred Years of the Post-Gazette*, Pittsburgh: University of Pittsburgh Press, 2005, 174-75. Also, see Sally Kalson, "Chickens Had Role in Sprigle's Pulitzer," *Pittsburgh Post-Gazette*, September 16, 1986.

10. Newman, *Hugo Black: A Biography*, 149.

someone in Alabama's legal system might stop an out-of-town reporter from carrying documents out of state, used the *Post-Gazette* to give the Esdale family an all-expenses-paid trip to New York City.

All they had to do was smuggle the documents in their luggage. They did; Sprigle met the Esdales at their hotel, took possession of the papers, and on September 13, 1937, the *Pittsburgh Post-Gazette* and the *Toledo Blade* splashed a huge exclusive across their front pages under the headline, "Justice Black Revealed as Ku Klux Klansman."

Sprigle, a master of what we today might call purple prose, began his lead story by writing "Hugo Lafayette Black, Associate Justice of the Supreme Court, is a member of the hooded brotherhood that for ten long blood-drenched years ruled the Southland with lash and noose and torch, the Invisible Empire, Knights of the Ku Klux Klan."

Moreover, he reported, Black was a life member of "the mysterious super-government that once ruled half a continent with terror and violence."

There was much more, including photocopies of letters and documents signed by Hugo Black that proved his Klan membership. Paul Block also contributed a signed editorial, headlined "Klansman on Court Insult and Danger to Country."

To his credit, the publisher began, "We cannot believe that Mr. Roosevelt knew that Senator Black was a member of that horde of narrow-minded bigots," but went on to say that "after the many rumors" surfaced following the nomination "would it not been fair to have had a hearing so all information could have been brought out?"[11]

Franklin D. Roosevelt himself might well have agreed. "The Klan thing hit me like a clap of thunder," he told Lister Hill, an Alabama congressman who soon would follow Black to the U.S. Senate. "It knocked me out of the damn chair."[12]

While there were many reasons to be aghast at the thought of a Klansman on the nation's highest court, Paul Block made it clear in his editorial that the hooded order's murderous record of violent racism came first. This was soon after the U.S. Supreme Court had twice reversed the convictions of the 'Scottsboro Boys," nine Black teenagers who now are acknowledged to have been falsely accused in 1931 of raping two white women on a train in Alabama. "Only a short time ago, inflamed race prejudice in a southern town, Scottsboro, was about to railroad a group of colored boys, some held on very flimsy evidence," Block wrote.

---

11. *Toledo Blade*, editorial page, Monday, September 13, 1937.
12. Newman, *Hugo Black: A Biography,* 250.

"The Supreme Court intervened and set aside the verdict of the state – holding the trial had not been fair because colored people had been barred from serving on the jury. "Would a Klansman have taken the same firm stand for equal civil rights for the colored race?" he asked, clearly implying the answer was no.

The story went on for day after day as Sprigle presented more documents and evidence. Paul Block had announced three days earlier that he had a major blockbuster story on Hugo Black coming, and it ended up on the front pages of virtually every newspaper in the country. Black was on a European vacation when the story broke, where he spent much of his time avoiding the hordes of reporters who pursued him.[13]

When his ship finally arrived in Norfolk, Virginia, on September 29, it was mobbed by reporters. William Mylander, a reporter in Block's Washington bureau, came on board and approached the justice with copies of all the articles from the *Post-Gazette*.

"Mr. Justice, would you care to look them over?" he asked.

"Suppose you take them back to Mr. Block," he said, and closed his cabin door.[14] The Gallup polls showed that after the *Post-Gazette* articles, 59 percent of the American people thought Black should resign from the court.

But the next night Hugo Black made a nationwide speech in which he said only "I did join the Klan. I later resigned. I never rejoined," and provided no explanation.

He also said that his record in the U.S. Senate "refutes every implication of racial or religious intolerance." The speech, which was only eleven minutes long, won the country over, including the famous irreverent and iconoclastic journalist H.L. Mencken.

Ever the reporter, Ray Sprigle had returned to Birmingham, Alabama, to listen to the speech with a few former Klan leaders. According to Roger Newman, Hugo Black's biographer, when Black finished one of them said with a grin, "That ain't the way we heard it the night he almost kissed our feet in gratitude for making him senator, is it?"

But while the new justice had denounced what he called a "planned and concerted campaign against him," he denied nothing that Sprigle had written.

The next year, Ray Sprigle won the Pulitzer Prize for "his series of articles, supported by photostats of the original documents, exposing the one-time membership of Mr. Justice Hugo L. Black in the Ku Klux Klan."

---

13. When one reporter did manage to ask him about the stories Hugo Black said, "I don't see you, I don't know you. And I don't answer you," which didn't help his image.

14. Newman, *Hugo Black: A Biography*, 255.

Paul Block had to have been proud – especially because he was directly responsible for making the stories happen. Back in Pennsylvania, the local Ku Klux Klan was less happy; they burned a huge cross near the driveway that led to Sprigle's farm and added a tombstone that said "Kastigate the Kallous Kallumniator Ray Sprigle."[15]

Nobody knew it then – but Ray Sprigle would go on a decade later to write an even greater story, one that went far beyond anything a major newspaper had ever done to expose the nature and scope of racial bigotry in much of this nation.

Sprigle's award for the Hugo Black stories would be the only Pulitzer Prize Paul Block's papers would win in the publisher's lifetime.

Less than four years later, he fell ill and was found to be in the final stages of both pancreatic and liver cancer. The immigrant boy who had been astonishingly successful in the world of newspaper publishing would die on June 22, 1941.

That was the day Nazi Germany invaded the Soviet Union. That, it is worth noting, is where Paul Block was born, and he would likely have been murdered along with most of Europe's Jews had his parents not come to America.

Hugo Black went on to serve on the high court until eight days before his death in 1971, outliving both Block and Sprigle, who survived many risky reporting adventures only to be killed in a taxicab accident one night in December 1957.

Conventional wisdom holds that despite his Klan membership, Black went on to become one of the U.S. Supreme Court's most liberal justices. But that wasn't completely true. He wrote the majority opinion in *Korematsu v. United States,* the infamous 1944 case that upheld the internment of Japanese Americans during World War II.

While he was part of the unanimous 1954 *Brown v. Board* decision outlawing school segregation, Hugo Black also maintained that there is no such thing in the Constitution as a right to privacy, and thought warrantless wiretapping was legal.

Whether the *Pittsburgh Post-Gazette's* exposure of his Klan past had any effect on his later rulings favoring civil rights can't be known. What is certain, however, is this:

Within weeks after taking up his duties as an associate justice, Hugo Black appointed a Jewish law clerk, hired a Roman Catholic secretary, and

---

15. Bill Steigerwald, *30 Days a Black Man: The Forgotten Story That Exposed the Jim Crow South,* Guilford, CT: Lyons Press/Globe Pequot, 2017, 17.

had an African-American messenger. Whether calculated or not, those three appointments would have been anathema to the Invisible Empire – sent a clear signal to the nation that Hugo Lafayette Black was completely done with the Ku Klux Klan.

8

Changing Leadership in
a Changing World

Though Paul Block's health had been rocky throughout the 1930s, Block's sons, Paul Jr. and William, had little time to prepare to take over the company.

Though he had long since become a skilled businessman, the Great Depression slowly took more and more of a toll. William Block, usually called "Bill," noted in his privately published *Memoirs of William Block*, "1938 was probably the worst year of the depression for the newspaper industry."[1]

There's little doubt that business worries added to Paul Block's stress. By 1940 he had sold all of his newspapers except the *Toledo Blade* and the *Pittsburgh Post-Gazette*. Though his sons were then fully adult, they likely had little sense how tough things were.[2] "Father was not one who confided his difficulties. He was not a person who would talk frankly to the family about things like that," Bill Block remembered.

Nor was their father candid with his sons about his health, though it may not even have been clear even to him how ill he was until very late. What was

---

1. Though the worst effects of the Depression had begun to improve by the time Franklin D. Roosevelt became president in 1933, an ill-advised tightening of fiscal and monetary policy caused a severe "recession within the Depression" in 1937-38.

2. William Block, *Memoirs of William Block*, Toledo Blade Communications, 1990, 52-53.

clear was that World War II was raging and the United States was likely to be drawn into it, sooner or later. Universal conscription had begun, and in early 1941 Bill Block, who had always wanted to be in the newspaper business, was in the process of working a series of jobs in both Toledo and Pittsburgh that would teach him all phases of the business.

He was about to start a stint in the editorial department of the *Blade*, when he was notified that he was about to be drafted.

His older brother, who would eventually become the senior publisher in the family firm, was also destined to become a newspaper man, but his first love was science. In early 1941 Paul Block, Jr., was working on a doctorate in organic chemistry at Columbia University in New York City, which put him physically closer to his parents.

On March 12, 1941, Paul called his younger brother in Toledo and told him that he had learned that their father had cancer. He began failing fast, and toward the end Bill obtained a ten-day furlough so that he could be home when his father died.

Barely three months later the brothers found themselves co-publishers of the *Toledo Blade* and the *Pittsburgh Post-Gazette*. Not only were they not ready to take up their duties, they were in a world that was being ripped apart by war.

World War II would change many things and challenge many assumptions, including ideas about race. The new publishers were their father's sons and revered his memory – but they were also members of a new generation, born in a new century.

Their father had no real opportunity for higher education, but thanks to his success both his sons had been educated at two of the nation's finest institutions – the Hotchkiss School in Connecticut and Yale University.

The elder Paul Block, as his grandson Allan noted, "clearly had a basic sense of fairness that was passed on to my father and uncle, a sense of fairness and decency unusual in a publisher of his day."

When it came to racial justice, that sense would be tested soon. It may now seem hard to believe, but the U.S. Armed Forces were strictly segregated during World War II, to the absurd extent that a white soldier who had been wounded and had lost blood was not supposed to be given a transfusion if only African-American blood was available.[3]

---

3. President Harry Truman finally issued an executive order ending segregation in the U.S. Armed Forces on July 26, 1948. He issued the order because he believed, almost certainly correctly, that a bill doing the same would be filibustered and killed by southern Democrats in Congress.

Following his father's death, Bill Block had returned to the U.S. Army. After the attack on Pearl Harbor less than six months later, he was assigned to an anti-aircraft regiment in Camp Stewart, Georgia, which, as he said in his privately published memoir, "was the army's first small step towards racial integration. It had all Black enlisted men, Black warrant officer, Black chaplains, but all the rest of the officers were white."

In fact, that pattern wasn't unusual at all. While enlisted men were rigidly segregated, it was informal army custom to place white officers – especially southern white officers – in command over Black soldiers, because it was believed they had more experience in "handling Negroes."[4]

Nor is it likely that anyone would have chosen a base in rural Georgia to conduct an experiment in integration. Bill Block, who had become a second lieutenant, got a lesson in the reality of tensions between the races one afternoon in the fall of 1942.

His anti-aircraft regiment had been alerted that it was soon to be sent overseas and, as a result, instead of eating in a separate officers' mess the officers were sent to eat with their enlisted men, though two tables were reserved for the officers and their chaplains. One day Bill Block came in and sat down with a Black lieutenant and two Black chaplains, and a captain from Mississippi came in and ordered them to move.

This troubled Block. When the Mississippian did it again the next day, he challenged him, saying "don't you think we ought to fight one war at a time?"[5]

This was observed by a colonel, whose solution was to transfer both the Black lieutenant and Bill Block out of the regiment, presumably as troublemakers.

"My uncle told me that's why he never got overseas while the fighting was going on," John Robinson Block said.

His father, Paul Block, Jr., was not drafted during the war. He was already in his thirties when it began and soon afterwards his leg was badly broken in a skiing accident. After he finished his doctorate in 1943 he went to Toledo, where he simultaneously headed the company and pursued original research into organic chemistry.

Though chemistry was his first love, he was the oldest son and felt the need to learn every facet of the newspaper business.

Though he was less outwardly demonstrative than his younger brother, Paul had a strong belief in being fair. According to family lore, when Second

---

4. Stanley Nelson, dir., *Soldiers Without Swords* (1999; Half Nelson Productions).
5. Block, *Memoirs of William Block*, 63-64.

Lieutenant Bill Block was transferred from a base in Georgia to one in California in 1943, he had to leave his car behind. The *Blade's* general manager sent a Black handyman, Theodore Spurlock, to Georgia to drive it home. However, anyone who knew anything about the Deep South should have known it wasn't safe for a Black man to be driving a nice car in rural Georgia.

Within a few miles Spurlock was arrested on suspicion of theft and thrown into a rural jail. Paul Block, Jr. (or PBJR, as many of his employees called him), either called, or possibly got Grove Patterson to call, Ohio governor John W. Bricker, whom Patterson knew very well.

Bricker called his counterpart in Georgia, Ellis Arnall, the nation's youngest governor and, fortunately, the closest thing to a liberal on race there was in deep southern politics at that time. The handyman was soon freed and on his way home.

"Father was so incensed at that manager's stupidity, and that he had risked that man's life, that he fired him," John Block told me.

On another occasion, there were rumors that a Black employee at the paper had syphilis and other employees demanded she be fired. Paul Block, Jr., angrily refused.

Grove Patterson, the legendary editor who had worked for his father for many years, remained a driving force behind the editorial page until his death in 1956. However, Paul Block, Jr., was conscious that it was a different era and began subtly putting his stamp on the paper. He authored a rare bylined story of his own, explaining how the atom bomb worked on the day of the Hiroshima bombing.

As the war was winding down, he hired the famous theatrical and industrial designer Norman Bel Geddes, the creator of the stunning Futurama exhibit at the 1939 World's Fair, to create *Toledo Tomorrow*, a stunning exhibit Bel Geddes called "an inspiration for future living" – a vision of the city in 1995.[6]

Bill Block's return to civilian life after the war was delayed. He ended up being sent to Korea, which had been occupied by Japan, and did not return to the States until mid-1946, when he moved to Pittsburgh. Almost by osmosis, it was decided that Paul Block, who was four-and-a-half years older, would be the senior partner, and each of the brothers would live in one of the cities where their father had left them newspapers.

"Paul had settled in Toledo and had been running the company from there for the five years since father's death. I thought it was probably logical that I go to Pittsburgh."

---

6. Though few in New York knew it, Bel Geddes was a native of nearby Adrian, Michigan, and had once lived in Toledo.

That arrangement continued for the rest of both men's lives.

But the world was changing rapidly and dramatically in many ways, including when it came to relations between the races. Not long before their father died, Bill Block was doing a stint at the *Toledo Blade,* and was trying to start an orchestra.

He helped bring Paul Robeson, the great baritone, in for a concert. Block called the Commodore Perry hotel, then the best in Toledo, and asked if they could arrange a suite for Robeson, who was already nationally famous.

But when he called the general manager, there was a long pause. Eventually, he said, "Yes, we can arrange a suite for Mr. Robeson, but we would prefer if he would eat in the suite and not the dining room." Bill Block, then twenty-five, was stunned.

Embarrassed, he called the great singer's manager, who said "That's all right; we accept that." Writing his memoir half a century later, Bill observed, "That's the way it was in 1940."

But that began to change dramatically and quickly, and both brothers were well aware of and highly sympathetic to the change. The next year, even before the United States entered the Second World War, African-Americans threatened a protest march on Washington – and won a major victory from the federal government.

African-Americans wanted an end to discrimination and segregation in the armed forces and threatened to rally 100,000 Blacks to huge march on Washington to pressure President Franklin D. Roosevelt to do just that.

FDR wasn't willing to go that far. But a protest march was the last thing he wanted, especially since it might easily have turned violent. And he was willing to negotiate a compromise: for the first time ever, he issued an executive order banning discrimination in federal vocational and training programs, and, more importantly, also banned discrimination in defense industries working on government contracts.

He also created a Fair Employment Practices Committee that was supposed to make sure the president's order was upheld. That was enough to get A. Philip Randolph, the leader of the March on Washington movement, to cancel the march.

Pressure for equal rights and equal treatment continued and accelerated throughout the war – and one of the main forces behind that change was in Pittsburgh.

But it was not the *Post-Gazette,* but the *Pittsburgh Courier,* which by that time had surpassed the *Chicago Defender* to become the nation's most influential Black newspaper.[7] During the war, the *Courier*, which had achieved a national circulation with editions in many cities, cleverly launched what it called its "Double V Campaign" – for victory over fascism abroad – and victory over racism at home.

The campaign was enormously popular nationally, and perhaps especially in Pittsburgh, where the Black population was steadily growing during the war.[8]

"You had Double V baseball games, Double V flag-waving ceremonies, Double V gardens… there was even a Double V song," Patrick Washburn, professor emeritus of communication at Ohio University noted in Stanley Nelson's documentary, *Soldiers Without Swords*. "The *Pittsburgh Courier*, which was looking for circulation, played this to the hilt." But it was more than an extremely effective promotional campaign.

"The Black press really was a catalyst for the Civil Rights Movement," Washburn added. "I mean you look at the Black papers in that time and they aren't talking about civil rights. They're not using those words, but the things that they're trying to get for the Black community and Black people *are* civil rights.

"If you had not had the Black press… and if you had not had World War II, the Civil Rights Movement would have started at a lot lower level," he later noted.

The *Pittsburgh Post-Gazette* had no involvement in the Double V Campaign, and neither did the *Toledo Blade,* where the Black population, while growing, was less than eight percent when the war ended. But Paul Block's sons knew the world was changing.

So did Grove Patterson, the legendary editor of the *Blade*, who had long served as somewhat of a mentor to Paul Block, Jr. Patterson, as noted earlier, had deeply admired his father, and turned down numerous opportunities for better-paying jobs.

But while he said that from his standpoint as an editor the first Paul Block was "the perfect publisher… mainly interested in one thing, the best possible newspaper that the best available staff could produce, whatever the cost," he wasn't perfect.

---

7. According to Patrick Washburn, a leading expert on the Black press during World War II, the Courier's weekly circulation grew from 190,000 to 350,000 during the war.

8. Pittsburgh's Black population, which had been only 8.2 percent in 1930, climbed to 12.2 percent, or 82,543, by 1950; see the U.S. Census publication, Historical Census Statistics On Population Totals By Race, 1790 to 1990, and By Hispanic Origin, 1970 to 1990, For Large Cities And Other Urban Places In The United States, February 2005.

"To be critical, I would say that his principal weakness was in the field where he thought he was particularly strong… he fancied himself an unusually keen judge of human nature." Patterson, however, thought the reverse was true, noting, "In my opinion, he was too easy with incompetents and even crooks… he would sometimes stick to an associate when other member of the organization knew the fellow was no good."[9]

To what extent Patterson gave Paul Block, Jr., management advice isn't known, but it is clear that he sometimes attempted to raise his conscience on ethnic issues. On July 1, 1938, he wrote to PBJR, then serving a stint in the *Blade*'s Washington bureau.

"I think you will be interested in the enclosed letter from the Japanese embassy," it began. A Japanese diplomat had objected to American newspapers using "Jap" in headlines, or in any other context. Patterson told the younger man that he never thought of it as racist, just as a "convenient diminutive." Nevertheless, he said, "I am forced to give recognition to the fact that an intelligent Japanese regards the terms as offensive, and therefore… I think we ought to discourage its use and I have done so."

One has to wonder whether either man remembered that letter three-and-a-half years later, when Japan struck Pearl Harbor on December 7, 1941.

Patterson was not known as a civil rights crusader –but he was active in Republican politics in a way that would be unimaginable for a newspaper editor today; he nominated U.S. Sen. Robert Taft for president at the 1940 GOP National Convention and was the sort of Republican who remembered that Abraham Lincoln freed the slaves; he still believed his party needed to do what it could for the people Lincoln freed.

Patterson likely suggested to Paul Block that he attend a Kiwanis Club event in Toledo with him on February 12, 1930, to celebrate race relations week. African-Americans were a mere 4.6 percent of Toledo's population then, but an effort was being made to raise funds to build a Blacks-only branch of the YMCA on Indiana Avenue.

Block had already given $25,000 to Toledo's YMCA, but according to Grove Patterson he was deeply inspired by two Black ministers, The Revs. Channing Tobias and B.F. Williams, who spoke eloquently about how greatly African-American kids needed recreational facilities.

When he finished, Patterson later wrote, "Mr. Block sent a note to me: 'After I have left the room, please say that I will give another $5,000 in tribute to the great speech this man has just made.'"[10] That is the equivalent of

---

9. Grove Patterson, *I Like People,* New York: Random House, 1954, 132-33.
10. Patterson, *I Like People*, 134; *Toledo Blade,* February 13, 1930.

$75,690 in 2019 – a sizable sum.

This was also at a time when the Great Depression was beginning to deepen and ad revenue was declining, and Block had his hands full trying to keep his newspapers in Ohio, Pennsylvania, Minnesota, and New Jersey afloat.

Grove Patterson never hired any Black editorial staffers prior to World War II; it is unknown whether he ever considered doing so, though it seems unlikely.

But as the war wound down, he knew the world was changing. In his nationally syndicated column, *The Way of the World*, he noted that while social equality and complete integration might be only a dream… "Economic equality – that's something else again. If a member of the colored race, man or woman, proves just as competent in whatever job as a white man or white woman, (they) ought to precisely have the same opportunity for upgrading, for promotion, for the fulfillment of ambition as a member of the white race."

"There should not be one iota of difference in the manner of selection, placement and respect," he concluded. That was in 1945. The next year, the war over, Paul Block Jr. moved to do something to show that he agreed.

The *Toledo Blade* hired its first Black reporter.

This was, at the time, almost revolutionary. There were then almost no Black reporters in any newsrooms apart from the strictly Black press. The *New York Post* had hired investigative reporter Ted Poston in 1936,[11] but he was almost alone.

The *New York Times* had briefly hired a Black reporter, George Streator, in 1945, something that Arthur Sulzberger had called an "experiment," but it didn't work out. His work was seen as substandard and managing editor Turner Catledge soon fired him.[12]

The *Times* had made a mistake in hiring its first Black reporter; he did not understand journalism's "tradition of objectivity."[13]

Even in the 1950s, a Newspaper Guild survey found that there were only thirty-eight Blacks among the 75,000 people who worked in America's newsrooms. And some, perhaps most, of those were there to cover exclusively

---

11. Poston (1906-74), who spent thirty-three years at the *Post,* complained that tryouts there are elsewhere were rigged to prevent most Black reporters from having a chance. See his obituary in the *New York Times,* January 12, 1974, 36.

12. Susan Tifft and Alex Jones, *The Trust: The Private and Powerful Family behind* The New York Times, New York: Little, Brown and Co., 1999, 276-77.

13. Tifft and Jones, ibid.

"Negro news."

That wasn't the case with William "Bill" Brower, (1916-2004) the son of a South Carolina barber and traveling preacher who, despite poverty, had graduated from Wilberforce University in 1939, taught adult education, and then worked in a series of Black newspapers as a reporter and editor, finally serving stints as editor of the *Baltimore Afro-American's* regional editions in Virginia and Philadelphia.

Patrick Washburn, professor emeritus of journalism and communications at Ohio University, is a nationally recognized expert on the Black press and Black journalists' experiences with white majority newspapers.[14] "Newspapers really didn't start hiring Black reporters till the 1950s, and then only because the civil rights movement, and they found out there were stories they couldn't get otherwise," he said.

For a newspaper like the *Blade* to hire a Black reporter in 1946 was "highly unusual, really exceptional," he said in an interview. Nor was it easy for any of those pioneering Black reporters. "Blacks wanted to come (to the white-owned newspapers) both because of the higher salaries and the much larger audiences they could reach."

"But they often had trouble." *The New York Times'* experience with their first Black reporter was hardly unique. "The Black press was an advocacy press and wrote stories differently. They were often a mix of hard news and opinion" – they had a clear agenda, which was better treatment for members of their race.

On the other hand, he noted, the "white" press had a standard, going back at least to the 1920s, "of attempting to be free of bias, neutral in presenting the facts."

To succeed, a Black reporter had to be able to adopt the conventions of objectivity and do so in a climate where he or she would be under intense scrutiny.

Paul Block, Jr., like Branch Rickey, the baseball executive who brought Jackie Robinson to the major leagues in 1947, wanted to make sure that the first Black to shatter the invisible racial barrier was more than good enough to succeed.

Bill Brower was that man.

Though the details are lost to history, it seems likely that Brower was

---

14. Patrick Washburn's book, *The African-American Newspaper: Voice of Freedom*, Evanston, IL: Northwestern University Press, 2006, is invaluable for understanding the subject and the era.

recruited, or at least invited to apply. What is certain he was very thoroughly vetted.

"He had been thoroughly 'scouted' and we were quite certain we wanted him as a reporter," Paul Schrader, then the *Blade's* managing editor, wrote in 1951.

Bill Brower, however, wasn't so sure he wanted to come; as editor of the *Afro-American* in Philadelphia, he had one of the better jobs in Black journalism. As Schrader noted, he "didn't want to make a mistake and get professionally sidetracked."

Brower had good reason to be cautious.

"Many Black reporters who came from Black newspapers didn't have the greatest experience (when they were hired by major newspapers)," Washburn noted.

"They often felt ostracized, and if they were the only Black reporter, which was usually the case, they felt they had few people in the newsroom to talk to or hang out with," he noted. That may have not been a major concern for Brower, a quietly dignified and self-possessed man who already had a wife and son.

But something else was bothering him. "Black reporters often found themselves relegated to covering only stories about Blacks, or Black events. It was kind of what like happened to women reporters early on; they were confined to the women's pages and society news," Washburn said.

Paul Schrader, then an assistant managing editor, sensed that this was bothering Brower when he was interviewing him. Writing in 1951[15], he remembered "He was reticent until I said quite bluntly: 'If you come to work on the *Blade* you will do so as a general assignment reporter taking assignments from the city editor as they come. We have no intention of using you as the *Blade's* Negro News Editor. We deplore segregation in every phase.'"

"Bill visibly brightened, and enthusiastically replied, 'That's the kind of job I want. When do I go to work?'"

When he actually started isn't clear. Whether it was 1946 or as Schrader remembered it, 1947, Brower was a true pioneer.

True to their word, the *Blade* did not ghettoize Brower. They gave him the same kind of assignments any other reporter would have been given, including, as he continued to prove himself, assignments of gradually

---

15. Taken from a preface Schrader wrote for a reprint of a series Brower wrote for the *Blade* in 1951, "15,000,000 Americans: A personal inquiry into the status of the one-tenth of our population that constitutes what is called 'the Negro problem.'"

increasing complexity.

He covered crime and the courts and won notice for his nuanced and intelligent coverage of education issues; his wife, Louise, was a teacher who later became Toledo's first Black high school principal. As a mark of the newspaper's increasing confidence in him, Brower was sent to New York City in 1949 to cover one of that year's biggest and most sensational stories — the "Smith Act" trial of eleven top leaders of the Communist Party, a major event that was a key milestone in the opening phase of the Cold War.

However, he was also something very rare in America's newsrooms in the early 1950s — a highly skilled, professionally trained journalist who knew African-American issues as few other journalists did, because he was a Black man who had been born in the Deep South, lived in many places in many states in America, and was in a position and had the knowledge to report on that in a way almost no one else ever could.

The *Blade,* as we will see, would put those skills to work in a few years that would provide a series that was ahead of its time — and which the newspaper and Bill Brower would, astonishingly, repeat twice over the next half-century.

The *Pittsburgh Post-Gazette* didn't move as quickly to hire a Black reporter though it was still ahead of most newspapers when Regis Bobonis (1927-2016), a reporter for the *Pittsburgh Courier,* joined its staff in 1955. A Duquesne graduate and World War II veteran, he only stayed six years before moving on to become Pittsburgh's first Black television reporter,[16] and then to a career in public relations.

Other Black reporters and, later, editors would follow.[17]

But years before that, the *Pittsburgh Post-Gazette* and its best reporter would do one of the most stunning, difficult, and dangerous civil rights stories ever.

What is hard to believe is that it wasn't turned into a best-selling book and a movie. What's even harder to believe is that it never won a Pulitzer Prize.

---

16. For WIIC-TV (now WPXI), in which the Block family owned a 50 percent share from 1957 to 1964 when their share was sold to Cox Enterprises. Apart from the *Courier,* the Block family can thus say they hired both the first Black newspaper and TV reporter in Pittsburgh — and it was the same person.

17. By the end of 1952, the *Blade* had six Black employees. Besides Brower, there were two "proof boys" in the dispatch department, Theodore Spurlock, who was then working in circulation, and two women, one a secretarial aid in the marketing department and another who was a clerk in the business office. *Congressional Record,* March 15, 1954, appendix, PA 1982. The names of the Black employees appear as part of a tribute to National Negro Newspaper Week by Congressman Frazier Reams.

9

Pittsburgh: The Pulitzer that Should Have Been

For more than half a century generations of American students have grown up reading *Black Like Me*,[1] novelist John Howard Griffin's account of living as a Negro in the Deep South for a month in late 1959. The book was an instant best-seller, has been constantly in print, and has sold more than 10 million copies.

The author, who was white, underwent a series of chemical treatments to darken his skin, became an instant celebrity and a sort of cultural hero. His book was praised by the *New York Times* as an "essential document of American life," a national must-read.

Black Like Me is riveting. But what the author never mentions is that what he did had been done more than ten years before, in a time and in a way that made trying to pass as a member of a different race almost certainly even more dangerous.

What's more, the pioneer who was ahead of Griffin also authored a book that as Philadelphia author Hugh Gilmore noted in 2015, is by far "the superior work of journalism," but which until recently had been all but forgotten by history.

---

1. John Howard Griffin, *Black Like Me,* New York: Houghton Mifflin, 1961, and in many succeeding editions.

That man was none other than *Pittsburgh Post-Gazette* reporter Ray Sprigle, the reporter who, a decade before, had won a Pulitzer Prize for proving that Hugo Black had indeed been a member of the Ku Klux Klan.

His book was called *In the Land of Jim Crow*,[2] and while it may not have been written with quite the graceful novelist's prose of John Howard Griffin, it is a far richer account of the many faces and evils of racism in the segregated South of that time.

However, the book was in a sense, an afterthought. Sprigle, one of the greatest investigative reporters of his or, indeed, any day, originally did his work as a series of articles for his newspaper. The idea was his.

"I put the suggestion before William Block and Andrew Bernhard, publisher and editor of our *Pittsburgh Post-Gazette*," Sprigle later wrote in his book. "They're both the kind of newspapermen that a newspaperman likes to work for. I didn't have to do too much of a job of selling, and they finally gave me the word to go."

Not everyone at the paper thought this was a good idea. The editorial page editor, Frank Hawkins, himself a Southerner, later wrote that "I thoroughly disapproved of this silly venture into sensationalism, but it was out of my hands and I appreciated Bill Block's motives to combat racial injustice and at the same time, establish a public service reputation for the P-G (*Post-Gazette*.)"[3]

If Bill Block did have any reservations, they probably had to do with the fear that Sprigle might get himself killed, which easily could have happened had southern whites figured out who he was and what he was trying to do. Trying to pass as a Black man in the Deep South was probably almost as dangerous as trying to infiltrate ISIS would be today. But Block and his editors also had to know that when it came to undercover reporting, Sprigle was the best in the business.[4]

During the last months of World War II, he had posed as a black-market butcher to expose how easy it was to thwart rationing rules. He had also

---

2. Ray Sprigle, *In the Land of Jim Crow*, New York; Simon & Schuster, 1949.

3. Frank Hawkins, *That Was Hot Type*, privately printed; cited in "*Front Page Pittsburgh: Two Hundred Years of the Post-Gazette*, by Clarke M. Thomas, Pittsburgh: University of Pittsburgh Press, 2005.

4. As a precaution, Sprigle was to phone his editor at the *Post-Gazette* every two days to let them know he was alive; if they didn't hear from him, they would call the FBI. But as his biographer, Bill Steigerwald revealed, he also took his own precautions. Sprigle contacted a racketeer friend, "Pittsburgh Hymie" Martin, who gave him phone numbers for other friendly criminals who lived in various southern towns. Sprigle was, indeed, an authentic character.

worked as a coal miner during a bitter miners' strike and booked himself into a truly snake-pit-style state mental hospital to reveal the corruption and atrocities there.

He truly had nerves of steel and would need them in the Deep South.

Black Like Me, the book that everyone remembers, mainly shows vignettes of life in some of the South's major cities, as experienced by an author who just plunged in, without many connections, to try to see what life as a Black man was all about.

Sprigle, as was his habit, engaged in meticulous preparation. We now know just what he did and how incredible his achievement was, thanks to a much newer book, *30 Days a Black Man,* by Bill Steigerwald, a retired *Post-Gazette* reporter who came to the paper long after Sprigle's time, but possesses many of his same instincts.[5]

Steigerwald's book, which also serves as a biography of the great reporter, illustrates in fascinating detail how Ray Sprigle, a light-skinned white man, managed his feat of both passing as a "Negro in the Deep South" but also how he got Blacks from all walks of life to trust him when that easily could have gotten them – and him – lynched.

What he did was enlist the help of Walter White, then the executive secretary of the NAACP, who gave him perhaps the best companion and guide imaginable – John Wesley Dobbs, of Atlanta, a "bigger than life" figure who was a major power in Atlanta's Black community (the 'mayor' of Auburn Avenue) and in Black (Prince Hall) Masonic circles throughout the country.[6]

Dobbs was a man who could go anywhere in African-American society and who would be trusted, as would anyone he traveled with.

So it came to pass that Dobbs, driving his "enormous, dark green and chrome 1947 Mercury sedan," and an aging bald, light-skinned Black man named James Rayel Crawford, set off on their tour of the Black south in May 1948.

Except James Rayel Crawford was really Ray Sprigle, his head shaved and his fair skin darkened just a bit by a deep, sunburned tan.

---

5. Bill Steigerwald, *30 Days a Black Man: The Forgotten Story That Exposed the Jim Crow South,* Guilford, CT: Lyons Press/Globe Pequot, 2017. Steigerwald is himself no slouch as an investigative reporter. In an earlier, self-published book, *Dogging Charley* (2013), he exposed that the events in John Steinbeck's beloved classic travelogue *Travels With Charley* were largely fiction.

6. Steigerwald describes Dobbs as looking "like a cross between a movie star and the Ambassador of Ethiopia" who "played hardball with white politicians, taught black history to college kids, gave speeches on national radio, and had his own parking space" at baseball games.

A decade later John Howard Griffin would dye his skin deep brown before setting out on his journey of passing for Black. Sprigle tried, with the assistance of chemists at the Mellon Institute, but reported in entertaining detail that "in more than six months of searching I couldn't find any lotion or liquid that would turn a white hide brown or Black" without killing him.[7] Finally, he came to realize something.

Passing as Black in the 1948 segregated Deep South had very little to do with how you looked and everything to do with how you acted. "Black" people came in all shades and colors; Walter White, the NAACP leader, could easily pass for a white man, and sometimes did. Sprigle's Black guide and a number of other Negro friends gave him a crash-course in living like a Black man in the land of Jim Crow, and as he later said in his book, he had no desire to be a hero, much less a martyr.

"So I saw to it that I never got in the way of one of the master race. I almost wore out my cap, dragging it off my shaven (head) whenever I addressed a white man. I 'sirred' everybody… I took no chances. I was more than careful to be a 'good nigger.'"

John Howard Griffin used his own name when he tried living as a Black man in 1959. Sprigle, who relished working undercover, could not have used his own name when he was pretending to be Black, even if he had wanted to. He had gotten a fair amount of national attention for some of his past exploits, including both his Pulitzer Prize-winning exposé of Hugo Black's membership in the Klan.

Many of those who were still in what remained of the Klan in 1948 knew the name Ray Sprigle; Klansmen had burned a cross near his home after the Hugo Black stories. He would have been asking to be lynched, and he well might have been.

Even more than a decade later John Howard Griffin was beaten with chains and almost killed by a group of Klansmen who ambushed him on a country road in 1964.

Sprigle – perhaps miraculously – was never physically attacked after his stories and book were published. Could this have been because, as annoyed as they were, the racists didn't see his work as seriously threatening their way of life?

Consider that things were already dramatically changing in the South when the events in *Black Like Me* took place. The *Brown v. Board of Education*

---

7. "Walnut juice will stain the human skin, I am able to report. I am also able to report that a day or two later it will neatly remove the human hide," Sprigle wrote in the second installment of his twenty-one-part series in the *Post-Gazette*.

case, in which the U.S. Supreme Court had unanimously outlawed "separate but equal" segregation in public schools, was already more than five years old. President Dwight D. Eisenhower had federalized the Arkansas National Guard in 1957 to force the admittance of Black students to Little Rock's Central High School.

The murder of fourteen-year-old Emmett Till in 1955 had touched off the modern civil rights movement, and sit-ins at lunch counters were just months away. There would be plenty of struggles and violence ahead,[8] but it was clear to everyone by the time John Howard Griffin passed as Black in 1959 that change was under way.

That was anything but the case when Ray Sprigle made his journey in 1948. True, the U.S. Supreme Court that very month ruled, in *Shelley v. Kraemer*, that restrictive housing covenants weren't legally enforceable – but few realized that this ruling would instantly deal a death blow to segregation in housing.

Similarly, President Harry Truman would issue an order later that summer to desegregate the armed forces, but it wouldn't be implemented for years. At the time many, including top military brass, felt it would never be put into practice at all.

Truman was almost universally expected to be defeated that fall, anyway. His desegregation order helped lead southern "Dixiecrats" to bolt from the Democratic Party and run Strom Thurmond for president.

Southern whites, in other words, felt they had no reason in 1948 to fear that white supremacy and their way of life was facing any serious immediate threat.

And Ray Sprigle was anything but a liberal civil rights crusader. In fact, as his biographer Steigerwald has noted, "he was a staunch conservative Republican who hated FDR and the New Deal," and who would, later that same year, happily vote for Thomas Dewey, not the man who now is credited with desegregating the armed forces.[9]

Sprigle himself, though he admitted he had a lifelong sympathy for the underdog, said at the outset of his book, "I might as well be honest about this expedition of mine into the South. I wasn't bent on any crusade. All I saw at first was the possibility of a darned good newspaper story."[10]

That, however, made his reporting much more valuable, and it is clear

---

8. None of this is meant to disparage the bravery of Griffin, a World War II veteran who, as noted, was violently attacked and almost killed after *Black Like Me* was published. .

9. Bill Steigerwald, "Sprigle's Secret Journey," *Pittsburgh Post-Gazette*, August 9, 1998.

10. Sprigle, *In the Land of Jim Crow*, 18.

from his stories and his book, published four months after the series ran, that he was deeply affected, moved, and even shaken by the horrors he found.

And he was, Sprigle admitted, attempting to find them. "This is no complete and impartial survey of the race problem in the South... I deliberately sought out the worst the South could show me in the way of discrimination and oppression... I spent most of my time in Georgia, Mississippi and Alabama... I deliberately sought the evil and the barbarous aspects of the white South's treatment of the Negro.

"How can you correct evil until you find it?"

Find it, he did. Sprigle and Dobbs traveled for nearly 4,000 miles through the cotton fields and small impoverished towns of the South. Unlike Griffin, he reported not so much on how he was treated, but on what life was like for Black people in the South.

He told the harrowing story of Dr. P.W. Hill, a middle-class Black dentist in Clarksdale, Mississippi, whose wife went into labor, needed an emergency Caesarian section, and died along with their newborn baby, because no good hospital in the area would admit a Black person.

He told painful stories of separate and unequal schools, of sharecroppers systematically cheated by the landowners, and of Black war heroes who were cruelly murdered when they had the audacity to try and exercise their basic right to vote after returning from war.

Sprigle did also tell of a few decent white men, including one who paid his sharecroppers fairly and even gave them an exact accounting of how their wages were determined. Nor does he portray every Black as a hero or a saint.

But overall, this is a saga of monstrous unfairness and evil in America on a scale so large as to be almost unimaginable.

Many of the stories he reported are still deeply moving, such as that of Henry Gilbert, a hardworking Black farmer who was "murdered by the white folks of Harris and Troup counties, Georgia, May 29, 1947," even though he had done nothing wrong. "When a Negro kills a white man and escapes, another Negro – any Negro – has to pay," Sprigle reported. "Henry Gilbert just happened to be the Negro picked for slaughter."

Carolyn Gilbert, his heartbroken wife, sat in a parlor "in a haze of dull despair" and told Sprigle, who she thought was a Black man named Crawford, that "when the white folks gave him back to me he was in his coffin... I held his head in my hands when I kissed him. And I felt the broken pieces of bone under the skin... all down one side of him there were no ribs – just pieces that moved when I held him."

The reporter told how she had asked "James Crawford" to pray for her.

"Me, a white man, even though she thinks I am Black?"

"Who would listen?" he asks his readers – and himself.

There are a lot more similar profoundly moving vignettes in what became one of the longest modern daily newspaper series – twenty-one parts – and one of the most avidly read. The series, "I Was a Negro in the South for 30 Days," ran from August 9 to September 1, 1948.

Ray Sprigle summed up what he thought it all meant in the very first installment. "Don't anybody try to tell me that the North discriminates against the Negro, too, and seek to use that as a defense against the savage oppression and the brutal intolerance the Black man encounters in the South. Discrimination in the North is an annoyance and an injustice. In the South it is bloodstained tragedy."

That painted a too-rosy picture of the North; lynchings, as we have seen, *did* happen there, even in Duluth. Whites had savagely killed Blacks in race riots throughout the North, including a major one in Detroit just five years before Sprigle went south.

But what he reported about the South was all too true.

The series was a national sensation, and in addition to the *Post-Gazette* it ran in fourteen major newspapers across the nation – all of them in the North. The *Pittsburgh Courier,* the one leading Black newspaper with a truly nationwide reach, acquired exclusive rights to serialize it for the Black press, which it swiftly did.

The series was praised by *Time, Newsweek,* and no less a national icon than Eleanor Roosevelt, who wrote the paper that she had read the series "with the greatest of interest. They are certainly a contribution to the understanding of a bad situation."[11]

"I Was a Negro in the South for 30 Days," was likely the best-read series in the *Post-Gazette's* history. The paper aggressively marketed it and while it ran, sales of the paper soared as much as an extra 30,000 copies a day.[12]

Long before the series finished running, at least five publishers contacted Sprigle to try to get him to sign a contract to turn the series into a book. Walter White, the national leader of the NAACP, was thrilled with the series.

In a letter to the *New York Herald Tribune,* he said that "Mr. Sprigle's brilliant articles will do a great deal towards encouraging the growth of decent public opinion in the South... I profoundly hope that the Pulitzer Prize committee will see fit again to honor Mr. Sprigle because of his able series."

---

11. Steigerwald, *30 Days a Black Man,* 206.
12. Ibid, 199.

To many in journalism circles, a Pulitzer must have seemed almost a forgone conclusion given what Sprigle had accomplished. Exposing that Hugo Black had been a Klansman was a worthy achievement – but not one that seriously risked Sprigle's life or required him to successfully convince an entire region he was a Black man.

What he had uncovered seemed irrefutable. He had begun his series, as noted, by asking that nobody use discrimination in the North as "a defense against the savage oppression and the brutal intolerance the Black man encounters in the South."

But somebody did.

Slyly, skillfully, and persuasively.

That someone was not a Klansman, or a cigar-chomping bigot like Mississippi's odious Senator Theodore Bilbo, who had died the year before.

Instead, it was the most prominent and most respected white "moderate" in the South, Hodding Carter II,[13] the editor and publisher of the *Delta Democrat-Times*, in Greenville, Mississippi. Carter was widely seen as the "Spokesman of the New South."

More than twenty years younger than Sprigle, Carter himself had won a Pulitzer Prize for editorial writing in 1946. The jury was most impressed with a series he did on intolerance but tellingly his editorials didn't have to do with how Black people were treated, but how Japanese-American veterans were treated after World War II.

True, Carter had courageously denounced economic and social injustice in the South – but at this point, and for many years to come, he never questioned segregation.

It turned out he was also very provincial when it came to his region. It was all right for him to criticize it, but not for outsiders. "Defending, explaining and boosting the South in the northern press was Carter's second career," Bill Steigerwald noted.

That was echoed by legendary journalists Gene Roberts and Hank Klibanoff in *The Race Beat*,[14] their classic book on reporting the civil rights movement.

"Carter was defensive, sarcastic and prickly, taking issue with Sprigle's characterizations, word selection, and descriptions – everything except his findings. In a xenophobic voice... Carter essentially said that outside

---

13. Not to be confused with his son, Hodding Carter III, a prominent spokesman for the U.S. State Department during the Carter Administration.

14. Gene Roberts and Hank Klibanoff, *The Race Beat,* New York: Alfred A. Knopf, 2005, 44-45,

journalists had no business singling out the South for a focus on race relations."

When it came to attacking Sprigle, he made common cause with the worst racists of his region – and did so far more eloquently than they could have.

We know a lot more today than we ever did before about what happened after Sprigle's series started appearing, thanks to the diligent research conducted by Sprigle biographer Bill Steigerwald for his book, *30 Days a Black Man*. When the *Pittsburgh Post-Gazette* series began to appear Carter was on vacation in Maine, where he had gone to college. The publisher of the *Providence Journal*, a friend of Carter's, apparently suggested he write a rebuttal to Sprigle's "I Was a Negro in the South for 30 Days."

Carter eagerly jumped at the chance. While he liked to portray himself as a moderate on race relations, or as he put it, "a southern liberal" when the chips were down, Carter was first and foremost a defender of his region.

So Hodding Carter set out to discredit Ray Sprigle's work.

And when it came to fairness, Sprigle never had a chance.

Carter struck back, first by writing a six-part rebuttal, "The Other Side of Jim Crow," which ran in his *Delta Democrat-Times*.

Many other newspapers, in both the North and South, ran Hodding Carter's rebuttal, including the *Pittsburgh Post-Gazette* and two-thirds of all the papers that had printed "I Was a Negro in the South for 30 Days." Their readers could compare the two men's arguments.

But those who read Hodding Carter's newspaper could not do that.

Neither could any other newspaper in the South that published the famous southern editor's attacks on the series, for one reason:

They all refused to publish a single word of Ray Sprigle's series.

Remember, this was long before the internet.

For most readers in Mississippi, and most other southern states, it was essentially impossible to find and read out-of-town newspapers. The only way they might have been able to do that was to find copies of the nationally distributed *Pittsburgh Courier*. But very few white Southerners read, or even knew how to find, Black newspapers.

What they knew was what Hodding Carter told them – which was that "Sprigle's picture is one-sided and distorted. He has disregarded the South's own progress towards justice for the Negro." Things in fact had gotten a lot better, he argued.

Yes, he told his readers, certain things that Sprigle had reported were "tragically true." But he added that "there are equally valid proofs that the

South is rising above its traditional and tragic racial attitudes." And rather than making things better, he argued, those who write about what was wrong make things worse.

He actually argued that any movement towards a fairer and more equal society "is being immeasurably slowed down by the... lack of balanced approach which Ray Sprigle's articles in great part exemplify."

Today, this sounds contemptible – and it was. Hodding Carter wasn't willing to print the work of his fellow journalist and Pulitzer Prize-winning reporter so that his readers could decide for themselves. Yet he criticizes Sprigle for a "lack of balance."

Ironically, Ray Sprigle would have been the first to agree that he wasn't striving for balance in his stories, though he did argue – correctly – that every one of them was completely and appallingly true.

When his book based on the series, *In the Land of Jim Crow*, was published a few months later, Sprigle said in his very first chapter, "Let me make clear at the start, too, that this is no complete and impartial survey of the race problem in the South."

"I deliberately sought out the worst that the South could show me in the way of discrimination and oppression of the Negro. I spent most of my time in Georgia, Mississippi and Alabama. I ignored Virginia and North Carolina, where the greatest progress in civilized race relations has been recorded."

As previously mentioned, he also openly said why he did so, asking "How can you correct evil until you find it?"

Sprigle's approach needs no defending. What he did is what investigative journalists do. Nobody would author a story that said, "Even though President Kennedy's assassination was deplorable, most people visiting Dallas on November 22, 1963 were not murdered by Lee Harvey Oswald." What he did, as his biographer noted, was present "a blistering indictment of the evils of Jim Crow."[15]

Today, we know that conditions in the Deep South in 1948 were every bit as bad as Ray Sprigle said they were. Hodding Carter's claim that things were getting better was devastatingly shown to be a fraud less than seven years later in the summer of 1955 when a fourteen-year-old boy from Chicago named Emmett Till, visiting his grandparents in Mississippi for the summer, was kidnapped, horribly tortured, and murdered for the "crime" of whistling at a white woman in a grocery store.

His killers, who later happily admitted to the deed, were easily acquitted

---

15. Steigerwald, *30 Days a Black Man*, 282.

after a trial that received worldwide attention and which is commonly held to have been the spark that started the modern civil rights movement.

When the killers were acquitted Hodding Carter even more clearly disgraced himself. Incredibly, especially in his newspaper and before southern audiences, he seemed to put most of the blame for the acquittal, and even the boy's murder, on the NAACP. "He often seemed to consider the blot on Mississippi's name to be the real tragedy," Timothy Tyson concluded in his recent book, *The Blood of Emmett Till.*[16]

The *Chicago Defender* accurately summed Carter up as contemptibly trying to justify "the South's pernicious folkways," and "attempting to smooth over the facts."

Respect for Hodding Carter declined somewhat after that.[17]

But the Till scandal and the murder of Medgar Evers in 1963 and civil rights workers James Cheney, Andrew Goodman, and Michael Schwerner in 1964, sensational slayings that focused the nation's attention on Mississippi, were still years in the future when Carter set out to destroy the credibility of Sprigle's series.

The nation wasn't nearly as aware of what conditions were like in the Deep South as it would be in a few years. For one thing, very few people, and almost no one in the Land of Jim Crow, had television in 1948, and TV news was all but non-existent.

There were other reasons, too, that made it easier for Carter to persuade people that Ray Sprigle's series was, if not completely wrong, hugely exaggerated.

Hodding Carter was a skilled, graceful, and genteel writer who had honed his skills at Maine's elite Bowdoin College. Sprigle was, as *Time Magazine* once called him, a "hard-digging hell-for-leather" reporter.[18]

He had a roughhewn, sometimes sensational, writing style to match; *Post-Gazette* city editor Joe Shuman once said that he liked to "pick up the paper by the corner of the page and watch the blood drip out" of the stories he had written.[19]

---

16. Timothy B. Tyson, *The Blood of Emmett Till,* New York: Simon & Schuster, 2017, 182-84.

17. Later in life Hodding Carter managed to regain his reputation among white liberals after he abandoned what had been his near-fanatical support of segregation and became a fervent supporter of John F. and Robert Kennedy. Carter died of a sudden heart attack at age sixty-five in 1972.

18. *Time Magazine*, April 30, 1945. The reference refers to Sprigle's exposé of the wartime black-market meat scandal.

19. Newman, *Hugo Black: A Biography*, 247.

That made it easy for many to sympathize with Carter – especially those thousands of his readers who never got to read a word of what Ray Sprigle wrote.

But the story didn't end with both men publishing their stories.

They then went to debate each other in a variety of forums, often with other prominent journalists, including the ABC network's immensely popular radio program, "Town Meeting of the Air." During these encounters it was invariably the *Post-Gazette* reporter who was the gentleman. "Sprigle respected Carter as a writer and a journalist," and often complimented his critic in these forums, his biographer Steigerwald said.

"Carter never returned Sprigle's respect or publicly complimented him in the slightest way," he added. Indeed, the southern editor seemed almost obsessed with his critic, the man who had dared insult his region.

Hodding Carter even went on to write a sophomoric parody for *Look* magazine, describing a mythical southern reporter who was going to disguise himself as a New York drug addict and write a series called "In the Land of Grim Snow."

In contrast, the *Pittsburgh Post-Gazette* put out a booklet that reprinted both Ray Sprigle's series and Hodding Carter's rebuttal and sold nearly 10,000 copies of it.

They may have done this as part of their campaign to win Ray Sprigle a second Pulitzer Prize, which many felt he richly deserved. But they never had a chance.

For sitting on the jury that decided who would be awarded the Pulitzers for their reporting in 1948 was none other than Hodding Carter.

You might think, given that he was heavily involved in controversy over this very series, that he would have voluntarily recused himself from the jury – or have been asked to do so by his fellow jurors as he had a clear conflict of interest.[20] But he did not.

The Pulitzer board instead split the prize for National Reporting between a reporter who wrote about a state department security case for the *New York Herald Tribune* and a *Minneapolis Tribune* reporter who wrote about efforts by the Truman administration to impose secrecy about the affairs of civilian agencies in peace-time.

The award for Public Service went to the *St. Louis Post-Dispatch* for its coverage of a mine disaster in Centralia, Illinois.

Within a few years what Ray Sprigle had done was, tragically, forgotten.

---

20. The friend who suggested Hodding Carter write his rebuttal, Rhode Island publisher Sevellon Brown, was also on the jury, according to Bill Steigerwald.

In fact, years later, John Howard Griffin said he never heard of *In the Land of Jim Crow* before he wrote *Black Like Me.*

"There's no evidence Sprigle's series dramatically changed history," Bill Steigerwald said after authoring his book on what the great reporter had done. "But by exposing the cold heart and soul of Jim Crow to the entire country, Sprigle provided a priceless contribution to the embryonic civil rights movement. He'll go down in history as the first journalist – white or Black – to strike a serious blow against segregation on the mainstream media," Steigerwald believed.

Nevertheless, "In 1948 it was still too soon for the northern white press to practice civil rights journalism. It was too soon, politically and socially," he concluded, adding that it would "take the power of television to arouse the North's conscience for good."

Perhaps.

But might not a little more attention have been paid to what was happening had "I Was a Negro in the South for 30 Days" won the Pulitzer Prize?

If Ray Sprigle was bitter, he never showed it. He went on doing his patented brand of journalism, touring refugee camps in Europe the next year to write about displaced persons, those surviving victims of the madness of Adolf Hitler and World War II.

Even in his early seventies he was exposing police corruption, racketeers, and greedy Pittsburgh slumlords that victimized Black and white victims alike.

Working late on Saturday night, December 21, 1957, he decided to take a cab home after covering a trial that had gone on into the weekend.

A speeding car ran a red light and crashed into the cab. Ray Sprigle, who had always expected to die at his *Post-Gazette* desk, died early the next morning from his injuries.

Looking at the sweep of history it is hard not to feel that his reporting on the Jim Crow south deserves a posthumous Pulitzer Prize.

10

Toledo: Bill Brower's Remarkable Journey

I AM A NEGRO. I am writing this at the conclusion of a 3-month tour of 15,000 miles to all parts of the nation for a personal inquiry into the status of the 15,000,000 Americans who constitute what is called "the Negro problem."

The relationship between the Negro and his fellow American is one of the most disturbing issues in the country.[1]

— Bill Brower, *Toledo Blade*, December 1951

Those were the opening lines of what was the beginning of one of the most stunning, and perhaps most overlooked, series in American journalism.

For sixteen days William "Bill" Brower's reports ran on racial conditions across the nation, North and South, from housing discrimination to school segregation, from hypocrisy in the North to the first glimmerings of hope for an end to Jim Crow.

He had spent three months traveling throughout twenty-seven states and visiting and interviewing people of all colors and walks of life in more than

---

1. As previously noted, "Black" did not become the preferred term for African-Americans until the 1970s; Martin Luther King, Jr., for example, always referred to himself as a "Negro."

fifty cities.

Nothing like this – a nationwide look at racial conditions from the perspective of a Black journalist – had ever been attempted by a daily, mass-market newspaper.

Few newspapers, apart from the historically Black press, even had any Black reporters on their staffs in 1951; the *Toledo Blade,* as we've seen, hired Bill Brower, a seasoned reporter, more than four years earlier. The editors had, as noted, assigned him to cover everything from routine stories to the city's battles against the Licavoli organized crime syndicate to a story that was an international sensation: the "Smith Act" trials of American Communist Party leaders in New York.[2]

Brower, who had worked for papers in five eastern cities, from Philadelphia to Norfolk, had agreed to come to the paper only after he had been promised that he would not be pigeonholed and used to cover only "Negro News."

Indeed he hadn't. But who could resist a chance to tackle the nationwide race question, something that would soon be one of the biggest stories in the nation?

What isn't clear is exactly whose idea the series was – though it likely came from the publisher himself, Paul Block, Jr., whose ideas were often ahead of his time.[3] He thought, his son John Robinson Block told me,[4] "that while race might be a problem America would never get beyond, he was determined to do the best he could to try."

Other newspapers had, from time to time, reported on race and the condition of Blacks in America; Ray Sprigle, a white man disguised as a Negro, had after all, reported on the most terrible abuses in the Jim Crow South only three years before.

But again – as far as I can determine, no mainstream newspaper had ever sent a Black reporter across the country to report on the status of Blacks in America.

Bill Brower was the first.

---

2. William Brower, *Brief Biographies,* Net Industries, 2020.

3. Paul Block, Jr., as mentioned earlier, commissioned Norman Bel Geddes to create the futuristic Toledo Tomorrow exhibit in 1945, something designed to goad Toledoans to thinking about new horizons for their city in the post-World War II era. He also demonstrated firmly that the *Blade* was now a fully independent newspaper by endorsing Adlai Stevenson for president in 1956 and, in 1972, was one of the few publishers in the nation to realize the deeper meaning of the Watergate scandal and oppose the re-election of Richard Nixon.

4. John Robinson Block, interview by the author, May 9, 2019.

However, any reader who may have expected to find an investigative series even more searing and sensational than Sprigle's *In the Land of Jim Crow* may have been disappointed. Brower had a very different personality and a very different style.

He was cautious, reserved, judicious, and strove for balance, a style more in tune with that of Paul Block, Jr.'s philosophy of newspapering; Sprigle's brilliant but swashbuckling, sometimes sensationalist, prose was that of the fading jazz era.

Brower, who was thirty-five when he made his own racial odyssey across America in the fall of 1951, was a man of another generation. He had also grown up in the Jim Crow South, an upbringing designed to make a young Black man cautious – or dead.

He was young enough to have been the son of Sprigle (or "James Rayel Crawford"). But not only was he of another generation, the world had changed dramatically in three short years. The Cold War had become much hotter. The Soviet Union exploded its first atom bomb in 1949, a few weeks after *In the Land of Jim Crow* was published.

That same year communists completely captured all of China. The next year North Korea, with the full support of both giant communist nations, invaded South Korea, and Americans soon found themselves in an unexpected shooting war.

These events all helped lead to the rise one of the nation's most dangerous demagogues, Joe McCarthy, the junior senator from Wisconsin, who charged that hundreds of "card-carrying communists" had infiltrated the federal government.

Though he accused many people of "Red" ties and ruined many lives before his fall from power in 1954, he actually never proved that anyone in the government was a communist. However, there was a racial dimension to the Red Scare.

For years Moscow, and the few real communists and Soviet agents in the United States, had been using the oppression of Blacks in America in their propaganda. Since the 1920s they had been attempting to recruit African-Americans, noting that the communists had been the only party calling for an end to segregation.[5]

Though the Civil Rights Movement itself had yet to be born, as the Cold

---

5. In 1932 the U.S. Communist Party nominated James Ford, a Black candidate, for vice president. Their ticket got 102,785 votes, more than the Communist Party would ever again achieve, though this was likely due mostly to the desperate economic circumstances caused by the Great Depression.

War intensified many enlightened anti-communists, including Paul Block, Jr.,[6] became worried that if Black Americans felt that the "American Dream" was hopelessly closed to them, they might become vulnerable to recruitment by outside agitators.

How much of a factor this was in the decision to send the *Blade's* first Black reporter on a nationwide odyssey isn't clear. But Brower clearly understood that the Cold War battle for hearts and minds was an issue.

"Other Americans have a strong stake in seeing that democratic justice is achieved for Negroes," he wrote in the paragraphs of the last installment of the series. "This nation is locked in an ideological struggle with communism. Harmony and unity are vital. America can present a stronger front to the world the sooner it makes racial discrimination and intolerance expendable," he concluded.

The series, which began on December 5, 1951, was well-received in both Toledo and Pittsburgh. "William Brower, by conscientious fact-finding and fair-minded reporting, has revealed a heartening picture of the struggle of his downtrodden race for equality in our 'democratic' America... congratulations to the *Post-Gazette*," one S.W. Place of Philadelphia wrote in a letter that was printed in the Pittsburgh paper on December 27.

Toledo Blade managing editor Paul Schrader summed up the Toledo reaction by noting, when the series was republished as a five-inch booklet the next year, that it "has been applauded for its dispassionate objectivity, amazing facts, and calm conclusions."

Calm it was, certainly by comparison to Ray Sprigle's fiery prose. Nor did Brower's work invite the sort of attacks Hodding Carter II had delivered against Sprigle's work three years before. Brower's series, "15,000,000 Americans: A personal inquiry into the status of the one-tenth of our population that constitutes what is called 'the Negro problem,'[7] was nominated for a Pulitzer Prize, just as Sprigle's series had been.

And once again, it was passed over.

Instead, the Pulitzer for Public Service was split between the *Miami*

---

6. I know this from discussing the Cold War with Block when I was national correspondent for the *Blade,* sometime in the early 1980s.

7. One has to wonder if Brower was aware of something an irritated Frederick Douglass told a crowd made up largely of white hecklers at the Columbian Exhibition in Chicago in 1893: "Men talk of the 'Negro problem'. There is no Negro problem. The problem is whether the American people have honesty enough, loyalty enough, honor enough, patriotism enough to live up to their own constitution. We intend that the American people shall learn the great lesson of the brotherhood of man and the fatherhood of God from our presence among them."

Herald and the *Brooklyn Eagle* for their crime reporting during the year. Oddly, no prize for National Reporting, the other category into which Brower's work could easily have fit, was given at all for 1951, a year when attention was largely fixed on the Korean War.

Once again both Hodding Carter II and his friend, Sevellon Brown of the *Providence Journal,* sat on the Pulitzer board. Carter's attitude towards Bill Brower's series is not known.[8] But, ironically, it might have served Carter's interests as a defender of his region to have called favorable attention to it and given it the prize.

For Bill Brower made many of the same arguments that Hodding Carter had in his response to Sprigle, published as "The Other Side of Jim Crow." Like Carter, Brower portrayed a nation, including the South, where there was injustice, but where things were getting better. In fact, read today, with the hindsight of what we know now and what was to come in the bloody and turbulent years ahead, Brower's series often seems far too starry-eyed; his view of the ease with which gains would come optimistic.

Too starry-eyed, that is, on conditions and the likelihood of change in the South. But Brower was far more accurate than Ray Sprigle had been about discrimination in the North. The author of *In the Land of Jim Crow* absurdly represented prejudice against Blacks in northern states as an "annoyance and an injustice" at worst, and said that a Black victim of it "can take his case to court and he invariably wins."

Brower knew better. He found Chicago "the most disquieting city in the country," to be a hotbed of racism and noted, accurately, that there was "simmering racial antagonism in Detroit," where a ferocious race riot had broken out only eight years before, one in which, as he hints, many Blacks were killed by white policemen.

"The South never held the copyright on racial discrimination," he noted near the series' end. But overall, he was optimistic. "I came back reassured and hopeful," he concluded. "I heard many shades of opinion on Negro progress. Nearly everybody was agreed that the situation is getting better," he wrote in the series' first installment.

While there were still problems, Brower said, "the climate is clearing for improved race relations in most places. "Not only that, he felt that

---

8. Paul Block Jr. and Grove Patterson wrote to many newspaper editors across the nation urging them to reprint Brower's series. Only the *Newark Star-Ledger* did. Sevellon Brown 3d wrote to Block on Nov. 30, 1951, praising the series but adding "I am afraid we shall not be able to do anything with them ourselves because we are running such a very tight paper."

"segregation is on the ropes in the South… the sight of Negro students on hitherto all-white campuses will become commonplace. Some other aspects of segregation – on streetcars and buses, in public assembly and, perhaps, in all phases of public education – appear moribund."

More Blacks were voting, even in the Deep South, Brower said, and nationally Blacks were making more money and their standard of living was better than ever. In one installment, he argued that Blacks tended to be richer and live better lives in the South.

Hodding Carter II would likely have been pleased by that and might have nodded at many other places in Brower's series, including "one expert on interracial affairs in the South," whom he anonymously quotes as saying that the problem was "to strike a pace that a region clumsily ridden with hate… can stand.

"The pace may be too fast for whites, too slow for Negroes, but that is the only way in which it can be done democratically."

The anonymous sage added, "if only we can keep the wild boys on both sides quiet." Brower also quoted a "prominent, much-traveled Washington woman who stressed "patience and tolerance," and said things had changed a lot already.

This is not to imply that Bill Brower was what militant Blacks might later have called an Uncle Tom. Consider that he was writing at a time when nobody was yet even using the term "Civil Rights Movement." Emmett Till, whose murder four years later is commonly held to have started that movement, was still a ten-year-old boy living in Detroit. Martin Luther King, Jr., was an unknown, twenty-two-year-old seminary student in Pennsylvania. Malcolm X was in a state prison in Massachusetts.

Bill Brower was clearly striving to be a restrained, carefully objective reporter – something of a polar opposite to the flamboyant, swashbuckling Sprigle.

He would have had to be. Sprigle was firmly established as a Pulitzer Prize-winning journalistic giant when he made his undercover trip through the Jim Crow South.

Brower, by nature a very reserved, dignified man, must have felt under enormous pressure; in a sense, he was sort of a Jackie Robinson of the white newspaper world. He had to pave the way for other Black reporters.[9]

He must have known he could not afford to come across as a militant racial partisan, even had he wanted to, and he may have overcompensated to prove his fairness. But it is also clear that he wanted to think things were getting better in the United States of America.

On some issues, especially housing, which he called the "key point of segregation," Brower took a more openly tough stand. "It leads to discrimination in schools, employment, churches and recreation. It is one of the most provocative of racial tensions. Brower called out the "combination of real estate and financial interests" that made this happen. "Even the Federal Government is involved," he continued, noting that "the Federal Housing Administration has refused, in many instances, to approve loans for Negroes who desire to move into areas in which they are not wanted."

But, showing his even-handed philosophy at its best, Brower attacked "crafty real estate speculators (who) tell whites a neighborhood is going Negro and promise them fancy prices for their homes. They promptly inflate the price and sell to the first Negro taker. Though still in its infancy in 1951, such "blockbusters" would later be infamous nationwide. Brower charges, however, that "Negro manipulators are just as guilty of this practice as anywhere else," and also notes that "Some Negro businessmen, politicians and even clergymen have a vested interest in segregated housing" and "tacitly oppose the movement of Negroes into new neighborhoods."

Brower also made it clear that he had a hard time emotionally returning to anywhere Jim Crow laws remained in force. During his travels for the series, he wrote, "I was in and out of the South three times. I found that I had barely enough stamina to stand two weeks of Jim Crow at a time." While he felt things were changing, he "... came across too many reminders of the past to make my stay entirely pleasant."

Those reminders included a bathtub in the "best Negro hotel" in Raleigh, N.C., that was so filthy it "discouraged me from taking a bath" and colored rest rooms and drinking fountains, But unlike Ray Sprigle, he had no great desire to dive into and plumb the depths of the worst parts of segregation and report about it.

After all, Bill Brower had grown up living it.

---

9. Moderate though he was, the notion of even writing about race in America was too much for many newspaper editors. When The Blade offered Brower's series to Joseph Pulitzer Jr., publisher of the *St. Louis Post-Dispatch,* Pulitzer wrote Paul Block, "Unfortunately the *Post-Dispatch* cannot use them because of racial incidents here in the recent past. I will tell you about this when I see you." Letter to PB, Dec. 3, 1951.

Brower continued reporting for the *Blade* after his series ended, and his career made steady progress. In 1956 he returned to the topic of race with a series on Black voters in the Midwest and South.[10] He became rewrite editor, a position requiring considerable thinking-on-your feet skill, in 1957 and an assistant city editor in 1963.

Four years later he moved over to the wire desk, dealing mostly with national and international news, and then became news editor in the turbulent year of 1968.

Three years later he moved into upper management, becoming an assistant managing editor, in charge of the tricky and hugely important and demanding Sunday edition, which in terms of revenue was the most important paper of the week.

Twenty years had passed since his historic trip and his nationwide survey of racial attitudes and progress. The U.S. Supreme Court had unanimously outlawed mandatory segregation in schools. The Civil Rights Movement had exploded into being after the murder of Emmett Till in August 1955, followed by the Montgomery bus boycott, the lunch counter sit-ins, and all that followed.

Martin Luther King, Jr., had appeared out of nowhere to become one of the most famous men in the world and then was assassinated.

Congress had passed the Civil Rights Act of 1964, which outlawed segregation in virtually everything from employment to housing in both the public and private sectors, and the next year passed the Voting Rights Act and other legislation designed to mean that no state or community could prevent Blacks from voting any longer.

The nation, and the relationship between the races, had changed dramatically in twenty years – or so it seemed. But how much had things really changed?

To find out, the *Blade* sent William Brower out on the road again in late fall 1971. This time he didn't visit quite as many states – nineteen compared to twenty-seven – or quite as many cities – forty instead of fifty-plus.

Still, it was a mammoth reporting odyssey for a man who was now

---

10. Brower found correctly that while President Eisenhower had made inroads, most Blacks intended to vote Democratic as they had since the Great Depression. That election was notable for The *Blade's* decision to endorse Adlai Stevenson, the first time the paper had ever endorsed a Democrat for president, something that was seen as a clear signal by Paul Block, Jr., that the paper would be truly independent. The *Post-Gazette,* however, stayed with President Eisenhower, who was reelected in a landslide.

fifty-five and he examined more issues in a series that was actually three installments longer than the first. Nor were any previously covered topics ignored.

As the booklet the newspaper issued when it reprinted his second series noted, he "retraced his steps in virtually every region of the nation to put in perspective changes in Black-white relationships over two decades."

He did his best to do exactly that. The trip was not an exact replica of his first one; he went to some new places where, as he said, "newly important racial developments had occurred and where events are still stirring."

The world had indeed changed, as Brower noted with a sophistication that seemed far deeper than his writing had shown two decades before. "Twenty years have made a difference, no doubt about it," he noted in his very first installment on March 5, 1972.[11]

While he found that there had been "perceptible progress, both real and symbolic," he also concluded that "many of the basic problems remain," and added that "as a Black American moving about the nation, I perceived that the racial challenge in the seventies is far more complex than it was in the fifties, largely because of the change."

In other words, Black America was, thanks to the successes of the Civil Rights Movement, far less monolithic than it was in 1951. There were more Black millionaires, prominent artists, and recording stars. But there were many more still struggling and all were under relentless scrutiny of a kind fairly new to Black America.

Brower acknowledged this. He noted that this trip, unlike his first one, came "in an era when the national consciousness is centered on the struggle of Black Americans for civil rights and equality like no other time in history."

Though he didn't acknowledge it in the series, there had been a fairly significant linguistic change as well. Only a few years before Bill Brower would have described himself as a Negro. Now the preferred term was Black.

"Black America – 20 Years Later" was far more clearly divided into consideration of various issues than his series two decades before. Brower, then *The Blade's* news editor, analyzed how politics were changing in the South (he interviewed, among other officials, an interesting young governor of Georgia named Jimmy Carter). He took on tough issues, including that of police brutality against Blacks, and the ugly reality of continued housing segregation.

He looked at the growing success of Blacks, including in politics. Twenty

---

11. William Brower, "Black America – 20 years Later," *Toledo Blade,* March 5-23, 1972.

years before he had somewhat lionized U.S. Representative William Dawson (D-Ill.) one of only two Black congressmen in the nation. Twenty years later, he realized that Dawson, who by then was dead, was mostly just a compliant cog in the vast Chicago city hall Democratic machine, like many other Black Chicago officeholders.

Looking at the complex issue of lingering segregation in schools, he wrote one installment about an issue largely ignored elsewhere, that of the great number of Black teachers who were losing their jobs as school systems merged.

Over the years Brower's writing had evolved and become more fluid, but he still had a largely formal and occasionally stilted style. There were a few odd omissions: when he noted that one Mrs. Louise Brower, the principal at McTigue High School, was the only Black administrator in a mostly white school, he didn't mention that she happened to be his wife. Curiously, he also didn't mention that while more than two-thirds of all Black Americans lived in the South in 1951, by 1971 nearly half lived in the North.[12]

Overall, however, his second series is well-written, solid, occasionally fascinating, and much more layered than his first. Read today, "15,000,000 Americans," his 1951 series, offers a description of life so different from our time that it is stunning to realize that millions are still alive who actually lived in and remember that world.

But much of "Black America – 20 Years Later" still seems stunningly relevant today. "There is great polarization today, physically and psychologically. Whites have surrendered the inner city and fled to the suburbs," Bower noted in the first installment.

"Middle-class, elite, more affluent Blacks are enjoying much improved social, economic, and leisure time conditions over their status twenty years ago. Some are following the relentless flow of whites... to the suburbs."

On the other hand, "I sensed a mood of despair and frustration, sometimes anger, among the ghetto masses. The consequences of substandard and congested housing, spiraling unemployment, swelling welfare rolls, embittered police-Black relations and sprawling poverty are poisoning the atmosphere."

William Brower admitted that some things have changed for the better

---

12. According to the U.S. Census Bureau, 68 percent of African-Americans lived in the South in 1950; only 53 percent did by 1970. Ironically, the percentage of Blacks living in the South later began increasing again and reached 55 percent in 2010. See also James Gregory, *The Southern Diaspora: How the Great Migrations of Black and White Southerners Transformed America,* Chapel Hill: University of North Carolina Press, 2007.

faster than even he had hoped. For example, Blacks could no longer be denied access to public accommodations such as hotel rooms or restaurants (thanks to the Civil Rights Act of 1964) and he noted that "I thought that Jim Crow public facilities (toilets and drinking foundations) would be the last degrading custom in the old South to go."

Yet all that was gone by the time of his second trip. He concluded with a gentle admonition to both races: "in setting standards for Blacks, it must be remembered that they have been exposed to a long history of deprivation and cultural disadvantages, and still have to overcome social, economic, and political obstacles."

But in the series' very last words, he added, "One thing I haven't said and should say, however, is that as Blacks claim their rights as citizens, they should be willing to accept the responsibilities for them."

While a Black journalist writing about civil rights was no longer novel in the 1970s, this series did get recognition, winning a citation from the Robert F. Kennedy Memorial Foundation journalism awards. Later in the 1970s, Brower became an associate editor and part of the *Blade's* editorial board, than a senior editor.

In 1977, five years after his second series, he reported and wrote a seven-part series, "The Black Athlete." Soon afterward, Brower wrote a column three times a week on subjects that ranged from politics to baseball; from Toledo's mercurial Mayor Carty Finkbeiner to Chicago's infamous Cabrini Green housing project.

But he wasn't quite done with reporting on his nation and race.

Bill Brower had joined the *Blade* almost exactly half a century after the U.S. Supreme Court's infamous *Plessy v. Ferguson* decision that made segregation legal.

Plessy came twenty years before William Brower was born. The *Blade's* first Black reporter was at the paper when *Brown v. Board of Education* reversed that decision in 1954 and made segregation in public schools illegal and destroyed the entire myth of "separate but equal." On that day Brower wrote in his second series, "I jumped for joy."

Nearly half a century later in 1996, a full century after *Plessy*, Bill Brower, who would be eighty that fall, was still a columnist for the *Blade*.

Forty-five years had passed since his first cross-country trip to take the nation's temperature on race; a quarter-century since the second. And for a number of reasons the editors of the *Blade* decided it was time to do it again.[13]

Relations between the races were as important a story as ever, the editors knew. Bill Brower's first two series had each ended on an optimistic note but in the mid-1990s there were new outbreaks of racist incidents.

"Americans see smoldering embers from torched churches of predominantly Black congregations and wonder what progress had been made" they noted in the introduction to the third series.

The internet was just beginning to cut into newspaper revenue and the *Blade,* like other papers, was beginning to feel the pinch. But it still was willing to spend thousands on an important story – and few were more important than race.

So they decided to send Bill Brower to do a third series – but this time he didn't go alone. He was accompanied by Eddie B. Allen, Jr., then newspaper's smart, twenty-three-year-old urban affairs reporter, a recent graduate of Wayne State University in Detroit. That collaboration wasn't a guaranteed success.

Brower could have resented having to travel with a colleague who wasn't even born when he did his second series, let alone his first. Some younger reporters might have rolled their eyes at having to play understudy to "grandpa."

Thankfully that didn't happen here. The men seemed to genuinely respect each other. Eddie Allen, who had recently returned from covering the Million Man March in Washington, D.C., said that when he was asked to work with Bill Brower on his third trek across the country he "… considered it a high honor."

For his part, Brower said he was happy to work with Allen, since "younger eyes and ears lend a fresh perspective to the issues and conditions still challenging the nation's Black-white relationships." He noted that the young man's native Detroit, which had been torn by two destructive riots in his lifetime, "has long had a reputation as a hotbed of racism… so, as you can see, Eddie Allen brings to this series a background of having lived through some intense racial dynamics… far different than a generation ago."

This series was called "America in Black and White." This time the geography covered was somewhat less than the previous two trips – fourteen states and twenty-four cities. The series that resulted was slightly shorter as well – a dozen installments in that many days.

Some of the territory covered was familiar – the second-to-last installment

---

13. The reporting began in the fall of 1995; the series itself ran from June 16-27, 1996.

dealt with discrimination, poverty, and police corruption. There were updates on Black elected officials and a look at Black colleges' struggle to survive.

Some were new – a look at the role of museums in preserving Black and civil rights heritage; a perhaps overdue look at the role of Black women in the community, and, finally, in politics. One story, written by Allen, would have been unimaginable in 1951 and unlikely in 1972 – a look at the double discrimination Black gays and lesbians faced. When it was over, Eddie Allen wrote that the experience was "a combination of journalism, history, sociology, and comedy." While at times his companion was "deadly serious in his approach to examining the issues that have affected his life" at other times he was like "the fun-loving mischievous child in the back of the classroom."[14]

It had, however, given him "a greater understanding of the problem and its origins; a beneficial look through his eyes as well as mine."

Bill Brower retired after the series' end. Belatedly, he finally began to be honored and recognized for his remarkable career.

His final series won him and his colleague an award for best minority coverage from the Ohio chapter of the Society of Professional Journalists. NABJ, the National Association of Black Journalists, gave him a lifetime achievement award and cited him as one of the century's most influential Black journalists.

Perhaps symbolically Toledo's city council named a highway bridge after him. He was a bridge, after all, between not only generations, but eras.

Soon after he retired, his health began to fail. He moved to Washington to be close to his only child, Bill Jr., who had become an important figure in the jazz world, where he died on May 28, 2004. His wife Louise had died the year before.

Both were buried in Toledo, their adopted home. Weeks before, his newspaper had finally won the Pulitzer he and Ray Sprigle had been denied for its stories documenting atrocities committed against Vietnamese civilians by soldiers in Vietnam.

Bill Brower never knew that when he was reporting his first series there was a nine-year-old girl in Kansas who would someday be mother to the first Black man ever to sit in the Oval Office. Nor did he know that during his second series there was a ten-year-old African-American boy in Hawaii who

---

14. Bill Brower was not a playful writer, but he didn't lack a wry sense of humor. Once, emerging from a fellow reporter's home in an all-white neighborhood, he noticed neighbors staring at him, so he reached over and shook his colleague's hand, saying loudly, "Thank you very much for letting me see your home. It's pretty much what we want. We'll give it some serious thought."

one day would occupy the White House. Barack Obama won the presidency four years after William Brower died. On election night he cinched victory with a big win in Toledo and a solid one in Ohio.

Maybe, just maybe, Brower's conscience-raising reporting played a part in getting America's first Black president there.

11

Covering the Civil
Rights Movement

*The only sane response – the only moral and just response – is swiftly
to dismantle the barricades still barring the progress of Negro citizens
from their rightful place in American life.*
                                                    – *Toledo Blade* editorial on the murder of
                                                                  Medgar Evers, June 13, 1963

Though the modern Civil Rights Movement is commonly thought to have
begun with the murder of Emmett Till in August 1955 and the sensational
publicity that followed, it had been building for some time.

Patrick Washburn, who wrote a highly regarded book on the Black
press,[1] believes the role of Black newspapers during World War II was a
major catalyst – especially in their promotion of things like the *Pittsburgh
Courier's* "Double V Campaign", in which one "V" stood for victory over
our enemies abroad; one "V" for victory over racism and discrimination at
home. "You look at the Black papers of that time and they aren't talking
about civil rights," Washburn said.

---

1. Patrick Washburn, *The African-American Newspaper: Voice of Freedom,* Evanston, IL:
Northwestern University Press, 2006. Patrick Washburn is professor emeritus of journalism
at Ohio University.

"They're not using those words, but the things they are trying to get for the Black community and the Black people are civil rights. And if you had not had World War II… the Civil Rights Movement would have started at a lot lower level," and years later.[2]

Neither Toledo nor Pittsburgh had especially large Black populations when the war ended, though they had been gradually growing, as the Great Migration continued and more Blacks came for better jobs in the auto factories and steel mills.

Pittsburgh's Black population increased from 62,216 in 1940 to 82,543 ten years later, rising from just over 9 percent to 12.2 percent of the total. Toledo's Black population nearly doubled during the decade but was still small by 1950; 25,026 people, or barely 8 percent of the city's total.[3]

It also seems likely that they were an even smaller percentage of subscribers to the newspapers Paul Block's sons still owned in those cities, the *Toledo Blade* and the *Pittsburgh Post-Gazette*. Most were financially less well-off than their white neighbors, and poorer people are less inclined to subscribe to newspapers. Pittsburgh Blacks who read newspapers preferred the *Pittsburgh Courier*, then the strongest and largest circulated African-American paper in the nation.

In both cities most Blacks were crammed into what were essentially ghettos. In Toledo these included neighborhoods near the central city and in the Lower Hill, or "Little Harlem" district in Pittsburgh, an area of which Ray Sprigle once sagely wrote, "Nobody gives much of a damn about the Hill."[4] That was surely true in part because the district was then overwhelmingly Black. White inhabitants in many places – like the newspapers they read – often paid little attention to the Blacks who shared their cities.

But that began to change everywhere on Monday morning, May 17, 1954, when the U.S. Supreme Court unanimously ruled that segregation in public schools was unconstitutional.[5] The *Blade* was then an afternoon newspaper and the ruling that morning dominated the newspaper's front page under a

2. Patrick Washburn, interview with the author, December 2019. Also as quoted in the 1999 Stanley Nelson film, *The Black Press: Soldiers Without Swords*.

3. Campbell Gibson and Kay Jung, *Historical Census Statistics on Population Totals by Race, 1790 to 1990 … For Large Cities and Other Urban Cities in the United States,* Suitland-Silver Hill, MD: U.S. Census Bureau, February 2005.

4. Steigerwald, *30 Days a Black Man,* 287. Sprigle's quote came at the end of a series he did about Pittsburgh slums in 1954.

5. Though that decision is universally referred to today as *Brown v. Board,* or more formally, *Brown v. Board of Education of Topeka, Kansas,* most media at the time, including the *Toledo Blade, Toledo Times* and the *Pittsburgh Post-Gazette* did not refer to the case by name at all, and only concentrated on the court's overall ruling.

five-column headline:

Public School Segregation
Declared Unconstitutional
In Supreme Court Decision

Beneath the headline was a smaller subhead that made what turned out to be a wildly overoptimistic prediction: "Months Likely to Elapse Before Practice is Ended."

In fact it would be years, and a considerable amount of blood would flow first. The newspapers instantly realized the importance of the story. The next day the *Blade's* front page featured a long analysis by George Zielke, one of the paper's Washington correspondents, as well as other wire service stories about its potential impact.

Curiously, however, the coverage does not include any column or analysis by Bill Brower, who less than three years before had traveled across the nation for his first series on Black America and wrote much later that he "jumped for joy" when he heard of the Supreme Court's *Brown v. Board* ruling.

Nor were there any stories in which the *Blade* interviewed Black residents of Toledo to get their reaction to the decision. This may have been because Toledo schools weren't legally segregated, as they were in most of the South.

There may also have been a lack of understanding on the part of local news editors to how far-reaching the implications of the decision were likely to be for all of society. However, the *Blade's* editorial writers did see that – instantly.

The newspaper's lead editorial the next day, "An End to Segregation," proclaimed the court's decision "struck a killing blow at segregation" and added that "because the system of public education is the keystone of the American system, ending segregation in the nation's schools undoubtedly means ending it in all its other applications."

Yet no Toledoans were interviewed as to their thoughts on the matter, though a wire story told them what the press in Great Britain believed about it.

Bizarre as this may sound, it is worth noting that at many papers there was a considerable gulf between those handling national news and those covering foreign news. Plus, paying any attention at all to the Black community was still something fairly new for most mainstream newspapers in 1954 and the *Blade* in this era seldom, if ever, did "man on the street" reactions to major news events.

Editorial reaction to the decision in the *Toledo Times,* the *Blade*'s more conservative and far smaller morning counterpart, was less enthusiastic.[6]

While its editorial the next morning did congratulate "The Negroes of America" for having won "a long and historic fight for equal rights and privileges" guaranteed them by the Fourteenth Amendment, it seemed to question the wisdom of the Supreme Court's unanimous decision, saying it "could have held that it was a decision for the legislature, not the courts. "That would appear to contradict the same editorial's argument that the *Brown v. Board* decision recognized a constitutional right.

The *Times* also correctly predicted the South would engage in massive resistance and hinted that the highest court's decision might prove impossible to enforce.

Pittsburgh's coverage was not much different. Following World War II, both papers had begun slowly to cover news events – other than crime – involving Blacks.

The *Blade,* for example, weighed in as early as December 1945, editorially praising a local church's efforts to set up what was called a "clinic" to try to promote equal employment opportunities for Black veterans returning from duty.[7]

How well that turned out isn't known, but the next July the newspaper also supported the establishment of a Board of Community Relations, which was supposed to try and identify and hopefully head off any sources of racial tension.

Paul Block, Jr., likely was fully aware that Detroit, a larger city with a similar industrial profile barely fifty miles away, had been engulfed in a major race riot in June 1943, just three years before – a riot that had to be stopped by the U.S. Army.

Less than a year before the *Brown v. Board* decision, there was open hostility and the threat of violence when public housing in East Toledo was desegregated. That was a section of town inhabited largely by blue-collar workers of Hungarian and Polish descent.

---

6. Paul Block bought the *Toledo Times* in 1930, largely to eliminate competition for advertising with the *Blade*; it also had a Sunday edition, which the *Blade* did not. While the *Toledo Times* never had as many resources or subscribers as the *Blade,* it was allowed to compete for stories with its sister paper and take its own editorial positions. In 1960, for example, the *Blade* endorsed John F. Kennedy and the *Times,* Richard Nixon. As newspaper economics changed it became harder to justify two newspapers in one medium-sized city, and The *Times* shut down in July 1975.

7. John Harrison, *The Blade of Toledo: The First 150 Years,* Toledo: The Toledo Blade Co., 1985, 337.

The area was not known for a welcoming attitude toward racial minorities. John Harrison, a former Iowa publisher and journalism professor, noted in his 1985 history of the newspaper that in this and other racially charged postwar incidents, "The *Blade* has stood its ground in defense of racial equality through the exercise of restraint in situations where the public clamor seemed to invite a strategic retreat to another position."

He added that following World War II "reason and restraint have always characterized the *Blade*'s approach to racial relations within the Toledo community."

Clarke Thomas, a longtime *Post-Gazette* newsman, came to a similar conclusion about the family's newspaper in Pittsburgh, though he was not quite as charitable.

Writing about this era in his 2005 history of the *Post-Gazette, Front-Page Pittsburgh*,[8] he concluded that "after William Block took over the *Post-Gazette* in 1946, the paper gradually became more responsive to African-American concerns."

While things may have gotten better in Pittsburgh they did so, to borrow the words of the Supreme Court's *Brown* decision, "with all deliberate speed," and mainly by comparison to the other newspapers, especially Scripps-Howard's *Pittsburgh Press.*

Prior to William Block's taking charge, coverage of Black Pittsburgh was basically limited to stories in which they figured in a crime or occasional sports stories, as when Jesse Owens won his epic four gold medals in the 1936 Olympic games.

Even then, the language was sometimes jarring, especially by today's standards. When it was clear that Owens and other Black track stars were likely to shine in the Berlin games, a *Post-Gazette* sportswriter wrote, as if they were another species, "Dusky shadows are being cast athwart the coming Olympic games by the greatest crop of colored track and field athletes ever developed in the United States." [9]

Ten years later, however, the *Post-Gazette* was beginning to change. In December 1946, during the height of the Christmas shopping season, the Urban League launched a campaign – complete with pickets of both races to pressure big downtown department stores to begin hiring Black women as salesclerks.

That was all-important in an era when there were no suburban shopping

---

8. Clarke Thomas, *Front Page Pittsburgh: Two Hundred Years of the Post-Gazette,* Pittsburgh: University of Pittsburgh Press, 2005, 203-25.
    9. Ibid, 211.

malls. Today that would almost certainly be a front-page story, especially because of a large number of biracial pickets. Incredibly, however, the *Pittsburgh Press,* then the largest-circulation daily in Pittsburgh, entirely ignored the story.

However the *Post-Gazette* did cover it with a story and picture, not on the front-page, but on an inside page on December 10. (The smaller *Sun-Telegraph,* which would be bought by the *Post-Gazette* and merged with it in 1960, also reported the story.)

That was better than nothing, although the white papers then dropped the story, leaving coverage of this intense labor dispute to the *Pittsburgh Courier.* In the end, the department stores held firm to their whites-only employment practices during that holiday season, but quietly began hiring some Black salesclerks early in 1947.

Change came slowly. "The treatment of African Americans by Pittsburgh's newspapers was not much improved in the years that followed," Clarke Thomas said.

For years, he added, quoting a prominent Black attorney, whenever a Black person was charged with committing a crime, he or she would be noted in the papers as "coming from the Hill district," regardless of where the accused actually lived.

True, in 1948 the *Post-Gazette* did publish Ray Sprigle's series on living as a Negro in the Deep South – but that did not include reporting on African-Americans in Pittsburgh; instead, it presented the Jim Crow South as virtually another world. Discrimination in the North, Sprigle essentially said, was merely an inconvenience.

Meanwhile, the *Pittsburgh Courier* was sending a young female reporter, Edna Chappell McKenzie, to try to eat at whites-only restaurants in Allegheny County in the early 1950s; she wrote about being snarled at, refused service, and thrown out.[10]

But neither the *Post-Gazette* nor the other papers paid much attention at first. Gradually, however, the paper and its white population began to take notice. Pittsburgh passed a Fair Employment Practices ordinance in 1952; three years later, in 1955, city government, then very much under the control of legendary Mayor David Lawrence, began a Commission on Human Relations to look into citizen complaints.

Times were changing and later than year the *Post-Gazette,* prodded by

---

10. Edna Chappell McKenzie, "I was just so hurt I would cry myself to sleep. But I knew to be a hard-nosed reporter and to do my share for the cause." in Stanley Nelson, dir., *The Black Press: Soldiers Without Swords,* 1999.

William Block, hired its first Black reporter, Regis Bobonis, a thirty-year-old World War II veteran who had already had a distinguished career with the *Pittsburgh Courier.*

Though Pittsburgh had a considerably larger Black population than Toledo, Bobonis was the first African-American hired by a Pittsburgh paper.

Even though that was eight or nine years after Bill Brower started working for the *Blade,* for a Black reporter to be hired by a major paper in 1955 "was still rare enough that it was covered in trade journals when it happened," noted Professor Dave Davies, an expert on race and the American press.[11]

Bobonis (1925-2016) would go on to have a solid, if not stellar, career at the *Post-Gazette*, covering various city and metropolitan stories before leaving at the end of 1962 to become Pittsburgh's first Black television reporter.[12] A cheerful, modest man, he later had a career in public relations after "realizing I was not the stuff of Pulitzer prizes." He later devoted countless hours to seeing that the Tuskegee airmen, the Black fighter pilots of World War II, were adequately remembered; Bobonis helped get a memorial to them erected in Sewickley, the Pittsburgh suburb where he lived and is buried.

But the year he was hired – 1955 – was the year of two bombshell events that many see as marking the true beginnings of the modern Civil Rights Movement.

One involved a brash teenage boy; the other, a dignified, middle-class woman. They were not people anyone outside their families and a few friends ever knew.

Today, their names are a permanent part of American history, one as a symbol of the triumph of justice and the other as an example of the worst of racism's evil and horror.

The horror came first.

Emmett Till was a fourteen-year-old, born in Chicago, but whose mother was originally from Mississippi. That August in 1955 he went to spend a few days with his great uncle and cousins in the tiny town of Money, Mississippi, where he bought candy at a small local store, Bryant's Candy and Meat Market.

Carolyn Bryant, the twenty-one-year-old wife of owner Roy Bryant, was alone in the store when Till came in. Something – no one knows for sure what – happened. Most likely, the teenager looked at her, a woman later described in the press as a "backwoods Marilyn Monroe," and let out a wolf whistle. His terrified cousins dragged him away.

---

11. Dave Davies, interview with the author, August 29, 2019.

12. At WIIC-TV, which at the time was part-owned by the Block family, who owned the *Post-Gazette.*

Several nights later several white men showed up at his uncle's house in the middle of the night and took Emmett away. He was beaten, tortured, mutilated, and murdered, then weighted down and thrown in the Tallahatchie River.

Three days later, two boys discovered his body. The lynching of a young Black man in Mississippi was scarcely a unique occurrence. Though this murderous practice had been declining for years, more than five hundred Blacks had met a similar fate since 1882.[13]

Typically no one was even arrested in these cases. But this time something was different. Mamie Till Bradley, Emmett Till's mother, managed to get the body sent back to Chicago, where she insisted on displaying it in an open-casket funeral.

Thousands saw her son's horribly mutilated head and face –and photographs of it appeared in the Black press, including the *Chicago Defender* and *Jet Magazine,* as well as some national publications. *Time Magazine* later called it "one of the most influential images of all time."

The photo caused a nationwide sensation, even in the Deep South. Even most segregationists drew the line at murdering children, and Mississippi governor Hugh White urged a "vigorous prosecution."[14] Roy Bryant and his half-brother, J.W. Milam, were duly arrested, charged with capital murder, and put on trial – a rare event.

For the first time since perhaps the 1925 *Scopes* trial, a significant number of national news outlets sent reporters. The *Toledo Blade* and the *Post-Gazette* did not,[15] but prominently featured stories from the Associated Press every day.

The verdict was likely a foregone conclusion; no Mississippi jury was going to convict two white men of murder in such a case, especially since the law didn't allow them to find them guilty of a lesser charge. The jury deliberated a little over one hour; one juror later said they only took that long because they stopped to drink some soda.

The next day, Saturday, September 24, 1955, the verdict inspired a rare banner headline in the *Toledo Times*:

13. Tuskegee Institute Archives. Between 1882 and 1968 a total of 539 African-Americans (including Till), and 42 whites were lynched in Mississippi.

14. The Wikipedia entry, "Emmett Till," is well-sourced and -documented. Perhaps the best book on the case is *The Blood of Emmett Till,* by Timothy Tyson, New York: Simon & Schuster, 2017. Incidentally, it claims that reporters from Toledo were among the press contingent covering the trial; I can find no evidence of that.

15. During the 1980s Paul Block, Jr., told me he felt it was his paper's mission to cover any nationally important story within a 150-mile-radius of the *Blade.*

PAIR ACQUITTED IN SLAYING OF BOY.

The *Blade* analyzed what the verdict had meant in a thoughtful editorial, "A Verdict in the Till Case" on Monday, September 26. "Could justice have been done in such an atmosphere?" the newspaper asked. "It is still possible to assert, without reference to the fairness of the trial or the verdict, that the State of Mississippi did not do justice to itself or to Emmet(sic) Till." That was because, the newspaper said, it had turned into "The People of Mississippi vs. Northern Agitators."

Historians today agree that is exactly what happened.

The Emmett Till case soon vanished from the nation's headlines for one major reason: President Dwight D. Eisenhower suffered a massive heart attack while on vacation in Colorado one day after the verdict, and it dominated the news for weeks.

But the fallout from the case was just beginning. The Emmett Till murder case is worth recounting in detail here because of the massive effect it had on the nation and the nation's newspapers, then still very much the dominant force in media.

The ugly reality of racism was brought home to millions by that famous open-casket photograph in a way mere words could never convey. Suddenly, the "15,000,000 Americans" Bill Brower had written about all had reason to be outraged.

This wasn't just a regional problem; a northern child had been kidnapped, tortured, and murdered while on a visit to the South. But the outrage even extended to southern whites, many of whom were deeply embarrassed.

Though Mississippi may have circled the wagons when they were put on trial in the press, many regarded Milam and Bryant as "peckerwoods"[16] and white trash, a feeling that increased when, after the verdict, they admitted what they had done and sold their story to William Bradford Huie and *Look* magazine.

They did so knowing that the rule of double jeopardy meant that having been acquitted they couldn't be tried for the same offense again. Though few kept up with the case, both men were both ostracized by Mississippians of both races, financially ruined, and essentially driven out of town and then out of state.

Carolyn and Roy Bryant eventually divorced. Many years later, long after

---

16. "The last thing I wanted to do was defend those peckerwoods," the local sheriff later said.

he was dead, she admitted in an interview what had been long suspected, that much of what she said on the witness stand wasn't true and that Emmett Till had never touched her.[17]

Suddenly there was a new feeling that, as Bob Dylan later famously sang, the times were indeed a'changin' when it came to race in America. In Pittsburgh that fall the *Post-Gazette* took a firm stand against segregation in sports for the first time.

On November 23, 1955, the University of Pittsburgh Panthers were chosen to oppose the Georgia Tech Yellow Jackets in the Sugar Bowl, played in New Orleans. Pittsburgh had gotten there principally because of its star player, Bobby Grier –a fullback who was the only African-American on the team. Then, on December 2, Georgia Governor Marvin Griffin, a particularly rabid segregationist, demanded that Grier not be allowed to play.

The *Pittsburgh Post-Gazette* didn't mince words. The newspaper ran a furious editorial the next day, "Governor Griffin's Bigotry. It read, "Good people everywhere, North and South, should ignore the rantings of Georgia Governor Marvin Griffin … . Surely the majority will have the courage to tell Gov. Griffin to take his bigotry back into the piney woods from which he came."[18]

Two days later, the *Gazette*'s famous cartoonist Cy Hungerford drew a cartoon showing Griffin as a braying "All-American Ass." *Post-Gazette* sports columnist Al Abrams denounced "narrow-minded, bigoted and vicious groups" the same day.

In the end, Griffin was humiliated. Georgia Tech's regents refused his demands and Grier played. Pitt lost 7-0, mainly because of an interference call against Grier that was widely seen as unfair.[19] That Sugar Bowl game, on January 2, 1956, was long-remembered as a milestone in the successful integration of college sports.

But something else had happened the day before Marvin Griffin demanded that Georgia Tech not play an integrated team – something that would be far more important.

One hundred and sixty miles away from Griffin's office in Atlanta a quiet, almost mousy forty-two-year-old seamstress was asked to give up her

---

17. Timothy Tyson, *The Blood of Emmett Till,* preface.

18. Thomas, *Front-Page Pittsburgh*, 216-18.

19. Some suspected racial motivations behind the pass interference call but there is no evidence of that. Indeed, Rusty Coles, the referee who made the call, was coincidentally from the Pittsburgh area and readily admitted after seeing the game films that he had made a mistake.

seat and go to the back of a bus in Montgomery. Alabama, so that a white person could sit down.

Rosa Parks, as the world now knows, refused. "I thought of Emmett Till, and I just couldn't go back," she said. The police were called and she was arrested.

What followed led to the first major victory in what some would soon be calling the Civil Rights Movement. After Rosa Parks was bailed out of jail and paid a $14 fine for her "offense,"[20] Black ministers, who were effectively the leaders of the community, held a meeting to discuss strategy. They decided on a total boycott of the city bus system and picked the twenty-six-year-old pastor of the place they met, the Dexter Avenue Baptist Church, to lead it.

His name was Martin Luther King, Jr.

What followed was probably the first successful, long-term mass protest against segregation in history. The boycott lasted more than a year, from December 5, 1955, to December 20, 1956, and only ended after the U.S. Supreme Court, in *Browder v. Gayle*, upheld a lower federal court ruling that Montgomery's policy of segregation on buses violated the equal protection clause of the Fourteenth Amendment, and was therefore unconstitutional.

The *Toledo Blade* and *Pittsburgh Post-Gazette* covered the boycott sporadically, mainly through Associated Press copy and via occasional national columnists. African-Americans, however, likely paid far more attention, especially in Pittsburgh, where the *Courier* paid far closer attention to what was happening.

The boycott was not without its costs; Montgomery and Alabama officials did everything they could to harass the boycott and those supporting it, including people who ran carpools and taxi drivers who charged no more than bus fare to take people to work.

King's house was firebombed as was that of his close friend and ally, Ralph Abernathy, and four Baptist churches. King was jailed for trumped up charges of "conspiring to interfere with business," but this only brought more national attention –and sympathy –to the boycott.

The victory, when it came, was somewhat of a pyrrhic one for Blacks in Montgomery; harassment, intimidation, and incidents of violence continued. There was at least one lynching[21] and the city passed ordinances toughening segregation in other areas, even forbidding Black and white people to play checkers together.

20. $134.34 in December 2019 dollars.
21. J. Mills Thornton, *Dividing Lines: Municipal Politics and the Struggle for Civil Rights in Montgomery, Birmingham, and Selma*, Tuscaloosa: University of Alabama Press, 2006.

Rosa Parks lost her job, was threatened with death, and ended up leaving Montgomery for Detroit, where she lived the rest of her life.

But what the national media had reported on was the victory of the boycott, and the sudden emergency of the man who quickly was seen as the leader of embattled Black America, The Rev. Dr. Martin Luther King, Jr., who, when that court-affirmed victory came, was still a few weeks shy of his twenty-eighth birthday.

How much the bus boycott victory resonated with Blacks in Pittsburgh and Toledo is hard to say. The *Blade* ran a front-page Associated Press story the day the boycott ended, but there was no attempt made to ask residents about it, and no reaction on the editorial page. Nationwide, some African-Americans undoubtedly felt the way journalist Vernon Jarrett did when the movement registered its first successes.

"I'm not going to take what I used to take, I'm not going to let them insult my mother and father the way they once did because… we are going to fight back."[22]

Toledo, thanks to Paul Block, Jr., was ahead of the curve in one important way that may have helped avoid violence for many years, especially in times when there were severe racial tensions including over the desegregating of public housing in 1953.[23]

A bigger test was yet to come. Nine years before that, soon after Block moved to Toledo, the *Blade* had made an important change in racial policy: it stopped identifying suspects or alleged criminals by race, creed, or color.

The wisdom of that would pay off in September 1957 when the daughter of a minister told police that three young Black men had raped her, and a waitress and nurse soon said they'd been raped by Black men as well.

The *Blade* did not identify the alleged assailants by race, though the newspaper did say the nurse's attacker had been a "dark brown man. "The community," John Harrison noted his history, *The Blade of Toledo*, "was in an uproar, and the *Blade* was attacked for covering up a 'Negro crime wave.'"[24]

The newspaper, which faced threats of subscription cancellations and loss of advertising, nevertheless courageously continued to call for citizens to not accept rumors as automatically true. Whether the newspaper knew

22. Stanley Nelson, dir., *Soldiers Without Swords* (1999; Half Nelson Productions).

23. John Harrison, *The Blade of Toledo,* Toledo: Blade Publications, 1985, 338. In some cases Paul Block, Jr., clearly believed the proper policy was to try and create a cooling-off period in times of racial strife. When tensions were high over the 1953 housing crisis, according to historian John Harrison, the *Blade* "limited its coverage of the controversy to a minimum, and even excluded letters to the editor on the subject.

24. Ibid. Single quotes above are mine.

the women's stories sounded fishy isn't clear, but in the end, the women had admitted they had lied.

The newspaper then responded with a front-page editorial – rare in the Paul Block, Jr., era – noting that "all of us have seen that racial identification in a crime story… clearly plays into the hands of those who would stir up animosity."

Had the *Blade* not adopted a statesman-like stand it is easy to imagine violence, rioting, and even murder breaking out; even flimsier rumors have been behind many of the nation's most savage race riots, including Detroit's in 1943.

That same month it became clear to the nation, including Toledo and Pittsburgh, that the battle over civil and equal rights for African-Americans was not going away.

The U.S. Supreme Court had ordered schools desegregated with "all deliberate speed," and the Board of Education in Little Rock, Arkansas attempted to follow that ruling by deciding to begin to integrate that city's previously all-white Central High School in the fall of 1957; nine high-achieving back pupils were chosen to integrate the school when classes began. Governor Orval Faubus, a clownish segregationist and demagogue, called in the Arkansas National Guard.

While he said he was doing so to preserve peace and order, it soon turned out that he had ordered them to prevent the Black students from entering the school, which they then did. President Eisenhower, while privately was not enthusiastic about integration, warned Faubus not to defy the federal government or the U.S. Supreme Court.

Curiously, on its editorial page, the usually more conservative *Toledo Times* was faster to correctly assess the situation than the *Blade*.

On September 6 the paper's lead editorial began: "The idea of progress and justice seems to be intensely obnoxious to one Orval Faubus, brought out of the depths of the Ozarks to be Governor of the state of Arkansas … he has opposed himself to law and order, to the Constitution of the Republic, the Federal Government and its Courts… ."

The editorial, "Who Backs Down, Faubus or Ike?" was stunning in its vituperative contempt for the rogue governor, who it more than once called "arrogantly stupid." It concluded, "The U.S. Government and the Eisenhower administration "must act quickly and peremptorily, even if Faubus is stewed in his own gravy."

President Eisenhower was, as usual, not eager for a confrontation and called Faubus to a meeting and warned him not to defy the U.S. Supreme

Court. Ike, who was on vacation, felt betrayed by Faubus when a mob formed to try to keep the Black students out of Central High.

There was convincing evidence that the renegade governor had been aware of the mob activity in advance. With that the president lost all patience with Faubus.

He federalized the Arkansas National Guard, taking their control away from the governor, ordered them to return to their armories (barracks), and then sent in elements of the U.S. Army's famous 101st Airborne division to make sure the students were admitted.

They were indeed, and the crisis, for the moment, passed. Both the *Blade* and the *Post-Gazette* devoted considerable space to the Little Rock crisis; at one point it was the lead story on the front page for five straight days.

Most days saw multiple stories about it though, again, there were no local stories in which Toledoans were interviewed. Curiously, the *Blade* had reservations when Eisenhower made the decision to send in the 101st Airborne. A September 25 editorial asked, "Was it really necessary for the president, who had appeared to dillydally with the situation, to send paratroopers into a state in order to escort nine children to a school? Had things gotten so out of hand at Little Rock that the military might of the United States Government had to be employed to enforce civil law?"

Well, in fact they *had* gotten out of hand; Eisenhower was almost certainly prudent in not relying on even a federalized Arkansas National Guard, and probably no one knew the reliability of the U.S. Army better than the man who led the Allied forces in Europe during World War II barely a decade before.

While the *Blade* editorial was a rare misreading of the situation, it made it clear that the newspaper had no sympathy for segregation or the behavior of Faubus and the mob he had helped stir up noting, "these scenes of brutality and hatred were a shame to the nation," and worrying that this would give "aid and comfort to our enemies the whole world over" like the Soviet Union and its Cold War allies.

Little Rock quickly faded from the headlines after that, though Faubus, who bizarrely remained an enduring presence in Arkansas politics for decades,[25] would manage to close all the public schools in Little Rock for a year in 1958.

The coverage of the crisis in Little Rock set the tone for much of the *Blade* and *Post-Gazette*'s reporting and analyzing of the national Civil Rights

---

25. Faubus lived from 1910 to 1994. His last hurrah was losing a primary challenge to Arkansas governor Bill Clinton in 1986.

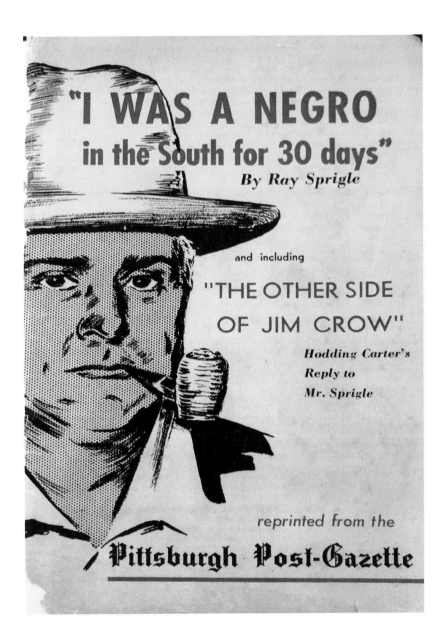

Sprigle's blockbuster series as reprinted
by the *Post-Gazette* – with segregationist
Hodding Carter's rebuttal.

Ray Sprigle, the *Pittsburgh Post-Gazette's* legendary
undercover reporter, with his trademark corncob pipe.
(All Sprigle photos courtesy of the Senator John Heinz
History Center, Pittsburgh)

Sprigle in disguise as a Black man, "James Rayel
Crawford," as he looked while spending a month
in the segregated Deep South.

At left, publisher Paul Block at meeting he arranged in May, 1925 between President Calvin Coolidge and an uncomfortable-seeming Tom Lee, Memphis hero of a Mississippi River disaster. (Harris & Ewing, courtesy of the Library of Congress)

Paul Block, founder of Block Communications, and his wife Dina, celebrating the *Toledo Blade's* 100th anniversary in 1935. (*Toledo Blade*)

William "Bill" Block, the founder's younger son, led the *Pittsburgh Post-Gazette* into the modern era, and was always proudly liberal on civil rights. (*Pittsburgh Post-Gazette*)

Paul Block Jr., the head of the company until his death in 1987, was a publisher, a distinguished chemist – and a man who loved newsprint. (*Toledo Blade*)

Paul Block Jr. was a savvy publisher who nevertheless sometimes wore a lab coat in the office. (*Toledo Blade*)

Allan Block, shown here with his wife, Susan Allan Block, is the current chair of Block Communications, Inc. In addition to insisting on fairness, he pushed the family company to become truly multimedia. (*Toledo Blade*)

John Robinson Block, publisher and editor-in-chief of both the *Toledo Blade* and *Pittsburgh Post-Gazette*, has led each paper to win a Pulitzer Prize. (*Toledo Blade*)

Bill Brower's first two series on Black America, in 1951 and 1972, were reprinted by *The Blade* in booklet form. (*Toledo Blade*)

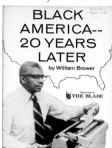

The *Toledo Blade's* Bill Brower, one of the first Black reporters at a predominately white newspaper, seen here at his typewriter in 1961. Also: in his home office with his wife Louise, Toledo's first Black public school principal, and son Bill. Jr. (*Toledo Blade*)

Eddie B. Allen Jr, left, accompanied Brower on his
last cross-country jaunt to report on race, in 1996.
(*Toledo Blade*)

Regis D. Bobonis became the first Black reporter on a
daily Pittsburgh newspaper when the *Post-Gazette* hired
him in 1955. A few years later, he became the city's first
Black TV reporter for a station co-owned by the Block
family. (*Pittsburgh Post-Gazette*)

Movement in the years to come. Looking back from the advantage of more than half a century the papers' news judgment was almost always reasonably complete and on the mark.

Editorially, the newspapers supported most, if not all of Black leaders' national aspirations, while stressing the need for nonviolence. When Medgar Evers was murdered in Mississippi on June 12, 1963, the same night that President Kennedy gave a nationally televised speech proposing a civil rights bill, the *Blade* responded in an editorial noting, "what a contrast there is between the bombings and shootings with which white extremists reply to Negro citizens' legal and moral demands, and the gospel of nonviolence preached by The Rev. Martin Luther King, Jr.," whose younger brother, The Rev. A.D. King, had spoken in Toledo the day of Evers' murder. In Toledo, where editorial pages were widely read and generally seen as having considerable influence, the newspapers' stand likely influenced people.

When, a little more than two months later, the historic March on Washington began (featuring King's "I Have a Dream" speech) at the Lincoln Memorial, the *Blade* devoted a great deal of space and the energies of its Washington correspondent, George Jenks, to providing balanced but essentially favorable coverage of it.

This time the *Blade* coverage included a local angle and a major local story on August 29, 1963. "100 from Toledo Area Off to March,"[26] interviewed local folks, both Black and white, said to be "in high spirits," who were boarding buses and trains to go to Washington.

The *Toledo Times* had been worried about the possibility of bloodshed, but happily admitted the same day that it was wrong.

"The worst fears that yesterday's Freedom March to the Lincoln Memorial might inadvertently erupt into violence have proved to be wholly unwarranted," the editorial said. "The leaders and participants in the parade demonstrated a remarkable restraint and capacity to avoid emotional disturbances under most trying conditions."[27]

The march, the usually conservative editorial page concluded, "certainly should convince the most skeptical that the Negro is fed up waiting for the same treatment white people get and has learned how to demand it through

---

26. The *Blade* in this era seldom used bylines on local stories, so it is impossible to know who wrote many pieces.

27. Interestingly, the first-day coverage of Martin Luther King, Jr.'s speech didn't emphasize the now-famous "I have a dream" sequence; an illustration of something that sometimes happens in journalism, the "first rough draft" of history. The *New York Times* coverage of Franklin D. Roosevelt's first inaugural address barely mentioned its now-famous phrase, "the only thing we have to fear is fear itself."

collective action."[28]

That was August 1963, and the Civil Rights Movement had up to that point been almost entirely peaceful – at least on the part of those fighting for their rights.

There had been plenty of violence committed against African-Americans but until then the movement had stayed faithful to Martin Luther King's philosophy of non-violence. The *Blade* had, however, warned that could change:.

The day after Medgar Evers' murder its lead editorial observed that "for while nonviolence is a noble concept of the way to right long-endured wrongs, it is far from an indestructible pattern... there are limits on Negro restraint that are being severely tested –criminally so by white violence; foolishly by white indifference."

The day was not far off when violence would indeed explode, like Langston Hughes' famous "dream deferred" reference in his poem, "Harlem." Something else lay ahead, too.

Except for a few demonstrations in Pittsburgh and Toledo, the Civil Rights Movement and the struggles of Black America had largely been played out in states many miles away from either of those cities.

That, too, would change, and test the newspapers that would cover it.

---

28. *Toledo Times,* August 29, 1963.

12

Two Newspapers, Two African-American Communities: 1950-1970

"We've been liberal in connection with civil rights; conservative on economics. That is my personal feeling, and the road we followed."[1]
— William Block, Sr. (1915-2005)

The way newspapers regarded the Black communities in their cities was indeed beginning to change in the 1950s, and both Bill Block in Pittsburgh and Paul Block, Jr., in Toledo were aware of the need to change the way their papers covered them.

They were probably ahead of most other publishers on this score; both papers, especially the *Blade,* hired Black reporters before most other newspapers did, though some of these papers were much larger and more nationally prominent.

They also began taking Black community concerns into account. This did not happen overnight, and there were times when the papers were not as sensitive as they might have been — as in the case of the "Pittsburgh Renaissance."

Urban renewal was very much in fashion in the 1950s. In Pittsburgh the

---

1. Clarke Thomas, *Front Page Pittsburgh: Two Hundred Years of the* Post-Gazette, Pittsburgh: University of Pittsburgh Press, 2005, 221.

major target was called the Hill District, much of which was undoubtedly badly blighted but which also contained what was often called "Little Harlem" – an area of vibrant culture, including the *Pittsburgh Courier* newspaper and lively jazz clubs such as the Crawford Grill, where artists like Dizzy Gillespie, Duke Ellington, and Art Blakey played, hung out, and often launched their careers.

Its days were numbered. Ray Sprigle was nearly seventy in 1954, but he had lost none of his zest for reporting. In April of that year his last major series, "Why Are There Slums?" took an eight-part look at the problem, which was especially acute in the Lower Hill District. Sprigle largely blamed greedy slumlords and a city government that had failed to provide even basic city services. He didn't blame racial discrimination, though most of the residents were Black. But as noted earlier, he did conclude quite correctly that "Nobody gives much of a damn about the hill."[2]

The city's leaders and editorial writers noticed his series – but they didn't respond by pouring resources into the Hill District, as New York City would do in the Bedford-Stuyvesant area of Brooklyn a little more than a decade later. They responded by bulldozing it.

"The Lower Hill was to be the first victim of a series of destructive redevelopment projects in poor neighborhoods later heralded as the 'Pittsburgh Renaissance,'" Bill Steigerwald, himself a longtime *Post-Gazette* reporter, observed in his excellent biography of Sprigle, *30 Days a Black Man.*

"The project would ultimately flatten nearly one hundred acres of the Lower Hill and displace eight thousand humans – 80 percent of them Black.

"A bustling, diverse, funky and admittedly rundown neighborhood alive with great jazz was replaced by the Civic Arena, the stainless steel home of the Civic Light Opera, and a sea of asphalt parking lots," Steigerwald added.

None of the newspapers, he complained, including the *Pittsburgh Post-Gazette,* cared about the project's steep social costs.

"They cheered it on from the start. They didn't write editorials questioning the project or write sad feature stories about its victims."

That was, in fact, true. Nor did the *Post-Gazette* or anyone else seem very concerned about where the displaced residents would go, in a city where housing still tended to be rigidly segregated with no laws forbidding discrimination. The vast majority of those who lived there were renters and would have received no compensation at all.

---

2. Bill Steigerwald, *30 Days a Black Man: The Forgotten Story That Exposed the Jim Crow South,* Guilford, CT: Lyons Press/Globe Pequot, 2017, 287-88.

Newspapers still were a long way in the 1950s, from taking minority viewpoints into consideration. However, it should be noted that there was little outcry of any kind against the demolition; slum clearance was seen as modern and progressive.

Even the Black Pennsylvania legislator who represented the Hill District fully supported the "Pittsburgh Renaissance" project. Much the same happened in many other cities, including Detroit, where a freeway was deliberately rammed through the city's historic Black residential and commercial districts, Black Bottom and Paradise Valley.

Eventually, there would be second thoughts. Ten years later, the year the landmark Civil Rights Act of 1964 was passed, the *Pittsburgh Post-Gazette* decided to take up the cause of discrimination against African-Americans in the housing market, one of the many injustices the bill was designed to remedy.

The paper ran a series of well-reported articles documenting the futile efforts of Kenneth Hawthorne, a young Black executive at the Gulf Oil Company, to purchase a home in Mt. Lebanon, an affluent Pittsburgh suburb. The stories led to an investigation by the Pennsylvania Human Relations Commission and court hearings in Allegheny County.[3]

Though the Black population in Toledo was smaller than that in Pittsburgh, both in total numbers and percentage, the newspaper may have been quicker to both begin covering and giving more weight to the concerns of the African-American community.

Bishop Robert Culp, the senior minister at the Church of God on Collingwood Boulevard in Toledo,[4] paused in 2019 to consider what he thought about the *Toledo Blade* and how it has covered race over the nearly sixty years he's been in town.

Culp, a tall, stately Pennsylvania native who has lived in Toledo since 1961, the year Barack Obama was born, has been deeply involved and a leader in the city's African-American community almost from the day he arrived. This was partly because the church he arrived to lead had gone through four ministers in five years, and he realized that he needed to give the congregation some time before making any changes.

Partly too, it was because he knew the world was changing. He had been a very young pastor in 1958 when he met another young minister a few years

---

3. Thomas, *Front-Page Pittsburgh*, 220.
4. The Church of God is a Pentecostal church similar to, but different from, the better-known Church of God in Christ (COGIC) – one of the largest African-American denominations.

older who, it was suggested to him, he might see as a mentor.

Culp, who was then almost twenty-four, remembered having some doubts as to whether he could really learn from a preacher who was also still in his twenties. Then he met the fellow, a Georgia native who had a church in Montgomery, Alabama.

His name was The Rev. Dr. Martin Luther King, Jr., and Culp, a former college basketball player, soon realized he was indeed special. He was deeply impressed by his style: "King never had an enemy, as least as far as he was concerned," Culp told me over a long and pleasant lunch meeting, more than half a century after the great civil rights leader was assassinated.

"Whenever there was an issue, King would hear everyone in the room out before making a decision," he said. Like him, Robert Culp became attuned to the fact that the world was changing, and that men of the cloth had a big part to play in leading it.

He quickly fell in love with Toledo and once he arrived, "I joined every committee in town," he said with a soft-spoken smile, "and as a result I became head of the NAACP and served from 1966 to 1968." In that capacity he had the chance to introduce his long-time friend Dr. King when he came to speak in Toledo in 1967.

Robert Culp, who was still in his pulpit more than half a century later, soon realized that as one of the city's major Black leaders he also needed to pay attention to the media in town, especially the dominant paper, the *Toledo Blade*.

He's been doing so ever since. "I have always regarded the *Blade* as kind of a mixed bag, and I still do," he said. "News coverage of the Black community, as of the community in general, has been excellent. But the editorial page has always been regarded as an enigma," by himself and the wider community, he said.

However, Culp said that John Robinson Block, grandson of the first Paul Block and editor-in-chief and publisher of both the Toledo and Pittsburgh papers, always had shown him and his views respect, even when they deeply disagreed.

"He's always asking me, 'What would you, what would your community, think about this or that?' He takes my concerns and the (Black) community's seriously."

The senior Block was not the first member of his family to do so. As already noted, by the early 1950s William Block, the younger of the founder's two sons, had begun pushing the *Pittsburgh Post-Gazette* to be more responsive to the Black community.

And in Toledo, Paul Block, Jr., had realized that the struggles for civil rights and the condition of Black citizens were going to be permanent major news stories. The *Blade* in the mid-1960s became one of the first papers in America to have a dedicated full-time civil rights reporter. Tom Gearhart, a young reporter "wanted that, pushed for it, and to his great credit, got it," said Tom Walton, a fellow reporter at the time.

Walton, who went on to hold a wide variety of beats at the *Blade* before finishing a fifty-two-year career at the company as editor (actually editorial page editor) of the paper, said "he got it, and did what I guess everyone would have said was a very good job."

While the exact dates are unclear, records and clipping files would indicate that Gearhart reported intensively on civil rights from 1966 to 1969, and occasionally after that until at least 1972. This included traveling to cover some national stories, such as a trip to New York City in 1969 to report on Bayard Rustin and the A. Philip Randolph Institute's efforts to persuade the Nixon Administration to launch a $185 billion-effort to achieve economic equality for African-Americans.

Gearhart also took a look at the "street academies" that were flourishing in Harlem for high school dropouts at the time.

But mostly, he did intensive, often hard-hitting reporting on Black issues, life and citizens in Toledo, including an in-depth piece on what he openly called Toledo's two Black ghettos in May 1968, just weeks after Martin Luther King, Jr.'s assassination.[5]

Gearhart's reporting was searing and didn't sugarcoat reality. It even included slightly veiled criticism of the media, which in Toledo in 1968, was mostly the *Blade:*

"Most white persons do not know any ordinary ghetto residents," he wrote. "Consequently, it is easy for white persons to get a distorted view of Negro life. They read only about ghetto Negroes only when something newsworthy occurs, and that something is often bad."[6]

Although Gearhart, who went on to a long career as an editor at the paper, was white, by that time the *Blade* had at least three Black reporters – Gloria Sneed, Wayne Graham, and Ben Wade, in addition to William Brower, who by then was news editor.

While there are apparently no available records listing past employees

5. "Toledo's Ghetto Looking to Youth for Improvements," *Toledo Blade,* May 12, 1968.
6. The term "Black" replaced "Negro" gradually, and became the preferred term for most African-Americans around 1969. By the early 1970s, the *Blade* and the *Post-Gazette* no longer used "Negro."

by race, after researching his 1985 history *The Blade of Toledo, the First 150 Years,* the late John Harrison concluded "The numbers of blacks on the editorial staff of the *Blade* have been greater than the national average, and a persistent effort has been made to recruit black reporters and editors."[7] Whether any consideration was given to choosing a Black reporter for that beat is unknown; the editors may have remembered the young Bill Brower's insistence that he not be pigeonholed as "the Negro news reporter."

In any event, the Black community seems not to have been chagrined that a white reporter was making a serious attempt to cover their issues. "We saw him as pretty good, pretty good and a fair writer – he was fair on the issues," said Culp.

The newspaper, and Paul Block, Jr.'s philosophy in the 1950s and '60s seemed to be rooted in the belief that Blacks needed to be given the same opportunities as whites, and all barriers to their progress needed to be removed so that they could fully take part in the American dream. Above all, the *Blade* wanted cooperation within the community and especially among its leaders, and to avoid violence.

"It is interesting to note how often the *Blade* proposed or praised dealing with racial problems with solutions based on mutual consent," Harrison observed.[8]

That was true in 1957, when Janet Quinn, who was Black, was elected football queen at Scott High School, and there was some threat of racial trouble. Students of both races met; tensions were lowered, and some hotheads apologized.

After the crisis passed, the *Blade* lauded the students, "who have shown their elders how people of different backgrounds (can) live together within the rules of a democratic society." A far more serious situation occurred in the fall of 1957.

In two separate incidents two women, a nurse working at a local hospital and a seventeen-year-old high school student, claimed they had been sexually assaulted by Black men.

The *Blade* reported the alleged assaults but held fast to the newspaper's policy of leaving out the racial descriptions of the assailant or assailants. The story was the talk of the town, and this caused a torrent of abuse to be leveled at the newspaper.

"We've received any number of letters and phone calls... denouncing

---

7. John Harrison, *The Blade of Toledo,* Toledo: Blade Publications, 1985, 337.
8. Ibid, 339.

us for not identifying persons accused of crimes by race and saying all sorts of unprintable things about us," then-editor Michael Bradshaw wrote in an unsigned editorial.[9]

Suddenly the story changed. Both women admitted that, for whatever reason, they had made up the story about their assaults. "The policy of the *Blade,* needless to say, will remain unchanged," Bradshaw wrote, adding,. "we do not believe race matters when the crime is the same regardless of who commits it."

Overall, the paper's attitude towards racial tensions locally in those years may, as Harrison noted, have been best summed up by a headline of a July 1964 editorial:

RESTRAINT – AND HELP

Restraint, that is, on the part of any hotheads of any color; help for minorities who had been unfairly disadvantaged. The topic at hand had to do with bad behavior by some local Black youth at the YWCA – teen-age boys evidently unable to find jobs.[10]

Help was on the way, at least nationally; that was the very month in which the most sweeping civil rights legislation since Reconstruction took effect – the Civil Rights Act of 1964. But pleas for restraint were not as successful.

The month before three civil rights workers, Andrew Goodman,[11] Michael Schwerner and James Cheney, disappeared in Mississippi where they had been attempting to register Blacks to vote. They were found in August buried in an earthen dam; all had been murdered and at least one of them, Cheney, who was Black, was tortured.

When their broken bodies were found, the *Blade* said of the young civil rights workers, two of whom were only twenty, "they were embarked on a crusade for justice in an American version of a police state. They lost their lives in an effort to bring light."[12]

Republican presidential nominee Barry Goldwater, one of only six GOP senators to oppose the Civil Rights Bill of 1964, went down in a crushing defeat three months later. Not only did neither Block paper endorse him,

---

9. "A Lesson for This Community," *Toledo Blade,* reprinted October 31, 1971. The *Blade* that Sunday reprinted a number of Bradshaw's more memorable editorials; he had died of a heart attack in Cambridge, Massachusetts, two weeks before.

10. Ibid.

11. Goodman, a twenty-year-old New Yorker, had received his field training for civil rights work on the campus of Miami University in Oxford, Ohio, not far from Toledo, earlier that summer, though the *Blade* doesn't seem to have realized that.

12. *Toledo Blade* editorial, August 6, 1964.

after he lost the *Blade* denounced his thinly veiled appeal to southern racists, calling it "dangerous demagoguery," and comparing it to the racist, anti-immigrant Know-Nothing movement of the 1850s.

The next year on February 21 Malcolm X, who had dramatically broken with King's philosophy of racial reconciliation, was assassinated by a rival faction of the Nation of Islam, generally then called the Black Muslims by the media.

The *Blade's* editorial on the killing was far more thoughtful and sophisticated than most reaction nationwide; many other editors had been deeply offended by Malcolm X's assertion that President Kennedy's assassination barely a year before had been a case of "the chickens coming home to roost," and somehow related to the many years of largely unpunished murders of innocent African-Americans by whites.

Many white Americans felt simply that Malcolm X, a former street hustler from Lansing, Michigan, had gotten what he deserved. But the *Blade's* editorial writers saw him and his death as far more complex.

"It would be much too glib, however, to dismiss Malcolm X's assassination merely as the violent death of a violent man," the newspaper said, two days after he died.[13] "… he was a man of some brilliance and power who, from beginnings as a Harlem racketeer, had made himself conspicuous not only in this country and abroad as a militant advocate of Negro rights against white oppression."

The newspaper noted that Malcolm X had also "in his last metamorphosis" repudiated racism and had praised "the brotherhood of men of all colors."

The *Blade* concluded by saying that his killers had to be brought to justice, because "justice was the one thing that this man did not expect from the society of which he was a victim as well as a foe."

Coincidentally, on the very day Malcolm X died, the *Blade's* Sunday Magazine carried a story by Seymour Rothman, a longtime feature writer and columnist for the paper, called "The First Lady" celebrating Ella Stewart, a longtime fixture in Toledo's Black community who, as the cover lines said, had been quietly "fighting (and) winning battles for integration long before the civil rights war in the U.S. was declared."

One wonders if readers thought about the contrast between the elderly, quiet woman pharmacist and the internationally famous firebrand, who was easily young enough to have been her son.

A month later, the newspaper went on to praise those who took part in

---

13. *Toledo Blade* editorial, February 23, 1965.

the historic march from Selma to Montgomery on March 25, 1965, and to deplore the murder of Viola Liuzzo, the white woman from Detroit who took part in the march and was murdered by the Klan. To those who scoffed that the march itself was only symbolic, the newspaper said:

"What did raising the flag on Iwo Jima actually achieve – except to give every American a symbol of ultimate victory?"[14]

But violent events far away were one thing. As the 1960s wore on, and the Vietnam War worsened and a newly energized Black America grew impatient, American cities began exploding in riots that were part racial, part economic.

Race riots were nothing new in America, of course, but most of the earlier riots began with whites attacking Blacks, or at least primarily violence directed against Black citizens and neighborhoods. These riots were different; they mostly involved explosions within Black neighborhoods or ghettos, with loss of life and enormous property damage.

New York erupted in 1965; the mostly Black area of Los Angeles called Watts blew up, leaving thirty-four dead. Smaller disturbances, nearly all of them labeled "riots" by the media, took place in other cities in 1966.[15]

Newark, where Paul Block owned a paper from 1916 to 1939, suffered an incredibly destructive one that included twenty-six deaths from July 12 to 17, 1967.

Then, a week after Newark burned itself out, Detroit exploded in the worst and most destructive urban disturbance of the 1960s on the night of July 23-24.

The riot started innocently enough, with a police raid on an after-hours drinking joint known as a blind pig. Before it ended five days later, forty-three people were dead, thousands injured, thousands more arrested, and two thousand buildings destroyed.

In the end, President Lyndon B. Johnson had to send paratroopers in from the U.S. Army's 82nd and 101st divisions to restore order, much as President Franklin D. Roosevelt had done in 1943 during an earlier Motown race riot. That riot found no echo in Toledo. This one did.

The Detroit disturbance started in the wee hours of Sunday morning (July 24). As the day wore on, conditions steadily worsened in the city. Toledo was barely fifty miles away and many people in both cities knew each other.

---

14. *Toledo Blade*, March 26, 1965.
15. It has now become fashionable, if not politically correct, to refer to what happened in Detroit in July 1967 as "the rebellion." At the time, however, and for many years afterwards, both Black and white citizens called and thought of it a "riot."

Though Toledo's Black population was still smaller than most major cities, it was approaching 50,000 people by 1967, twice the 1950 figure; nearly all of them packed into two downtown inner-city neighborhoods.[16] That night, almost a day after violence began in Detroit, fires, looting, and sporadic violence broke out in Toledo.

No one was killed, but extra police were called into duty; 500 Ohio National Guard troops were called up and roadblocks were set up "to prevent a possible influx of outside agitators,"[17] though none came. The rioting lessened but continued for a second day. Seventy-nine fires were started by what were called "firebombs," dozens were arrested, and a speech by Martin Luther King, Jr., was postponed until the fall.

Though frightening at the time, it was pretty small as 1960's disturbances went. After the lawlessness died down the *Blade,* which intensively covered Toledo's upheaval, ran an editorial, "Plaudits for the Police," which praised the city's men in blue for handling the situation "with skill, firmness and a keen sense of responsibility."

"Probably not the least of the factors... has been the presence of more than a score of Negroes on the force... they symbolize the joint interest of both Negro and white Toledoans in law, order and sound enforcement policies."[18]

These words were written while murder and arson still raged in Detroit, in a riot that was clearly made worse by the actions of a racist and nearly all-white police force.

But if anyone in Toledo – or anywhere in the nation – thought the moment of danger had passed with the end of the Detroit riot, they got a rude awakening nine months later when Martin Luther King, Jr., was shot to death on the balcony of Lorraine Motel in Memphis, Tennessee, on Thursday night, April 4, 1968.

With that, cities across the country erupted.[19] Toledo was not untouched, though things were not nearly as bloody or destructive as elsewhere. Several days later, Tom Gearhart reported that it was likely that "peace was preserved in the city by an extraordinary amount of hard work, much of it behind the

---

16. Campbell Gibson and Kay Jung, *Historical Census Statistics on Population Totals by Race, 1790 to 1990 ... For Large Cities and Other Urban Cities in the United States,* Suitland-Silver Hill, MD: U.S. Census Bureau, February 2005.

17. Harrison, 339.

18. *Toledo Blade,* July 26, 1967.

19. Two notable exceptions were Indianapolis where Robert Kennedy, the champion of Black America who was campaigning in that city's ghetto, urged calm, and Detroit, which was possibly still traumatized from the largest urban riot of the decade.

scenes, by concerned city officials and citizens, both Negro and white."[20]

There were close calls. On Friday, April 5, Black students at Toledo's Scott High School demanded that administrators fly the American flag at half-staff.

They unwisely refused.

Enraged, the students took to the streets, were joined by others, threw rocks, vandalized cars, and destroyed property. They were apparently heading for a nearby junior high school when police summoned Reverend Culp, then both one of the city's leading pastors and the head of the NAACP, to see if he could do something to stop the violence from escalating further.

He managed to do that. Later he told the *Blade* that he had done so by assuring the youths that he would see to it that there was a more organized march from a church on Dorr Street in the heart of Toledo's Black community to the city's downtown.

However, during an interview more than half a century later, Culp told it slightly differently. Yes, he did tell them about the march. But what really made a difference was a lucky accident. "By God's grace, the two ringleaders (of the protest) were grandsons of members of my church. Both their grandmothers were members of my congregation," Culp said.

"So I told them, now, you knock this off or I will tell your grandmothers what you've been doing," he chuckled before explaining that in their families, the grandmothers were the ones who laid down the law. The student demonstration quickly ended, though not before five people were injured. "The police regarded me as something of a miracle worker after that," Bishop Culp said, grinning softly. The march Culp promised did happen that night, and between about eight hundred people participated in a mostly peaceful demonstration that only turned ugly after it was over, when some of the marchers returned to the site and broke plate glass doors and display windows on Madison Avenue.[21]

Bishop Culp was praised by the *Blade* too. But according to John Robinson Block, a teenager at the time, his father, Paul Block, Jr., had become deeply disillusioned by urban rioting, especially in nearby Detroit.

"He was dismayed," John Block said. Paul Block, Jr., came to feel that "race was a problem America would never get beyond, though he did his best."

John C. Straub was a 28-year-old Toledo lawyer when he decided to run

---

20. Tom Gearhart, "Inner-City Residents, Police, Team Up to Prevent Spread of Violence Here," *Toledo Blade*, April 1968.

21. "Toledo Under Curfew Following Disorders," *Toledo Blade*, April 6, 1968, 1.

for the Toledo Board of Education in 1969. "I was told all candidates would have fifteen minutes to make their case to the publisher," he said more than a half century later.[22]

When Straub met Paul Block Jr., the older man wanted to know what he thought was the biggest issue facing the schools and society. There was no question about what Block thought it was: Race.

"Now this was at a time when the schools were only about 19 percent Black," said Straub, now retired and living in Washington, D.C. and Vermont, "but he thought it was the biggest issue facing the country in the long-term, and it was important for anyone to be on top of it."

The men talked for an hour and a half. Straub won the newspaper's endorsement – and the election.

The newspaper remained committed to gradual and peaceful change. What happened in Pittsburgh after the King assassination was far worse than in Toledo.

Genuine riots broke out and raged off and on for a week until April 12, when the Pennsylvania National Guard was called out to enforce a curfew on a community seething with anger. Before the rioting was over there were more than 500 fires, $620,000 in property damage ($16 million in 2020 dollars), 1 death, and 926 arrests.[23]

The *Post-Gazette* covered the rioting as the major story it was, deploying reporters to cover every aspect of it, handicapped only in not having a Sunday paper (the newspaper gave it up when it entered into a Joint Operating Agreement with the *Pittsburgh Press* in 1961). The newspaper covered it as a straight news, essentially a crime and disaster story.

Most of the coverage was even-handed, with the exception of a front-page story by business editor Jack Markowitz on April 9, "Moving Out Like Refugees – Hill's White Merchants Sad, Bitter." The story was a sympathetic feature on the white businessmen in the mostly Black Hill District, who had their stores burned out or vandalized in the looting and destruction that followed Dr. King's death.

Markowitz, writing about one man he assumed could speak for all such businessmen, wrote, "he was disgusted with a system that seemed to protect young looters while being unable to shield an eighty-year-old business; he

---

22. Personal interview, July 21, 2020. Straub became a member of the board of directors of the BCI, The Blade's parent company, in 2020.

23. Randy Fox, "Pittsburgh's Hill District: Death of a Dream," *Huffington Post,* September 15, 2012.

was bitter, he was angry... .[24] The story did mention a few "Negroes" who were appalled by and condemned the destruction.

There was, however, no attempt to interview Black residents about the grievances that had driven them to riot, with the exception of one man, depicted as sort of a shiftless lout in a "billiard room," who said it was because "the white man makes his money here and then he takes it out of here."

He did, however, condemn the riot, saying "We should have organized and bought 'em out... this was stupid." The story concluded by depicting (Black) rioters as believers in "a completely naïve idea; that all that has to be done is the removal of white businessmen and non-whites would be able to take over. When the burnt smell is gone, the militants would find that business doesn't work that way."

The *Post-Gazette's* editorial page the next day showed considerably more sophisticated understanding: "However ill-treated they may have been, most black people do not turn to criminal acts to get revenge.... As Pittsburghers consider the disorder and destruction that have come to their own city, they should avoid blanket condemnation based on skin color. They should recognize that gross racial injustices still exist here, and they should greatly intensify their efforts to equalize opportunities in employment, education and in housing – not as a reward for the vocal hostility and violence of the few, but as the just due of the majority of black people who have tried to keep their faith in our system and who, for the most part, suffer in silence."[25]

Racial tensions simmered throughout both cities and across the nation throughout the balance of the year. Two months to the day after Martin Luther King's assassination Robert F. Kennedy, the presidential contender seen by most Blacks as the only candidate who really cared about African-Americans, was assassinated after winning the California Democratic primary. That fall, running for president on an openly segregationist third-party platform, Alabama Governor George Wallace would win nearly ten million votes.

Paul Block, Jr., and his editors were clearly concerned in that nightmare year that American society was fragmenting along racial lines, and that the white majority had very little knowledge of the very real contributions Blacks made to society.

To help counter this the *Blade* produced a series that was remarkable for any newspaper, especially a medium-sized one in the Midwest: "Negroes in

---

24. *Pittsburgh Post-Gazette*, April 8, 1968, 1, 21.
25. "Racial Conflict in Pittsburgh," *Pittsburgh Post-Gazette,* April 9, 1968

American Civilization," which ran daily from June 16 through July 7, 1968.

Block, a noted research chemist as well as a publisher, believed strongly in expertise, and frequently hired experts in a given field who could write and understand journalism. The project began with and was anchored by six articles by Harvey Ford, the paper's longtime education editor, a scholar with a Ph.D. in American history.

Ford looked primarily at Black history from the origins of slavery to the Great Migration to the now-infamous 1896 *Plessy v. Ferguson* U.S. Supreme Court decision that legalized segregation, until it was overturned by the *Brown v. Board* decision in 1954.

Other staffers turned out solid, well-researched stories on everything from African-American religion to discrimination in unions and in business; from literature to politics, education, the military, women's issues, show business, music, and the arts.

William Brower, who in three years would be making his second nationwide trek reporting on the condition of Black America, did a major piece on Blacks (then still "Negroes") in sports. Four of the reporters contributing pieces were Black in an era when few major newspapers had that many African-Americans on staff.

Later the *Blade* reprinted all twenty-two articles as a thick booklet,[26] which its promotion and public service department made available for free to the public and school groups.

In an introduction to the series an anonymous editor noted that it wasn't enough for newspapers to cover breaking news; journalism meant "in-depth" reporting to help readers make sense of it all. Acknowledging that newspapers had long neglected most news about African-Americans, "The *Blade* concluded that as part of its commitment to in-depth reporting of contemporary affairs it has an obligation to its readers to place today's news about racial turmoil into a more intelligible and meaningful context."

Context, that is, "of what has gone on during the past 300 years of an evolving American civilization." The series was well-received, though it is impossible to know how widely the various articles were read.

The year 1968 was, scholars have long agreed, one of the most dreadful years in modern American history; the assassinations of Kennedy and King were followed by what has been called a "police riot" at the Democratic National Convention in August.

---

26. Tom Gearhart, *Negroes in American Civilization,* Toledo: *Toledo Blade* publication, 1968). Gearhart, who was extremely helpful in furthering my understanding of this era, kindly lent me his copy.

The next month, racially tinged broke out on Toledo, when on September 14, for no apparent reason, a crowd of nearly a thousand "rampaged" along Dorr Street in the heart of Toledo's Black ghetto. Toledo police shrewdly restored order with a dozen Black officers and an African-American youth group called the Black Deacons. There were about fifty arrests and a score of injuries according to the *Blade*, but no one was killed.

Violence, however, was never far from the surface in coming years, especially after the Black Panther Party expressly repudiated the idea that non-violence was the only way to make progress. The party was small but popular among African-Americans in Toledo who appreciated its free clothing and free breakfast programs.[27]

After various police clashes with Panthers in other cities in 1969, the Toledo chapter, along with those in some other cities, adopted the name National Committee to Combat Fascism, or NCCF, in early 1970. Things were about to get uglier.

On September 15, there were two major shootouts between police and NCCF members in a now-defunct housing project named Desire in New Orleans.

No one was killed but a number of Panthers were shot, and they thought they were the victims of unprovoked police aggression. Tensions were high, and as a *New York Times* story later reported, "So after New Orleans, it seemed inevitable that another clash would occur within a short time. And it did, three days later, in Toledo, Ohio."[28]

What nobody disputes is that early that morning a man, in the words of the *Times* article, "walked up to a patrol car, stuck a gun through the window, and shot and killed a policeman (Patrolman William Miscannon), the father of four children."

The shooting occurred near Toledo's NCCF office and within minutes the dead man's partner arrested an NCCF member, chapter leader John McClellan, who was later charged with murder. As the *Times* story put it, "Within an hour after the arrest, the Toledo police descended on the NCCF office and started pumping bullets into it, until it resembled a hut on a battlefield that had been shot up by an infantry company."

The police said there had been a gun battle, that they had been so violent

---

27. Derek Ide, "Serving the Community: Toledo's Black Panther Party," on the blog "Black Then: Discovering Our History," February 6, 2019, https://www.africanamerica. org/topic/black-then-discovering-our-history (accessed February 13, 2020).

28. Martin Arnold, "Police and Panthers: Urban Conflict in Mutual Fear," *New York Times,* October 26, 1970.

because NCCF members had been shooting at them. The *Toledo Blade* called it a gunfight between the Panthers and the police, and so did all other Toledo media.

"Within seconds after Patrolman Miscannon was shot, gunfire erupted from the Panther headquarters ... a half block from the fatal shooting," the *Blade* reported the day of the murder on September 18, 1970.

But that was almost certainly not true.

The evidence indicates that regardless of who murdered Miscannon, what happened at the NCCF headquarters was an unprovoked attack by police who were no doubt enraged by their comrade's murder.

"There was not a single bullet hole or pock mark to show that an NCCF bullet had been fired back at the police," the *New York Times* reported six weeks later. Meanwhile two *Blade* reporters had come to the same conclusion.

"Al Goldberg and I worked on a big story that showed that all the firing had been done by the cops," Tom Gearhart, the paper's civil rights reporter, told me in an interview almost half a century later. "But the publisher decided not to run the story."

That was Paul Block, Jr. Why he refused to run it was never made clear to the reporters, who insisted their reporting was solid. Was he afraid it would inflame tensions and possibly lead to a major civil disturbance, possibly a riot, in Toledo?

We cannot know, but that seems the most likely explanation.

Nobody else was killed in the September 1970 shootout, though Troy Montgomery, a sixteen-year-old who was in the bullet-riddled Panther headquarters, was seriously injured. Leroy Hardnett, the ambulance driver who took him to a hospital, claimed he disobeyed police orders to "leave him in the streets to die."[29]

John McClellan, the NCCF member arrested for the slaying of the policeman, was never convicted of the crime. Two trials ended in hung juries. McClellan was later honored by the Panthers with a "Community Day of Justice." He then mostly stayed out of the news until he was convicted of forgery in 2007 and sentenced to prison.

Was Paul Block, Jr., wrong to suppress the story of what now seems to have been out-of-control police attacking the NCCF/Panther headquarters?

Looked at from a strictly fact-finding point of view, yes.

But he plainly saw his role as a civic leader in addition to being in charge of its most important journalistic outlet. He had a difficult decision to make.

---

29. Ide, "Serving the Community: Toledo's Black Panther Party."

Looked at only through a purely journalistic prism he made the wrong one. But the man making it was also a publisher who might have been blamed had enraged Blacks rioted or attacked more police officers if they became aware of what really happened. This was an extremely tense and increasingly violent time in America, and that outcome was fully conceivable.

The truth didn't remain completely suppressed; weeks later, the *New York Times* clearly indicated that the police were to blame.

The failure of two juries to convict McClellan, despite huge city-wide outrage over the slain officer, was also a strong indication that the police had arrested a man for murder simply because he was Black and in the vicinity.

Neither Block nor his paper nor his city was perfect.

The publisher was, however, dedicated to ending racial discrimination – though doing so through a philosophy of "reason and restraint."

When he surveyed the paper's civil rights record for his 1985 history, *The Blade of Toledo*, John Harrison concluded, "In some instances… The *Blade*'s attitude toward the struggle for racial equality has resulted in editorial positions that have seemed less than heroic, or even moderately forceful to some… . But there has never been any serious reason to doubt the *Blade*'s substantial service to the achievement of liberty and justice for all, along the lines it believes to be most likely to promote those ends."[30]

---

30. Harrison, *The Blade of Toledo*, 340-41.

13

Busing and Beyond: 1970-2000

Americans tend to think of eras as being neatly encompassed by decades, and few have been as tumultuous as the 1960s, the decade of the Kennedys and Camelot, of Vietnam, of Rock 'n' Roll and drugs and vast changes in American culture.

Perhaps most of all it was the decade of the Civil Rights Movement and of dramatic and often violent changes in race relations. Legally African-Americans won tremendous victories: The Civil Rights Act of 1964 and the Voting Rights Act of 1965 being perhaps the two greatest. By 1970 no hotel or restaurant owner could deny service to Blacks, something that would have been scarcely imaginable a decade earlier.

African-Americans could also register and vote anywhere in the country without risking their lives, something else that, again, would have been unthinkable in rural Mississippi or Georgia and most of the Deep South in prior years.

Laws that had forbidden intermarriage between Blacks and whites in seventeen southern and border states had been unanimously overturned by the U.S. Supreme Court.[1]

There was more legal equality than ever in American history.

---

1. *Loving v. Virginia*, 388 U.S. 1 (1967).

But the decade had also been marked by the assassinations of three of the most prominent Black civil rights leaders – Medgar Evers, Malcolm X, and Martin Luther King, Jr. – and of President John F. Kennedy and his brother Robert, who had been the overwhelming choice of Black America for president when he was killed.

Many others had died too, and the bright promise of the early decade was soured by terrible, racially tinged violence, including civil disorders that had devastated cities like Newark, Detroit, and Los Angeles. Pittsburgh had seen considerable property destruction, though not much loss of life in its Hill District in the aftermath of King's murder.

Toledo, as we have seen, had been more lightly touched, with brief flare-ups that included broken windows and a few fires both at the time of the July 1967 Detroit civil disturbance,[2] and after King's death in April 1968.

There was still a vast economic gap between Blacks and whites as the 1970s began. But by that time major protest demonstrations of the kind covered by the media were far more likely to be about the Vietnam War.

For many, especially white citizens, the struggle for equal rights seemed to have been a battle that had been fought and won. Blacks, however, saw it differently.

True, when it came to race, segregation by law was dead, but in practice there were few integrated communities anywhere; Blacks lived in Black neighborhoods and whites in white ones. Besides tremendous economic inequality there was still wide disparity in educational and professional achievement.

And in many cities this had its roots in the public schools.

Those in Black neighborhoods were perceived as inferior, and test scores tended to indicate that. Many of these schools were in older, less affluent neighborhoods and looked run down and shabby compared to newer ones in better neighborhoods.

And that was what led to the major explosive civil rights issue of the decade: busing.

Many reasoned that if Blacks were ever going to catch up to whites in terms of economic and professional success, their children were going to have to get good educations and that they were entitled to equally good schools.

Even before the decade began, the NAACP's Legal Defense Fund had

---

2. In recent years it has been seen as politically correct in some circles to refer to July 1967 in Detroit as a "rebellion," though at the time, it was universally called a "riot" by both Blacks and whites.

sued the school board in Charlotte, North Carolina, demanding that a remedy be found to insure racial balance in that city's public schools. The most logical one, many felt, was to bus children to schools that wouldn't necessarily be in their own neighborhoods.

How the U.S. Supreme Court would rule was never in much doubt. In a series of rulings since *Brown v. Board* in 1954 it had indicated that it wasn't enough to outlaw segregation– public school districts needed to take steps to integrate.

Earl Warren had been replaced as chief justice by the more conservative Warren Burger, but that made little difference. On April 20, 1971, the court unanimously ruled in the Charlotte case that busing was an appropriate remedy to end racial imbalance in schools.[3] The ramifications were immediate, and nationwide.

There was resistance – sometimes violent – from parents and white supremacists in many cities. In Pontiac, Michigan, a city north of Detroit, Ku Klux Klan members dynamited ten school buses on August 30, 1971, just before a court-ordered busing plan was due to go into effect there.[4]

Not all the opposition was racial in nature though some clearly was, or was based on racial fears. Many parents merely worried about their young children spending a lot of time on a bus every day or being forced to attend a school far from their own neighborhood, possibly without any of their friends.

Many whites were fine with the idea that Black students needed better education but worried that their own children would end up at an inferior school. Black spokesmen, however, often dismissed white concerns as merely racism.

That meant that some whites who had been staunch supporters of civil rights suddenly found themselves bewildered and at odds with their former allies.

Covering the busing issue posed a challenge for newspapers, including the *Toledo Blade* and the *Pittsburgh Post-Gazette*. The situation in each of those two cities was different – and different from that in many other places.

Neither city had to contend with a federal court order to use busing to desegregate their schools; though there was busing, and it was bitterly controversial.

Toledo largely dodged a bullet, because "no one ever sued us," and hence

---

3. *Swann et al., v. Charlotte-Mecklenburg Board of Education,* 402 U.S. 1 (1971).
4. William K. Stevens, "5 Ex-Klansmen Convicted in School Bus Bomb Plot," *New York Times,* May 22, 1973.

there was never any court order to desegregate, Merrill Grant, a former superintendent of Toledo Public Schools, said in a 1998 interview.[5]

Toledo Public Schools had also moved to further integration in the mid-1960s but adopted a voluntary, open-enrollment plan that allowed students to transfer from their neighborhood to any school in the district if doing so would help make the new school more racially balanced. That was an admirable idea, but apparently few students transferred.

There was busing in Toledo as early as 1967, years before the U.S. Supreme Court gave it the green light. Not, however, to achieve racial balance – at least overtly, though the schools there were as *de facto* segregated by housing patterns as they were in most cities. It was done because some schools were more crowded than others.

Though only a few students were bused at first, in the fall of 1968 the decision was made to bus the entire fourth grade at Fulton School, about 200 students, to four other different elementary schools. One class of Fulton fifth graders was also bused.

Parents of Fulton students were incensed and organized a vigorous protest, which was well covered by the *Blade*. The parents voiced many of the same complaints parents of bused students elsewhere in the nation had: their children couldn't easily participate in after-school activities because they had to get back on a bus as soon as classes ended.

They felt like strangers in the new school and did not mingle easily with other students. After a few months, it also became clear that busing hadn't helped either the students' academic performance or their behavior.[6]

What made this situation different and fascinating, however, was that in this case, the students being bused were largely Black, and were being bussed to largely white schools. On its editorial page, the *Blade* asked a logical question:

"How do the authorities meet the situation when it is the minority that formally and openly opposes the busing?" the newspaper asked in the fall of 1971.[7]

Earlier that spring when the busing plan was announced and parents began to object, the *Blade* noted that some of the parents had told the school board they thought "overcrowding is not the real reason for busing at Fulton. The school administration is actually trying to make its integration record

5. Vanessa Gezari, "School Integration Ends Up On a One-Way Street; Racial Balance Remains a Dream," *Toledo Blade,* February 15, 1998.
6. *Toledo Blade* editorial, September 5, 1971.
7. Ibid.

look a little better for the federal inspectors."[8] By that time Toledo Public School administrators were backing off and busing only a third as many pupils.

Busing to relieve overcrowding in Toledo soon ended. Possibly because Black students were the ones being bused nobody ever took the Toledo Public Schools to court. By this time the *Blade,* which long-supported integration, had become thoroughly skeptical about busing.

Remarking that some parents thought that busing was always secretly meant to accomplish integration, the newspaper noted:

> *Suppose, for a moment, that the charge were true. It would mean Toledo had tried busing to achieve racial balance on a test sample basis, but the parents of the children were dissatisfied with the experiment and found it to be a failure. What, then, could be achieved by busing a large number of children all over the city to achieve racial balance in the schools? Would not the same objections cited by the Fulton parents hold true, only on a much larger scale? This is a question that cannot be ducked by those who see universal busing as the instant solution to the integration problem, and their answers must take into account the reality of angry and hostile parents.*[9]

Other communities across the nation would soon learn precisely how true that was. Paul Block, Jr., had strongly supported integration and every civil rights measure since he had become publisher of the *Blade.* But busing was different.

Allan Block, who was fourteen at the time of the Fulton School busing controversy, remembers discussing the issue with his father. "I wouldn't let you be bused," the publisher said, "and I am not going to support busing other people's children,"

This "had nothing to do with race," said Allan Block, who is now the chairman and chief executive officer of Block Communications, Inc. "It had to do mostly with the fact that it isn't good for kids to be on a bus for two hours a day and that in some cases the kids would be sent to inferior schools."

Chuckling, he added, "the irony was that my brother and I were bused anyway, to Maumee Valley Country Day, a private college preparatory school in Toledo.

Choosing to attend that school and ride those buses was, however, a

---

8. *oledo Blade* editorial, March 26, 1971.
9. Ibid.

completely voluntary choice, at least on the parents' part. Allan and John Block had, however, begun their education in the Toledo public schools.

Pittsburgh's busing situation was considerably different.

Brown v. Board hadn't had any legal impact on the city schools; school segregation had been outlawed by the Pennsylvania Legislature on July 4, 1881.

But of course *de facto* segregation based on where people lived was very much in place on February 2, 1968, when the Pennsylvania Human Relations Commission, just three years old at the time, ordered the Pittsburgh schools to desegregate.

This was clearly not seen as a major news story at the time; there was no mention of this whatsoever in the *Post-Gazette* in the days that followed. Granted, this happened when the surprising Tet Offensive was raging in South Vietnam and that year's presidential campaign was beginning to dramatically unfold.

The Human Relations Commission gave Pittsburgh five months to come up with a desegregation plan. When it did the plan, which largely relied on voluntary measures, was rejected as showing a "lack of commitment."[10]

What followed were years of the school district coming up with plans, all of which were rejected by the commission. It was becoming increasingly clear that busing was the only practical way school integration could happen.

The *Post-Gazette* supported the goal of integration, but eventually took a philosophical view of the delay. When the Pittsburgh school board came up with yet another plan in February 1973, the newspaper noted that it was inadequate and labeled it a "mark-time plan."[11]

"The Pennsylvania HRC has called for total school desegregation of the Pittsburgh system within three years. The plan approved Tuesday is scheduled to put only 75 percent of the city's students in desegregated schools… and even that won't be achieved until 1980." But Pittsburgh residents shouldn't worry, the *Post-Gazette* said.

The newspaper predicted that the issue would depend not on anything happening in Pennsylvania, but by a series of decisions that the U.S. Supreme Court was expected to make before long about school integration. Pittsburghers "might as well take it easy in the meantime," the editorial said.

The newspaper was largely wrong. One of the high court's decisions, *Milliken v. Bradley,* was nationally significant in that it essentially ended

---

10. Liz Reid, "An Unsuccessful 30-Year Effort to Desegregate Pittsburgh Public Schools," WESA-FM Radio, October 19, 2018.

11. "Integration Decision Elsewhere," *Pittsburgh Post-Gazette*, February 22, 1973.

attempts at "cross-district busing" in which students could be bused to schools in different districts to try and achieve racial balance. But that wasn't what was happening in Pittsburgh.

At that point, the Pennsylvania legislature upset everything by passing the bizarre "Act 372," which required any school system that bused its own students to also bus students to private schools, even ones as far as ten miles outside Pittsburgh!

That was a powerful incentive not to bus anyone. The *Post-Gazette* accurately summed things up in a 1974 editorial: "It is ridiculous to ask a city system hard-pressed to hold white students to achieve any sort of racial balance to be required to subsidize the undermining of its goals."[12] What the act meant, in other words, was that parents who didn't want their kids in an integrated school could pull them out, put them in an all-white private school, and the Pittsburgh Board of Education would take them there.

Ten years later, the *Post-Gazette* did a story on one family who lived in Pittsburgh but put their children in a Christian school outside the city limits, and whose transportation cost the schools $14,000 a year.[13] Indeed, the newspaper's editorials on busing in these years were usually more concerned with the absurdity of Act 372 than with integration. Eventually, after the Human Rights Commission ran out of patience and threatened to get a court order, a desegregation plan was put in place in the fall of 1980.

The *Post-Gazette* exhaustively covered the first day of integrated schools with news stories, feature stories, and maps showing which students were going where. An editorial the day after it started[14] praised the community for "smoothly coping with the first day of an extensive desegregation plan," but then oddly contradicted itself a few sentences later.

"To be sure, the desegregation plan was not all that extensive... but the plan does make it possible for every child in the system to have experience at an integrated school, usually at the middle-school level... perhaps as some of its critics contended, a more extensive plan could have been implemented. But the happy outcome is that the board's plan *did* succeed," the editorial concluded.

That was a premature conclusion – unless the *Post-Gazette* meant that forcible integrating some schools wasn't met with violence. Before long, whites began pulling their kids out of the system, helped in this by the district's willingness to bus them to all-white private schools at city expense.

12. *Pittsburgh Post-Gazette*, March 11, 1974.
13. "Private Busing Drains Public Purse," *Pittsburgh Post-Gazette,* March 8, 1984.
14. *Pittsburgh Post-Gazette,* September 3, 1980.

Two years later, again prodded by the Human Relations Commission, the Pittsburgh school board tried a more comprehensive integration plan, which was again endorsed by the *Post-Gazette*.[15]

That didn't solve the situation either. In Pittsburgh, as nationally, busing proved a failure. Editorially the newspaper, like the school system itself, was slow to realize this, but to its credit the *Post-Gazette* never pushed for busing, though it was open to it as a means of ending segregation and hopefully improving education.

Finally, the newspaper undertook a major project. "For Blacks and Whites in Our Region, School Desegregation Gets A Failing Grade," which was published in the Sunday paper on April 21, 1996. Written, edited, and reported by a "race education team" of nearly a dozen journalists, it showed that integration had largely failed, since many whites had fled rather than attend integrated schools.

For those who remained in the public schools, academic achievement didn't greatly improve. One story, "Pair has Mixed Memories of Integration,"[16] centered on a pair of thirty-somethings, one white, one Black, who as eighth-grade friends had been bused to schools outside their neighborhood. The white man, Joshua Silverman, said he had been "beaten up continually" by Black children in his elementary school. His Black friend, Melvin Moten, blamed busing for what he felt was an inferior education. "You don't put kids in a warehouse and chain the doors shut and say, 'get along,' he said.

Three months later, on July 12, 1996, then-Governor Tom Ridge, a Republican, came to Pittsburgh to sign a bill that returned the city to a system of neighborhood schools.

Surrounded by mostly Democratic lawmakers in an elementary school auditorium, Ridge got a standing ovation when he called busing "a well-intentioned but failed experiment." That ended forced school integration in Pittsburgh.

Curiously, the newspaper had no editorial comment on either the newspaper's own look at school desegregation in April or the bill the governor signed in July.

That was probably not because the *Post-Gazette* was reluctant to change its mind on a racial issue. Nine years before, publisher Bill Block had helped lead a dramatic reversal of the paper's longstanding policy in favor of electing all city council members at large, mainly because it had resulted in no African-American members.

---

15. *Pittsburgh Post-Gazette* editorial, October 26, 1982.
16. *Pittsburgh Post-Gazette*, April 21, 1996, 13.

"Block felt it was wrong for a group that composed 24 percent of the city's population to have no representation on council," Clarke Thomas, a longtime editorial writer for the *Post-Gazette,* later wrote.[17] The newspaper called for a switch to electing council members by district, both because it would open the door to the "possibility of having a Republican or independent opposition after five decades of none, and for better assuring that there will be black members on council."[18]

The newspaper's support was likely crucial and as a result Pittsburgh soon had a Black representative on council and later as many as three.

By that time the *Post-Gazette* had begun to get more serious about hiring minorities, something that long had been a priority for Bill Block, but which hadn't gotten very far under Frank Hawkins, the paper's longtime editor and himself a Southerner. He had opposed allowing Ray Sprigle to pose as a Black man in the South in 1948, calling it a "silly venture into sensationalism."[19]

However, in 1977, Hawkins retired and was replaced as executive editor by John Craig, who almost immediately began intensifying efforts to diversify the staff. As Thomas put it in *Front Page Pittsburgh,* "Craig set upon a deliberate path of bringing minorities onto the staff by drawing from an Urban Journalism Workshop for minorities run by Professor Samuel Adams of Kansas State University, using a program of newsroom internships, and working to promote copy messengers into copy-reading or reporting tasks. (He also) hired Al Donalson, an African-American reporter from the Press, to be an assistant city editor."[20]

That was evidently the first time the *Post-Gazette* had a minority in newsroom management, and this, plus a feeling of greater acceptance, helped lead to an increase in African-Americans on the staff. Tony Norman, a young Black man from West Philadelphia, ended up in Pittsburgh in the late 1980s and got a job in the newsroom of the *Post-Gazette* in November 1988 – not as a reporter, but as a clerk.

"I answered phones, typed letters into the (computer) system and changed the toner on the copy machine. One day in December, Bill Block, Sr., called me into his office. My hands and shirt were covered with ink but he still insisted on shaking hands.

---

17. Thomas, *Front-Page Pittsburgh*, 271. Thomas (1926-2009) makes an error in asserting that the referendum passed two to one. In fact, voters approved *both* going to a new system and staying with the old, but council by districts got more yes votes, and prevailed.

18. *Pittsburgh Post-Gazette* editorial, May 18, 1987.

19. Frank Hawkins, *That Was Hot Type,* privately printed.

20. Thomas, *Front-Page Pittsburgh,* 280.

"He asked me what my goals were. I figured, 'Oh man, he must have heard that I was really bad at answering phones,'" Norman told me.[21]

"I said, well, I would like to be a reporter, to write about music and culture." And he said, "You have to decide what you want to do, and set your face in that direction." Laughing, Norman told me, "I still thought this was a nice way of saying, 'you are lousy at answering the phones.' But a few days later, I was covering pop music."

Today, Tony Norman is one of the *Post-Gazette's* best-known columnists. He has won numerous awards and was a prestigious Knight-Wallace Journalism fellow at the University of Michigan.

Today, looking back at the conversation with Bill Block that essentially launched his journalism career, Norman said "It may have been paternalistic, but not in the derogatory sense – he came across sort of like 'Dad.' (Block was then seventy-three; Norman twenty-eight.) But he cared about you – cared about your development," Tony Norman said.

Bill Block also cared passionately about the newspaper's development, as he had ever since he had returned from World War II. But there were ominous clouds on the horizon – especially in Pittsburgh. The senior Block's life was complicated somewhat in that he had become, at that point, heavily involved in the affairs of the *Toledo Blade*.

His elder brother, Paul Block, Jr., had developed Alzheimer's Disease a few years earlier and had died March 15, 1987. While Paul's sons, John and Allan were adults and involved in the business,[22] they were still in their twenties, and Bill was the senior member of the family. The *Blade*, however, was financially stable in the 1980s and 1990s; it was the only major daily newspaper in its metropolitan area.

The *Post-Gazette,* however, was the junior partner in a Joint Operating Agreement with Scripps-Howard's larger *Pittsburgh Press,* an agreement that was scheduled to run out in 1999.

That meant that it wasn't at all clear whether there would even be a *Pittsburgh Post-Gazette* after that, since Scripps-Howard controlled everything from the printing presses to advertising sales and delivery of the newspapers.

However, that all changed dramatically when the Teamsters Union suddenly went on strike against the *Pittsburgh Press* in May 1992. That meant that neither it nor the *Post-Gazette* could be printed or delivered. After several

---

21. Tony Norman, telephone interview with the author, March 10, 2020.
22. Paul Block, Jr.'s oldest son, Cyrus Block, was not involved in the newspapers. Bill Block's son, Bill Block, Jr., was in his thirties and had just become general manager of the *Blade*.

bitter months Scripps Howard, in a startling decision, chose to sell the assets of the *Press* to the Block family.[23]

Suddenly the *Pittsburgh Post-Gazette* was the only newspaper in town, and it resumed publication on January 18, 1993, with more readers and a larger staff.

The future looked bright. No one knew that less than four years earlier a young British computer scientist working in a particle physics laboratory in Switzerland had invented something that would change our lives – and newspapers, forever.

His name was Tim Berners-Lee, and his invention was called the World Wide Web.

---

23. The story of the events that led to the demise of the *Pittsburgh Press* and the emergence of the *Post-Gazette* as the dominant newspaper in Pittsburgh are reasonably fully told in Chapter 15, "The 1992 Strike," of Clarke Thomas's *Front-Page Pittsburgh*.

14

Affirmative Action and its Aftermath

You do not take a man who for years has been hobbled by chains, liberate him, bring him to the starting line of a race, say 'you are free to compete with the others' and still justly believe you have been completely fair… this [affirmative action] is the next and most profound stage in the battle for civil rights."
– President Lyndon B. Johnson, June 4, 1965

The way to stop discrimination on the basis of race is to stop discriminating on the basis of race.
– John Roberts, Chief Justice of the U.S. Supreme Court, 2007

Outside the Deep South there was overwhelming support for most of the aims of the Civil Rights Movement, at least in the form presented by Dr. Martin Luther King, Jr.

Even in what the *Pittsburgh Post-Gazette's* Ray Sprigle had called "the land of Jim Crow," resistance to Blacks being able to vote, to have the right to stay in any hotel or eat in any restaurant crumbled surprisingly quickly, even in the South, after landmark legislation passed in the mid-1960s. Nor was there much resistance to outlawing segregation in schools, though whites bitterly opposed forced busing.

By the 1970s, virtually no one in mainstream political, intellectual, or public policy circles was seriously challenging any of the original goals of the Civil Rights Movement, from ending segregation to legal equality in the fullest sense of the term.

But what became controversial – even bitterly so – was what came to be called *affirmative action*. The term seems to have been coined by President John F. Kennedy and was used in an executive order he issued just six weeks after taking office.[1]

The order created something called the Committee on Equal Employment Opportunity and charged it with seeing that projects paid for with federal funds "take affirmative action" to make sure that racial bias wasn't used in hiring or employment.

Exactly what form affirmative action was to take wasn't spelled out, nor were any penalties prescribed for failing to do so. Whether it actually had any effect isn't clear.

The act also contained a loophole (Section 303) large enough to allow anyone to get out of any requirements if the committee agreed they could be exempted.

However, Lyndon B. Johnson, the vice-president at the time, was assigned to chair the commission, and by the time he unexpectedly became president on November 22, 1963, he became convinced that affirmative action was necessary to overcome racism.

He explained why in the Howard University commencement speech quoted at the beginning of this chapter, adding "We seek not just freedom but opportunity... not just equality as a right and a theory, but equality as a fact and a result."

Within a month following that speech Johnson got Congress to replace the old equal opportunity commission with a new, more powerful federal agency – the Equal Employment Opportunity Commission, or EEOC– which had real enforcement teeth.

And he issued a new, tougher executive order[2] requiring most contractors who worked for the government to take specific measures to increase the number of minorities in their work forces and to document their hiring practices.

Should the government determine that minorities were underrepresented,[3] they would have to immediately come up with an affirmative action plan to

1. Executive Order 10925, 3 C.F.R, March 6, 1961.
2. Executive Order 11246, 3 C.F.R., September 24, 1965.
3. Women were added to the executive order in October 1967.

increase their minority numbers if they wanted to continue doing business with the government.

This was, again, not highly controversial, and neither the *Toledo Blade* nor the *Pittsburgh Post-Gazette* took much notice. It was beyond dispute that Blacks had suffered the effects of wage and employment discrimination for more than a century.

Black men earned barely half of what white men did in 1965,[4] and the education gap was even greater, especially in the South where a majority of African-Americans still lived. More than twice as many whites as Blacks had graduated from high school in 1960. Nearly three times as many had graduated from college.[5]

Colleges and universities began affirmative action programs as well, aiming to increase the number of African-American students. There was broad bipartisan agreement on the need for affirmative action in the late 1960s and early 1970s, especially after the Nixon administration embraced it as part of its civil rights strategy.

President Richard Nixon, not usually thought of as a civil rights pioneer, actually made an attempt to fight discrimination in the construction and skilled trade unions when he issued what was sometimes referred to as his "Philadelphia Order," on September 23, 1969.

The order, also called the Philadelphia Plan, was designed to enforce what were, essentially, quotas for minority hiring in the craft unions, which were notoriously resistant to opening their ranks to African-Americans.[6] "The craft unions and the construction unions are among the most egregious offenders against equal opportunity laws," then-Assistant Secretary of Labor Arthur Fletcher said, adding that they were "openly hostile to allowing Blacks into their closed circle."

The University of Pittsburgh had taken a leading role in supporting Black demands for construction industry jobs, and the *Post-Gazette* ran a mostly sympathetic editorial the day Nixon issued his Philadelphia Order.

"We believe that most citizens are out of sympathy with construction

---

4. Amitabh Chandra, "Labor-Market Dropouts and the Racial Wage Gap: 1940–1990," *American Economic Review*, 2000. In 1940 the average wage paid to a Black man was only 48 percent of what a white worker earned. This rose to 70 percent by 1990.

5. U.S. Census Bureau, *Educational Attainment by Race and Hispanic Origin, 1960-1998*.

6. This included unions in most newspapers, other than the Newspaper Guild, which represented reporters and some editors. Long after Black faces were fairly common in America's newsrooms, the "back shops" where mailers, pressmen, and printers worked, were nearly all white. Even the *Chicago Defender*, once America's top Black newspaper, was forced to use white skilled trades workers to get the paper out.

union discrimination against Blacks, and want to see it ended," the paper said, before asking presciently how this was supposed to be accomplished. "Are the unions to establish a rigid quota system, and if so, what should that quota be?"[7]

That question – and the highly charged word *quota* – would haunt debates over affirmative action, and civil rights, for years to come.

President Nixon managed, after a stiff fight, to prevent Congress from outlawing his plan. But as he later wrote in his memoirs, "Getting the plan written into law turned out to be easier than implementing the law."[8]

The plan ended up setting goals and timetables, but not quotas – and it was not much of a success at diversification. After all, it only required contractors to make a "good faith effort" to employ more minorities.

But what it *did* do was fan the flames of growing resentment among white workers, especially those striving to improve themselves.

Many, even those who were not racist, came to feel that they were now the victims of reverse discrimination, thinly disguised by the phase "affirmative action."

The courts had rejected efforts to declare Nixon's attempt to desegregate the construction unions but, gradually, other legal challenges to affirmative action emerged.

University admissions were one key area. The first such case to reach the nation's highest court – *Marco DeFunis Jr. v. Odegaard* – is seldom remembered but was a harbinger for cases to come. DeFunis was a white man who argued that he had been denied admission to the University of Washington law school in 1970 while minority applicants who were less qualified had been admitted.

He claimed this violated the equal protection clause contained in the Fourteenth Amendment to the Constitution. The U.S. Supreme Court finally heard the case in 1974, but declined to rule on the merits and said the case was then moot. A lower court had ordered DeFunis admitted to the law school and by that time he was in his final year.

But in an indication of how big an issue this was going to become, Washington State Supreme Court Justice Robert Hunter noted that while he thought trying to increase the number of minority lawyers was "a laudable purpose with which I do not disagree," he added, "this must not be accomplished, however, by clear and willful discrimination against students

---

7. *Pittsburgh Post-Gazette* editorial, September 23, 1969.

8. "Philadelphia Plan" in *Encyclopedia.com,* https://www.encyclopedia.com/history/encyclopedias-almanacs-transcripts-and-maps/philadelphia-plan (accessed January 28, 2020).

of other races," as he thought this law school had done.

The case drew little notice in Toledo or Pittsburgh or almost anywhere else. The Nixon Administration was in its death throes that spring, and Watergate dominated national news coverage. The next case, however, would be very different.

Regents of the University of California v. Bakke, decided on June 28, 1978, is indeed the mother of all university affirmative action cases. Alan Bakke, a white man, had been repeatedly denied admission to the University of California medical school.

The school, which admitted one hundred students a year, had a policy of reserving sixteen of those places for qualified minority applicants. Bakke argued that this violated his civil rights. A deeply divided court agreed and ordered him admitted.

But Justice Lewis Powell, the swing vote in a muddy decision, wrote for the majority that affirmative action in admission decisions was allowable and that race could be a factor, but not the only factor – a decision that clarified nothing. The court's ruling was, in fact, unusually divided, with six justices writing opinions.

The *Pittsburgh Post-Gazette* wrote an editorial indicating strong support for affirmative action and tempered support for the Bakke decision, which the newspaper accurately called "a legal scholar's nightmare, and a monument to the ambivalence which the question of 'reverse discrimination' induces in legal as well as non-legal minds."[9]

The newspaper felt, the decision was a good one, however, because the bottom line was that affirmative action had been saved:

The danger… was that the U.S. Supreme Court might foreclose affirmative action programs before they could even begin to ameliorate the underrepresentation of Black Americans in higher education and the professions. And next to that welcome result, the ambiguities and scholarly shortcomings of the Bakke decision are as nothing.

The *Toledo Blade* took a week to weigh in on Bakke and while its editorial seemed to take for granted that increasing the number of minorities in the professions was desirable, it did not openly cheerlead for affirmative action.

Instead it took a sophisticated look at the problems the decision did *not* solve. It was all very well, the *Blade* noted, for Justice Powell to use Harvard University as an example of a school that didn't need to set quotas.

Schools like Harvard "and perhaps a handful of similarly prestigious

---

9. "Bakke: The Best of a Bad Job," *Pittsburgh Post-Gazette*, June 30, 1978.

ones can with minimum effort attract such a range of top-quality applicants
– Blacks and other minority-group members included," may not need to set
fixed numerical goals.

But what about less-famous schools like the University of California,
Davis, or for that matter, the Medical College of Ohio, "which are new and
still establishing their reputations"? They may not be overwhelmed with
high-level minority applicants.

"Yet they know that the Government is most unlikely to accept that
fact as a reason for their having what it considers too few Blacks or other
minorities among their student bodies." The article ended by quoting an
unnamed law school dean as saying, "I'll be very interested in how you take
race into consideration without setting up some kind of quota. The answer
may well be years in coming from the court – if it ever does."[10]

That was certainly an accurate prediction.

Locally, for years after that, both newspapers seemed to take it as a given
that affirmative action was an acceptable and likely necessary means of
increasing Black representation in government jobs they had too long been
prevented from filling.

The newspapers, especially perhaps the *Blade,* did still believe they had
a public watchdog function over this, as any other issue. When, in 1988,
the Toledo City Council suggested adding a second city affirmative action
office, an editorial took issue with this, but not the policy: "The issue is not
affirmative action, which is a perfectly reasonable effort on the part of city
government to redress discrimination in minority hiring. The issue is whether
municipal operations are effective in terms of the money spent on them… it
is utterly ridiculous." Ridiculous that the city should have two offices charged
with the same function, the article continued, adding, "If the city is serious
about affirmative action, let it install an agency that is directly answerable…
and hold it responsible for encouraging affirmative action in a fair and
effective manner."[11]

Support for affirmative action, however, gradually was tempered with
questions about how far it ought to go. When, a year and a half later, a federal
judge indicated that a new firefighting class needed to accept "all qualified
minority applicants," the newspaper noted editorially that "the *Blade* has
supported quotas in hiring people for city jobs, specifically in the police and
fire divisions, on the basis that otherwise, qualified minorities would continue
to be excluded unfairly."

---

10. "Bakke Issue Remains," *Toledo Blade*, July 5, 1978.
11. "Affirmative What?" *Toledo Blade,* March 15, 1988.

But a blanket order to hire all minority applicants with the proper credentials gave the newspaper pause: "it does raise a question as to the point at which fairness to one group becomes unfairness to another."[12]

Gradually the newspaper's editorials noted that affirmative action could sometimes be carried too far. Four years later, Toledoans voted to move to a strong mayor form of government and elected Carty Finkbeiner, a longtime local politician, to run it. Even before he took office Finkbeiner said he wanted a Black police chief.

The *Blade* took issue with that: "Toledo's next chief should be selected on ability and merit and not on any notion of political correctness... all Toledoans of any race want is a police chief who can improve the use of police resources, put more officers in the neighborhoods where they are needed and stem the rising tide of crime."[13]

Ten months later another editorial indicated that while "ideally, the racial and ethnic background of those who work for the city should reflect the city they serve," fair representation "is not quite the problem that some civic leaders believe."

While this may have been seen by some as an anti-affirmative action editorial it really was more measured. It noted that the population of Toledo at the time was 23.6 percent Black or Hispanic, and added that 18.5 percent of the city's top administrators were as well – "not an appreciable deficit" – and called for the city to make more of an effort to hire women and minorities for entry-level positions "to get a foot in the door."[14]

Opinions on the editorial page are one thing. But what kind of relationships have the papers owned by the Block family had with minorities in their communities?

How much did they try to have newsroom staffs that reflected the cities they served – essentially, Toledo and Pittsburgh?[15]

Locally both papers did strive for more diversified staffs in those years. To draw on my personal experiences: When I was an intern at the *Blade* in 1978 the newspaper, besides Bill Brower who was then an editor, had at least

---

12. "Discrimination and Quotas," *Toledo Blade,* August 28, 1989.

13. "The Search for a New Chief," *Toledo Blade,* December 10, 1993,

14. "Representation in City Hall," *Toledo Blade,* October 4, 1994.

15. Paul Block's sons, especially Paul Jr., knew their father had probably owned too many newspapers, not all of which were very profitable, and that he ultimately was financially stressed when the Great Depression arrived. Consequently they were very reluctant to expand their holdings. The only additional newspapers they ever bought were the tiny *Daily Register* in Red Bank, New Jersey (1965), which they owned for only a few years, and the *Monterey Peninsula Herald,* which we will examine later.

six full-time Black reporters, in news, features and sports, as well as several copy messengers and interns.

The late William P. "Bill" Day, a longtime editor who at that time had the title Assistant to the Publisher, was for years heavily involved in recruiting and hiring both interns and reporters. Years later, when I was the paper's national editor, he told me that it was difficult to both hire and retain top African-American talent.

Those who really had stellar ability tended to be recruited by top papers like the *New York Times* and *Washington Post*, he said. Some wanted to work in cities like Detroit, which had larger African-American populations. When the paper did manage to recruit good hires, they tended to soon move on to bigger newspapers," he complained.

To some extent that has always been true of journalists of any color; they tend to move from small papers to medium-sized papers to larger ones. Greg Moore, who worked at the *Blade* before going on to a distinguished career that included becoming executive editor of the *Denver Post*, said that Bill Brower had been an inspirational mentor.

In a speech to the American Society of Newspaper Editors, he described Toledo's pioneering Black journalist as a "hell raiser and an inside player. He taught me the importance of staying connected to one's roots, that my strength and my base—the place where I could always find stories—would be the African-American community."[16]

Not that every hire was an unqualified success. The *Blade* hired a young, talented feature writer in the late 1970s, a Toledo native named Janet Cooke, who later went to the *Washington Post* and, in one of modern journalism's biggest scandals, won a Pulitzer Prize for feature writing in 1981 for a story, "Jimmy's World," a profile of a young heroin addict that turned out to have been completely fabricated.

Ironically, her fraud was exposed in a sense by editors at the *Blade,* who, after Cooke won the prize, noted details in her published biography that they knew to be wrong. The *Post* had to return the Pulitzer and Cooke left journalism.[17]

That did not stop Toledo from continuing to recruit Black staffers when they could. Tom Walton spent more than half a century (1965-2017) working for the *Toledo Blade* in a wide variety of jobs, from city desk reporter to

---

16. "Greg Moore Delivers the Inaugural Robert McGruder Lecture at Kent State University," *American Society of Newspaper Editors,* November 22, 2004.

17. Cooke claimed to have been a graduate of Vassar, which the *Blade* editors knew wasn't true.

bureau chief in charge of government coverage in Columbus, Ohio.

Walton in 1975 became managing editor and then executive editor at a smaller paper in California that the Block family had bought in 1967, the *Monterey Peninsula-Herald*.[18] In 1989, he returned to Toledo to become editor (the title actually corresponded to editorial page editor) of the *Blade*, a position he kept until he retired.

Two years after his retirement he said of the owners, "It is primarily a family that rewards talent and loyalty and doesn't give a whit about race."[19]

"I'm talking about in-house," he added, meaning the staff. "Internally, I saw nothing but fairness and equality." He said that while he had talked to Paul Block, Jr., occasionally, he couldn't recall ever having a conversation with him about race or either the Monterey or Toledo paper's coverage of racial matters.

"Not that I can recall, and I took that as a good sign. I'm sure I would have if there were evidence of problems – I know I would have from John."

Walton said that his own consciousness had been raised by John Robinson Block, who was publisher and editor-in-chief by the time Walton came back from California to run the editorial pages. When he arrived the now-legendary Bill Brower, who had been at the newspaper for more than forty years, was a columnist and editorial writer.

"He was a pioneer in Ohio journalism, and really nationally – he was writing a column for the *Blade* before there were a lot of Black columnists, other than (William) Raspberry" at the *Washington Post*, Walton said.[20]

When Brower retired in 1996, both Walton and Block thought it important that the paper continue to have a Black voice as columnist and editorial writer. They selected Rose Russell Stewart, a longtime *Blade* reporter and feature writer.

Walton wanted to make sure she felt welcome. "We were having a crunch in terms of space, and we had the issue of where Rose would sit. I was able to offer her a little cubicle. I said 'Rose, why don't you settle in there?' Now, none of the other editorial writers had that. They were all [together] in a room behind the editor's office. Well, John (Block) heard about it, and had a fit. He was upset with me. He said, 'how does that look? You are isolating our Black writer over in the corner instead of having her mingle with the others.'

18. The *Monterey Peninsula-Herald* was transferred to Scripps-Howard in 1992 as part of the deal whereby the *Pittsburgh Post-Gazette* took over the assets of the defunct *Press*.

19. Tom Walton, interview with the author, June 3, 2019.

20. William Raspberry (1935-2012) began writing a column for the *Washington Post* in 1966. He won the Pulitzer Prize for commentary in 1994.

He was right and we fixed it."

Walton said that he would have welcomed the opportunity to further diversify the *Peninsula-Herald's* small staff during his years in Monterey, but opportunities were limited. "Nobody wanted to leave! It was a beautiful place to live," he chuckled.

"We did have one Black reporter, Sanford Chambliss. Very good guy, a good writer and a good reporter. We also had a Hispanic city editor for a time – Fred Hernandez, another great guy. We had a very large Hispanic population, much larger than the Black population, and everyone got along famously. I can't recall that we ever had an Asian staffer, but we certainly would have hired a qualified person if they had applied when we had openings – which, as I said, we hardly ever did."[21]

Tom Walton added that while he and he paper were in favor of ethnic diversity, they had another problem that seemed larger at the time – winning acceptance from the local community. The newspaper had been founded in 1923 by a local legend, Col. Robert Allen Griffin (1893-1981), who had been wounded in both World Wars, who sold it to the Block family in 1967 but continued to manage the paper for three years.

"The challenges we faced in winning acceptance were monumental," Walton said, adding that the residents were suspicious of outsiders, especially people from Toledo, "a place they had heard ridiculed. Heck, I was worried about fitting in, as a blue-collar kid who grew up in Toledo. It took ten years, but we did overcome it."

They did that, he said, partly by creating a Monterey County Science Fair, in which the paper sent the winners, a fair number of whom happened to be minorities, to Space Camp in Huntsville, Alabama. "We also launched a charity, and a project called Operation Christmas Cheer. We asked the Salvation Army to help us identify the ten neediest families on the Monterey Peninsula – they were almost all Black and Hispanic."

Walton thought that doing this helped bring different types of people together. "The outpouring of not only money, but love and help was amazing."

Meanwhile in Toledo, the newspaper during the 1980s began to work considerably harder at both covering the African-American community and

---

21. The 1990 census found that of a total population of 31,954 in the city of Monterey 27,696 were listed as white, 2,315 Hispanic, 2,336 were of Asian descent, and only 900 residents, slightly less than three percent, were Black. This from the *1990 Census of Population: Social and Economic Characteristics, California*, 78. The population ratios were similar for the entire county.

building bridges to it.

The newspaper didn't always do this as well as it should have.

It was clear to me as a young reporter working night police shifts in the late 1970s and early 1980s that the editors were often not as interested in crime and calamity in largely poor and Black areas[22] as they were in white ones.

But Black speakers and social events that would have been ignored by the newspaper a few decades ago *did* get covered. The newspaper also reached out to the community largely through the efforts of Laneta Goings, an African-American native of Toledo who worked at the paper from 1977 to 2000, beginning in classified advertising and eventually rising to become executive assistant to the publisher.

"They wanted to diversify themselves. They knew they needed to," she said.[23]

"I was told they were opening a position in the executive office, and they would close it, not fill it, if I didn't take it." In 1981 her supervisor suddenly died, and Goings became the top executive assistant, first to Paul Block, Jr., and eventually to John Robinson Block when he became editor-in-chief and publisher.

"They were very kind to me, they clearly respected me," she told me. She found, as many did, that Paul Block, Jr., was shy and introverted and not the easiest person to get to know. "But I never had any problem with any editorial they did on racial matters," said Goings, who eventually earned a bachelor's in journalism from the University of Toledo.

Eventually, she found herself acting as a trusted ambassador between the editorial department and the newsroom and also between the *Blade* and the Black community, in which she was very much involved. "Everything is built on relationships," she said.

Soon, Goings noted, she became the person to whom the Black community came when there were events they strongly felt should have been covered, "especially good news stories. Too often they felt that the only time

---

22. Toledo's Black population has grown steadily but relatively slowly especially when compared to a city like Detroit. It rose from 8 percent in 1950 to 13.79 percent in 1960, 17.41 percent in 1980, and 27.2 percent in 2010, according to the U.S. Census. However, as late as the 1980s, a higher percentage of Toledo's Black population remained packed into an older, inner city ghetto than in other Ohio cities, according to a 1985 University of Akron study, *Racial Residential Segregation in Ohio's Eight Largest Cities.*

23. Laneta Goings, interview with the author, August 22, 2019.

they were covered was when there was bad news, when there were crimes.[24] I did what I could," she said.

"Of course, there was always so much space, and now there's less than ever," she continued. "But I did what I could. The most important question was always 'are we treated fairly,' and I did what I could to help with that."

"She was very helpful to us in making contact with them," the Rev. Robert Culp said. "She was excellent at trying to make sure our side was heard."

The editors and the publisher came to trust her judgment internally as well as externally. When they decided in 1995 to send Bill Brower, then almost eighty, on a third and final journey to report on racial attitudes across America, it was recognized that he could no longer do it alone. The editors took Goings' recommendation that the staffer who should go with him was the paper's young urban affairs reporter, Eddie B. Allen, Jr.

"They never would have given me the opportunities I've had if they didn't have confidence in me," she said. Those included representing the *Blade* on numerous boards, planning and supporting annual goodwill and networking trips the senior executives made to Washington, D.C., and chairing the Toledo Zoo's centennial celebration.

The *Blade* also financially helped her complete her degree and paid for a three-week work-study program in Africa. "I will always love the Block family for what they made it possible for me to do," said Goings. Today, she runs Books4Buddies, a non-profit program designed to fight illiteracy by allowing disadvantaged young men, about two-thirds of them Black, the opportunity to read and love books.

The *Blade* and Buckeye Cablevision, another BCI company, are both corporate sponsors of her nonprofit, and the newspaper's mailroom has also become a depository for thousands of the books they gather to give out to kids.

Not all minority staffers had such positive experiences. Eddie B. Allen, Jr., the young reporter who teamed up with Bill Brower on his final cross-country survey, never felt that lower-ranking news executives understood minority coverage.

Allen, a Detroit native, spent four years at the *Toledo Blade,* joining shortly before he turned twenty-two, right after graduating from Wayne State University in 1994.[25] At first he did general assignment reporting but was

---

24. While Black readers in many communities have expressed similar sentiments, one of the most common complaints against newspapers by all readers is that the papers only cover bad news and ignore the good.

25. He had been a student of the author, who recommended him for the job.

soon given a new beat covering urban affairs.

But his conception of the beat – and the way issues of race ought to be covered – clashed repeatedly with the vision of his city editor, Dave Murray. "First of all I want to say that I had no problems with JRB," he said, meaning John Block.

"But I did with middle management, mainly Murray," he said.

"I absolutely believe there was a lot of ignorance – truly being ignorant of what the issues consisted of. Murray's idea of urban affairs reporting was to cover the NAACP chapter in Toledo, which had never been very forward thinking or aggressive, and by that point was just a bunch of old people, or just to 'cover some meeting Black people go to.' "I would go to these meetings, and they would bicker and posture. It came more and more clear to me that Murray was of the mind-set that as long as we write something about Black people, we are all right … . I guess what I am saying is that there was a real disconnect that I initially didn't realize was there – in terms of understanding the rabbit hole of racism and understanding the significance of the issue."

The breaking point came when a woman contacted Allen about her son Carl's murder. "She said that he had been a drug dealer, but was also a very talented boxer. He had reportedly left the drug scene and was in training for the Olympics.

"Then, he came home from training for Christmas, went to a gas station and got murdered." Eddie Allen saw this as a "fascinating, compelling human interest story – he had gotten it together and was about to do something with his life," and the police had no interest in the slaying of someone they saw as just another Black druggie.

Murray wasn't interested either. "One of the more painful moments of my life was having to tell that woman, 'I'm sorry, but the police don't care and we don't care either'," Allen said. Things soured further for him after that.

"They then moved me to three days urban affairs and two days night cops, which made it impossible to do the job the way it should be done," Allen said.

Looking back on the experience, he admits he didn't handle things perfectly either. "I didn't really talk to them in the way I now know I should have in terms of what the parameters of the beat were."

Some staffers there at the time said there was fault on both sides. Murray, who had grown up in a virtually all-white area, wasn't adequately sensitive to minority concerns in his first years as editor. Eddie Allen, on the other hand, was a brash reporter in his early twenties, and wasn't always diplomatic about pressing his points.

Nor did he realize that editors often needed to "feed the beast," in those days when there were far more news pages than now. There was pressure to produce a lot of daily copy, meaning few reporters could be spared for long investigative projects.

Eventually Allen left the *Blade* to pursue a career in non-profit communications. The newspaper, however, didn't see him as *persona non grata.* A few years later, when Allen's book *Low Road: The Life and Legacy of Donald Goines* was published,[26] the *Blade* favorably reviewed it. In 2015, after Rose Russell Stewart left the editorial pages, the *Blade* offered Allen a job as an editorial writer. He thought seriously about it but decided not to accept, mainly because he wanted to work on an idea he had for a documentary.

Dave Murray, however, would later become far more familiar with Toledo's Black community, as we will see in the next chapter.

Before that, however, the Block newspapers' foreign correspondent discovered another Black reporter in London who ended up at the *Blade* at the same time as Eddie Allen – but whose experience was much more positive.

Fernand Auberjonois, a respected journalist[27] who covered the world for the *Blade* and the *Pittsburgh Post-Gazette* for many years from the papers' bureau in London, was teaching a course in international reporting in the late 1980s when he noticed a very bright young Black woman in the class, a Michigan State University student studying in London for a year.

Ironically, she was from Toledo. Rhonda Sewell was born in Ohio and grew up largely in Toledo, but attended high school in Ann Arbor, which, she said, gave her a "strong social justice orientation."[28]

Auberjonois was so impressed by Sewell that he recommended her to John Block who interviewed her on the phone and told her "we want to offer you a position, and we want you to visit very many countries."

Sewell thought he meant eventually, perhaps after she became a seasoned reporter. Previously, she had worked only for MSU's student paper, and had done a stint at the *Lansing State Journal.* But Block "had me go to about six countries for the *Blade* before I ever arrived back in Toledo," she said, still

26. Eddie Allen, Jr., *Low Road: The Life and Legacy of Donald Goines,* New York: St. Martin's Press, 2004.

27. Fernand Auberjonois (1910-2004), a Swiss native who became a proud American citizen, was no stranger to discrimination. The author of many books and a former broadcaster for the Voice of America, he left the United States in response to U.S. Sen. Joseph R. McCarthy's assault on civil liberties in the early 1950s.

28. Rhonda Sewell, interview with the author, August 2019.

amazed.

Once she got to the paper, however, "I started at the bottom rung like everybody else, like every other new reporter. I did night police, I was a 'Neighbors' section reporter."

Sewell, who has a naturally warm and gregarious personality, said she never felt that she had encountered any racism from the staff, especially not from John Block.

"John wanted 'boots on the ground' – he wanted his reporters to cover stories anywhere. If I had a good idea, if anyone had a good idea, he went for it."

Nor, she said, did she ever get any pushback on a racially tinged story. "I expected some on a story I did about 'Wiggers'" – white youth who imitate Black urban and "hip hop" lifestyles. "But all I got were positive comments."

Sewell said she never experienced much racism in the community either. When she went to small, virtually all-white towns like Berkey, Ohio, to cover stories, "what I usually got was a sense of gratitude and wonder they were being covered at all."

Though she was a reporter, she added, she was also a part of Toledo's Black community. "A lot of times, I did hear complaints that not enough attention was being given to the community, that they weren't being covered enough."

Sewell relayed these concerns. She also heard that Black leaders felt the paper needed more Black staffers. One year, when she was covering an NAACP convention in Detroit, she and a white reporter met a Black reporter from Beaumont, Texas, named Clyde Hughes. "We told John Block and the senior management about him, and he ended up covering urban affairs for the *Blade*."

She stayed at the newspaper from 1988 until 2006, when she left to take a position at the Toledo-Lucas County library as media relations coordinator; she eventually became manager for external and governmental affairs for the library system. Sewell was by then a single mother of twins, and the job gave her more flexibility as a parent.

Sewell, a stylish woman who ended up covering features and fashion, concedes she may have had an easier time than some because she was sort of exotic – "part of the community and not part of it at the same time."

But "everyone, the editors – were all very helpful." She worried that the publisher might be upset when she left, but "John wasn't resentful, because I was going to the one institution he loved almost as much as the *Blade* – the library. For me, it was a wonderful experience."

15

New Century, New Challenges: America Elects a Black President

Dave Murray spent almost his entire career at the *Blade* before retiring as managing editor at the end of 2019. There is general agreement that in later years he became much more attuned to racial issues and minority concerns.

"Murray is an example of someone who has come a long way," said Bishop Robert Culp. "I've known him for a long time. He had these diversity sessions and came out of that more enlightened," he said a few months before Murray retired.[1]

That was a sentiment shared by the editor himself. "I've gone through a process of consciousness-raising," he said during a long interview shortly before his retirement.

"I grew up in nearly all-white Wood County.[2] I went to an all-white high school. I never knew any Black folks till I went to Bowling Green State University." When he became a journalist, he said candidly, "it was hard to understand their concerns at first because I was white and was raised in an all-white world."

"It took me a long time to understand the full impact of racism, but even before I did I was pushing for more inclusive coverage," he said. Early

---

1. Dave Murray, interview with the author, July 25, 2019.
2. Largely rural, Wood County was comprised of only 1.27 percent Blacks in 2000.

in his career at the *Blade* he worked on the now-vanished "Neighbors" sections – zoned weekly inserts – and didn't think it right that there wasn't a "Neighbors" section for the central city.

"My old city editor told me 'those people don't buy the paper.'" But years later, when Murray had the ability to do so, he created a "Neighbors" section for the central city. Unfortunately it, and all the other zoned sections, later vanished when the flight of ad revenue to the internet in the early twenty-first century meant the *Blade*, like nearly all papers, had to downsize.

By that time, however, Murray had begun to make friends and cultivate sources in the Black community. A turning point for him was when he began covering Bernard "Pete" Culp, the younger brother of the bishop, who "was forced out of a city job essentially for advocating policies that were right and fair."

Culp eventually became "both a friend, and an important source for understanding the community." This paid off in 2013 when many in Toledo's African-American community became troubled over a series the newspaper did on neighborhood gangs.

"Taylor Dungjen, then the police reporter, learned that the police were operating from a map they'd created showing where the gangs operated," Murray remembered.[3]

When the police refused to give the *Blade* a copy of the map, the newspaper decided to create its own – and then followed that with "Battle Lines: Gangs of Toledo," an extensive series about gang activity in the city.[4] "In Toledo, all the gangs are Black and Hispanic, there are no white gangs," Murray said. The editors were proud of their gang coverage, which was primarily handled by two white female reporters.

The reaction in the African-American community was something else again. The Rev. Robert Culp told Murray that a few friends would like to discuss the series with him. Murray gamely agreed to meet them at Culp's church, The First Church of God, on Collingwood Boulevard in Toledo's central city. He expected a handful of folks.

"But when I arrived, there were about seventy-five people there," he said. And some of them weren't too happy with the series. They felt it had been racist.

---

3. For a fuller account of this, and the way in which the *Blade* reported the story, see David Yaffe-Bellamy, "An Acclaimed Crime Reporter Leaves Her Newsroom for Police Work," *Columbia Journalism Review*, January 9, 2018.

4. When *Blade* reporters finally managed to get a copy of the police's gang map, they concluded it was considerably inferior to the one they created. See Yaffe-Bellamy, above.

This surprised the managing editor. "I told them that I thought our coverage of gang activity and crime wasn't racist – it wasn't racist to me."

Then something happened that Murray has never forgotten. "Pastor Culp told me that whenever he's shopping he doesn't touch merchandise in stores, because his mother always told him, 'white people don't want to buy anything a Black boy has touched.'"

The minister added that whenever he leaves his house he hears his grandmother telling him "You'd better take a pee before you go. There might not be any place to go."

"Pastor Culp then put his hand on my arm, gently squeezed it and said, 'David, this is racism. We live it. We live it every day.'"

Murray was shaken. "I was so moved by what he told me, so touched, and for the first time I had a glimpse of racism at a personal level. Yes, I knew what racism was – at least I thought I did. But that day I realized how much I didn't know, and that Pastor Culp was going to be a great teacher." Murray then went on to field questions from the group. "Towards the end, an elderly Black lady thanked me, saying it was the first time an editor from the *Blade* had come to meet with them. She said, 'thanks for listening to us and being open to our stories and how we see things.'"

Murray saw that more needed to be done. Culp asked if he would go back and see if the *Blade* would be open to sponsoring some community forums.

They were. The first, in September 2013, held at Woodward High School was called "Changing Minds and Changing Lives: Combating Racism," and focused on white privilege.[5] The *Blade* chipped in $5,000 to cover the costs," Murray said. The event was a huge success, more than filling the 575-seat high school auditorium.

Publisher John Block was quoted in the story as saying that newspapers needed to be "in the middle" of community conversations. He added that there was clearly "a need for an organization to help out, and we were happy to do that."

This was followed by several more – Murray thought four or five – similar forums, which then evolved into an ongoing "Dialogue for Change" series. The first meeting of that series was held at the *Blade* offices.

"'Dialogue for Change' represents a natural outgrowth of the community forums, an everyday attempt to educate the community about racism,"

---

5. Vanessa McCray, "Forum Calls for Action on Race Issues, Diversity," *Toledo Blade*, September 13, 2013. The speaker was Tim Wise, author of *White Like Me: Reflections on Race from a Privileged Son,* Berkeley, CA: Soft Skull Press, 2007.

Murray said.

He added that what he learned through the forums has had an effect on coverage: "The newspaper has moved away from suggesting the race of suspects, except in cases where the police provide very specific details about a particular suspect."

More than that, his vision of covering race and racial topics had been affected by his realization that "segregation has damaged both white and Black people – I firmly believe that – and has damaged Black people more. But everyone is damaged who hasn't grown up around people of different colors and ethnicities."

That ideally means a more diverse newsroom as well. "I concede that the editorial staff at the *Blade* is still not nearly diverse enough," Murray said. Taking a fast inventory of the newsroom in late 2019 he said, "currently there are two Black managers, the features and digital editors, one Black reporter and one longtime Black news assistant. This is out of about eighty-eight FTEs [full-time employees] in editorial."

"We have a problem keeping folks of color. After a couple years, they generally go on to larger papers." Another problem is that newspapers now have much smaller staffs – the *Blade* once had more than twice as many reporters and editors, and there is little opportunity to recruit. Newspaper salaries also haven't kept pace.

Newspapers and university journalism programs have found that African-Americans who have managed to graduate from college are often not eager to enter a profession where the pay is poor and job security virtually non-existent.

"But that doesn't mean we shouldn't be trying, and we are," Murray said.

Times have radically changed since the founding member of the newspaper family, Paul Block (1875-1941), first began running newspapers in the early twentieth century.

Though his editorial pages sometimes endorsed Democrats, most notably FDR in his 1928 campaign for governor of New York, they never endorsed one for president of the United States. Nor does it seem likely that Block ever could have imagined that a Black man would someday be elected president, much less as a Democrat – or that this candidate would have the enthusiastic backing of the Block newspapers.

But that is exactly what happened in 2008.

Neither the *Toledo Blade* nor the *Pittsburgh Post-Gazette* had supported George W. Bush in either of his campaigns for president; John Robinson Block, who has personally interviewed most presidential candidates over the last four decades never thought that the second President Bush was up to the job.

When Bush led the United States into war with Iraq after the terrorist attacks on September 11, 2001, the newspapers further soured on him. As his second term drew to a close the general expectation was that U.S. Senator Hillary Clinton, a Democrat from New York and a former first lady, would be the Democratic nominee.

Few thought, in early 2008, that a freshman senator from Illinois, a young Black man with an outlandish name, would present much of a challenge to her nomination.

However, both the *Blade* and the *Post-Gazette* thought otherwise. "Bush was a dolt," John Block said years later. "We needed something new. Clinton represented the past, the Vietnam War generation. Barack Obama was a fresh face, had a fresh outlook and offered hope."

Historically, with rare exceptions, neither paper endorsed candidates in primary election contests, especially for president. The philosophy was that it was up to the parties to choose their candidates and the newspaper to endorse in the general election.

But in 2008 both papers departed from that. They strongly endorsed Barack Obama prior to the Ohio and Pennsylvania primaries. "The *Blade* has a long-established principle of seldom endorsing a candidate in any primary election," the newspaper's editorial said on February 28, 2008. "It's easy to see, however, that this isn't a typical year. For the first time in history, the outcome of the Ohio primary may well determine the Democratic nominee for president of the United States… moreover, we believe that Mr. Obama's inspiring life story, keen intellect and his fresh and optimistic world view are what America needs after eight years of an administration that has repeatedly shown open contempt for the American people and the Constitution… America is badly in need of something new…. at this point, we feel free to break with tradition and enthusiastically recommend that on Tuesday, Ohio Democrats cast their primary ballots for Barack Obama."

Six weeks later, just prior to the Pennsylvania primary, an editorial in the *Pittsburgh Post-Gazette* sounded much the same:[6]

"Senator Obama has captured much of the nation's imagination for a reason: He offers real change, a vision of an America that can move past not only racial tensions but also the political partisanship that has so bedeviled it… the *Post-Gazette* endorses the nomination of Barack Obama, who has

---

6. *Pittsburgh Post-Gazette* editorial, April 16, 2008.

brought an excitement and electricity to American politics not seen since the days of John F. Kennedy."

Ironically, the editorials seemed to have little effect on voters in Ohio and Pennsylvania, perhaps because the Democratic parties in both states are not notably progressive. The *Post-Gazette's* editorial endorsing Obama referred to Pennsylvania as an "encrusted, change-averse commonwealth," an observation in many ways that was true of both its political parties, and of Ohio as well.

Hillary Clinton won both states by near-identical margins, 54 to 45 percent in Pennsylvania and 53 to 45 percent in Ohio. But Obama, of course, won the nomination, and breezed to victory in the November election, easily carrying both Pennsylvania and Ohio. Race was barely mentioned by either paper in their general election editorials. By that time Republican nominee John McCain's inept response to Wall Street's financial crisis and his choice of Sarah Palin as running mate had doomed his candidacy.

The *Post-Gazette* editorial mainly sounded those themes, and came closest to referencing race by referring to Obama as a man "whose story is a quintessentially American one of impossible odds overcome," and predicting, in a line made famous by Abraham Lincoln, that Americans would "heed the better angels of their nature."[7]

The *Blade* virtually ignored McCain in its final editorial, except to dismiss him as having demonstrated "his inability to show that he has a vision coherent enough."[8] As for Obama, it compared him to Franklin D. Roosevelt and John F. Kennedy as "leaders uniquely suited to their times," evoked the challenges presented in JFK's inaugural address, and added "Mr. Obama is ready to answer that summons."

By that time, although the polls showed Obama with a solid lead over his rival, some analysts thought there was a possibility of the so-called "Bradley effect," in which white voters supposedly tell pollsters that they plan to vote for a Black candidate, but then can't bring themselves to actually do so in the voting booth.[9]

Instead, Obama won by a solid margin in line with what polls had predicted. The *Blade* and *Post-Gazette* remained mainly supportive throughout his

---

7. *Pittsburgh Post-Gazette* editorial, October 12, 2008.

8. Actually the *Blade* had two editorials endorsing Obama, one on October 12 and a second on November 2, 2008, the Sunday before the election. The paper usually did major endorsements on Sundays because that was its highest circulation day.

9. The effect was named for Los Angeles Mayor Tom Bradley, a Black man who lost the race for governor of California in 1982 after consistently leading in the polls.

presidency. When he ran for re-election both papers again strongly supported him, saying in Toledo, for example, that his "steady, centrist leadership has been good for this nation and this region." While the newspapers mildly chided him for failing to do enough "on such issues as deficit reduction and entitlement reform" they were disdainful of his challenger, Mitt Romney, as an elitist whose "economic plan would shift tax burdens from the wealthiest Americans to middle-class families."

Romney had also opposed the federal assistance that saved the auto companies from going out of business, which was likely more than enough to doom his candidacy in older manufacturing states like Ohio and Pennsylvania.

Years later, interviewed about his newspapers' support for the nation's first Black major party nominee, John Robinson Block said that while Obama was the clearly superior choice for other reasons, there *had* been a racial factor.[10]

"Barack Obama offered hope. My father sent us to different schools – I remember that my brother Allan went to a Catholic school for first grade, and the nuns had pictures of JFK and Pope John XXIII on the wall as role models."

His hope, the publisher said, was that perhaps President Obama's picture would be put on the wall in inner-city schools and "inspire kids to learn, and get an education.

The hope was that he would be an inspiration to children."

The publisher remembered that for a while he and his brother Allan were in public school, but "father pulled us out of there, for a number of reasons, but one of them was working-class white kids who threw around the N-word. That was entirely unacceptable to him."

Paul Block may have been a self-made millionaire newspaper publisher but he, as well as his sons and grandsons, had to have been acutely aware that he was an immigrant who himself would have suffered discrimination because he was Jewish. But he was able to quickly learn English that was so unaccented and flawless that few of his friends and associates ever suspected he hadn't been born in New York.

That wasn't an option for most African-Americans. "My father once said that Americans always completely assimilated within three generations, except perhaps for religion. Blacks couldn't do that because of color," Block said.

Eventually, with the rise of Black power and ethnic identity movements,

---

10. John Robinson Block, interview with the author, March 5, 2020.

196 | REASON VS. RACISM

many Blacks and some other minority groups made it clear they didn't really want to completely assimilate even if they could have, which the publisher said presented another set of problems. "Do we really want to be hyphenated-Americans?"

The nation has drastically changed, he noted, and the kaleidoscope of racial interactions has become infinitely more complicated than it was nearly a century ago, when his grandfather was essentially driven out of journalism in Tennessee for lionizing a simple Black man who became a hero for saving white people's lives.[11]

How does a newspaper properly cover race?

"In these fraught times, with difficulty," the publisher acknowledged. "But as long as I am around, we are going to do it properly and with accuracy."

Unfortunately, newspapers no longer have as many resources, pages, or reporters to cover as many stories as they once did. That is a nationwide phenomenon.

In modern-day Pittsburgh, no leaders in the Black community with whom I spoke in early 2020 accused the *Post-Gazette* of overt or even covert racism. Many of them did say, however, there is a lack of in-depth coverage of their community.

"They do cover the African-American community," said Esther Bush, the longtime and highly respected president of the Urban League of Greater Pittsburgh. "But the coverage is not comprehensive, and the stories are almost never deep enough. When I read the *Pittsburgh Post-Gazette*, I find I also have to read the *Courier*[12] to get the full story. In the *Post-Gazette*, I often find that a lot of times a lot of details that might be pertinent to the African-American community are not included," she said.

Bush, a Pittsburgh native and former teacher, has led the organization since returning to her hometown in 1994 after stints running Urban League chapters in New York City and Hartford, Connecticut.[13] During an interview,[14] she said she thought the paper might provide better coverage if it had more Black reporters.

She praised Tony Norman, a popular Black columnist for the *Post-Gazette*

---

11. See Chapter 5, "Memphis: Recognizing a Black Hero."

12. The *Pittsburgh Courier*, which was the leading African-American newspaper in the nation during the 1940s, closed in 1966 and reopened in 1967 as the *New Pittsburgh Courier*, also a weekly. Its circulation is small – only 3,480 in 2012 – but it is still influential in black Pittsburgh.

13. Founded in 1910, the Urban League's official mission is "to enable African Americans to secure economic self-reliance, parity, power and civil rights."

14. Esther Bush, interview with the author, March 5, 2020.

who often writes about issues and personalities in the African-American community. "Oh, Tony's great," she said, as Mary Kay Filter Dietrich, the Urban League's vice-president for external relations, nodded approval. "But he is a columnist, not a news reporter."[15]

Bush did praise the *Post-Gazette* for the coverage it gave the Urban League when the organization held its national conference in Pittsburgh in 2003. Not only did she find the coverage fairly comprehensive, the newspaper collaborated with the *New Pittsburgh Courier* to put out a joint special section for the event.[16]

"It was an opportunity for us to show our accomplishments, as well as what we need to do to improve – and to see what a newspaper can do help us communicate these themes to a larger audience," she said.

Doris Carson Williams, one of the most influential voices in the Black business world in Pittsburgh, sounded similar themes. "They don't cover the African-American Chamber, or the Black business community, well," she said of the *Post-Gazette*.[17]

"Most of the time, they don't cover it at all. Now, they recently did a very nice article on me for Black History Month. But they seldom cover our members," said Williams, who founded the African-American chamber in Pittsburgh in 1998.

Twenty-two years later, it has grown to 562 members. "We send them press releases all the time and invite them to cover us," but they don't, she said.

Williams, who herself has had a notable business career, said she finds that puzzling and short-sighted. She has a degree in banking, has held executive positions in companies from Control Data Systems to Hartford Insurance, and, perhaps most impressively, is chair of the Federal Reserve Bank of Pittsburgh.

"I should say that once in a while they do cover us, and when they do, it is a welcome surprise. But they could do more – we are trying to do everything

---

15. Mary Kay Filter Dietrich, interview with the author, March 10, 2020.Tony Norman, who credited Bill Block, Sr., for launching his career as a journalist, believes the *Post-Gazette* is not as committed to covering minorities or understanding their concerns, or increasing their number working in the newsroom. "It's just not a priority for the *Post-Gazette*," he said. However, he said there had been no attempt to censor or kill any of his columns, including one on January 16, 2018, that seemed a direct rebuttal to "Reason as Racism."

16. The papers worked together to produce an eight-page supplement about the Urban League conference that ran in both the *Post-Gazette* and the *Courier* on July 26, 2003. The theme was "The Black Family: Building on its Resilience."

17. Doris Carson Williams, Interview with the author, March 29, 2020.

we can to support the African-American business community, and let people know about it."

But Dr. Joe William Trotter, Jr., perhaps Pittsburgh's leading scholar of African-American history, gives the *Post-Gazette* somewhat higher marks. Now a professor of history and social justice at the Carnegie Mellon University in Pittsburgh, he is working on a history of African-American urban life in America since the beginnings of the slave trade.

"I actually have done some work on [newspaper] reporting in Pittsburgh in the twentieth century," he said. In earlier decades, he said, the *Post-Gazette*, like most white-owned metropolitan newspapers, was inclined to "follow the trend of not giving the African-American community as much coverage as it deserves."[18]

"But in recent years, the paper has been very much better in covering the African-American experience," Trotter said. The paper, he added, "has done very well over the last decade or so, in picking up more of community life and offering stronger coverage. It has been become a more important source for information about African-Americans," thought not a completely adequate one. "The *Courier* still serves an important role," he said, as Black newspapers have always done. "You don't see the white dailies picking up on all the issues pertinent to the African-American community," he said.

And as a historian, Trotter noted, it is always a challenge to put all people and issues in their proper perspective. The irony is that while mainstream newspapers like the *Post-Gazette* are much more willing to cover Black issues, their circulations are dropping and they can afford fewer reporters and fewer pages because of sinking ad revenue.

Today the challenge the *Pittsburgh Post-Gazette*, the *Toledo Blade,* and all newspapers face in covering any community may have been most aptly put by a forty-six-year-old Lyft driver who took me to the airport in Pittsburgh one afternoon.

"Oh, I love the *Post-Gazette*" she said. "I used to deliver it, and the *Press* too, when I was a kid. But our family always took the *Post-Gazette*."

She went on to say that she still loved reading it online, but hadn't that day because she had used up her access to free stories for the month.

"Why don't you subscribe to it?" I asked. "I'm not about to *pay* for *news,*" she said with a touch of indignation. "You are supposed to get news for free."

I pointed out that all the customers she had once had on her delivery

---

18. Dr. Joe William Trotter, Jr., interview with the author, March 10, 2020.

route paid for news by subscribing to the newspaper. "I never thought of that," she said, then adding, "but that was before the internet. With the internet, you can get news for free."

I told her that it still cost money to gather it, to pay reporters to do their jobs and their expenses. I told her that, true, she could find a lot of national news online. But I said local communities like Pittsburgh depended on newspapers like the *Post-Gazette* to tell them what was going on. How, I asked her, did she think newspapers could afford to gather news if people wouldn't pay for it?

She seemed interested, but not really convinced.

Finding ways to overcome that attitude may be the biggest challenge any paper faces today, regardless of its politics, its style, or what it chooses to cover.

Note on coverage of Hispanics

Hispanic is an ethnic, not a racial, classification but they are often seen as an oppressed minority in the United States, with lagging income and education levels that are close to those of African-Americans in many places.

However, coverage of their communities is not dealt with systematically in this book, largely because the Hispanic populations of both the Pittsburgh and Toledo regions have been historically very small, much smaller than the national average. The U.S. Census Bureau's American Community Survey estimated in 2019 that less than 1 percent of the population of Allegheny County, which includes Pittsburgh, was of Hispanic origin.

The number in Toledo was higher –7.4 percent in 2010 and an estimated 8.96 percent today – but still far under the national figure of 17.8 percent.

But Northwest Ohio is also a destination for many Hispanic farm laborers – and it is also the home to Baldemar Velasquez and the Farm Labor Organizing Committee (FLOC), the union that he helped found in 1967, which successfully organized migrant workers in the Midwest. The *Blade* has always intensely covered FLOC.

"I'd say they've been pretty good to us, they've been fair," Velasquez said during an interview at FLOC headquarters. "Early on there I think there was one reporter we had some trouble with, but we've had no real complaints," he said.[19]

---

19. Baldemar Velasquez, interview with the author, August 9, 2019.

16

Broadcast Properties

Not only have the Block stations complied with all the federal regulations, I am not aware of any complaints being filed either on employment matters or coverage of racial issues. They have an extraordinarily good record in that regard.

— John Feore, Washington-based senior counsel
and broadcast regulatory expert, Cooley LLP

For most of the many years since the first Paul Block went into business for himself in 1900, the company he founded was primarily a newspaper company.[1]

The founder, who was farsighted in many ways, was absorbed in newspapers and his advertising business and did not understand the business potential of radio.

While he did acquire a low-power, 240-watt station in Pittsburgh in 1931

---

1. At various times his ventures were divided into as many as three holding companies, one of which was primarily concerned with advertising sales, but all revolved around the newspaper business. His heirs sold off the advertising business soon after his death.

(WWSW), he paid little attention to the medium otherwise.[2]

Following his death in 1941 the company did begin to diversify into broadcast media, albeit slowly. Besides the two radio stations, the Blocks acquired a half-interest in a Pittsburgh TV station, then WIIC (now WPXI), which went on the air in 1957.

But the company's key achievement was as the leading force and a founding partner in the creation of one of nation's pioneering cable television systems, originally called Buckeye Cablevision, Inc., which began broadcasting in parts of Toledo in March 1966.[3] Today Buckeye Broadband is a full-spectrum cable and telecommunications provider that serves customers in Michigan and Ohio.

Ironically, it was the only part of the company that has ever been accused of any form of racial discrimination – essentially falsely, as we will see.

But first, it is notable that starting Buckeye itself was seen as a daring and risky venture. Starting a cable television company in a fairly large and unserved market twenty years later might have been seen as a sure thing from a business perspective. But that was not the case in the mid-1960s. In the early years "Cable TV" flourished only in areas where mountains or atmospheric conditions made over-the-air reception difficult.

Elsewhere cable was scoffed at as "Pay TV" and despite the attraction of more channels and choices it was a hard sell to people used to getting television programs for free. "It wasn't widely accepted at first," said Allan Block, the board chairman of Block Communications, Inc. (BCI), the holding company for all the family businesses.

People had to be taught the advantages of cable, and much of the technology had to be invented as they went along. Ironically, while some may still think of Block Communications as a newspaper company, the *Pittsburgh Post-Gazette* and the *Toledo Blade* may still exist today only because of cable and broadcast revenue.

Though BCI is a privately held firm it is no secret that its newspapers, like newspapers nearly everywhere in the United States, have been losing money since the flight of readers and, especially, advertisers to the internet.

---

2. Tom Dawson, *Building Blocks: Buckeye CableSystem's Communications Revolution*, Lanham, MD: Hamilton Books, 2015, 7. WWSW was an AM station; there was no FM in 1931. An FM station was added in 1942. The FCC finally approved increasing its power in 1949.

3. The Block family's move into cable began with a chance meeting at the Democratic National Convention in Atlantic City, New Jersey, in 1964. For the full – and often fascinating – story of the seat-of-the-pants way the cable company grew, see Tom Dawson's book *Building Blocks*.

Buckeye Broadband, however, is clearly profitable, as is a newer sister company, MaxxSouth, which provides broadband and cable services in Mississippi. If newspaper revenue helped fuel the startup of Buckeye Cablevision in the 1960s, it is quite likely that broadband was keeping the papers afloat in the early twenty-first century.

By the mid-1970s the parent firm, then known as the Toledo Blade Co., had completed the process of buying out its partner, Cox Enterprises, to become sole owner of Toledo's cable franchise. Cox had bought the *Blade*'s half interest in WIIC, the Pittsburgh TV station, in 1964 though the deals were not directly related.

The parent firm then bought WLIO-TV, an over-the-air station in Lima, Ohio. Today Block Communications has diversified further and now owns, besides those in Lima, several stations in Louisville, Kentucky, and a station in Decatur, Illinois.

How have the non-newspaper Block media done when it comes to diversity?

John Feore is a highly seasoned Washington, D.C., communications lawyer who has represented major clients before the Federal Communications Commission (FCC) for nearly half a century, including the Block broadcast stations almost from the time the company first went into broadcasting.

His other clients have included major chains, including the Iowa-based Meredith Corporation and Media General, before its sale to Nexstar. He also represents a number of stations affiliated with the FOX and CBS networks.

When it comes to Block Communications stations and racial matters Feore said, "they have an extremely good record in that regard. Not only have they complied with all the federal regulations, I am not aware of any complaints being filed either on employment matters or racial issues. I see a lot of operations, and in this regard, Block is in very good company – they have a very good record."[4]

Had there been any such complaints Feore would undoubtedly have known of them. The FCC takes such complaints seriously and more than one station has lost its license for violating federal standards on fairness;[5] others have been reprimanded.

But there has apparently never been any whisper of any racial controversy with any of the Block broadcast properties. On the contrary, they were early trailblazers in a perhaps unique way. Not only had the *Post-Gazette* hired the

---

4. John Feore, interview with the author, May 18, 2020.
5. In the most notorious example, Lamar Broadcasting lost its license for WLBT-TV in Jackson, Mississippi for racist practices.

first Black reporter to work on a major market newspaper in 1955, six years later WIIC-TV, which was half-owned by the Block family, hired the city's first Black TV reporter.

That was unusual: for starters, it wasn't just that it was the same family who caused racial barriers to be shattered in both media. It was that the shattering was done by the *same* reporter, Regis Bobonis, who went to the *Post-Gazette* in 1955 and left for the bright lights of TV news in 1961.[6]

Circumstantial evidence suggests that the elder Bill Block may well have been involved in both hires; as we have seen, diversity was steadily and increasingly more important to him, and when Bobonis was hired Toledo had had a Black reporter for eight or nine years.

In the years that followed, whenever the *Blade* or *Post-Gazette* was criticized by readers over coverage of stories that had to do with race, it was usually white readers who were angry because they thought the paper was going too far in its support for Blacks.

So it was somewhat startling when a charge came in the early 1980s that Buckeye was, in effect, discriminating against inner-city (i.e., Black) Toledo by not wiring it for cable. In February 1982, a group of minority investors calling themselves Toledo Central City Cable Television, Inc., surfaced and claimed that portions of the poorer areas of central Toledo hadn't been wired for cable. They asked Toledo City Council to grant them a permit to build a system to serve those areas.

It *was* true that part of Toledo, including part of the inner city, had not yet been wired for cable in early 1982; some pockets in mainly white and suburban areas hadn't been wired either. Allan Block, today BCI's chair and chief executive officer, insisted that "this wasn't any kind of intentional redlining. We always intended to wire the entire city, but we were doing it as we could afford to pay for it. In fact, I remember my father telling me that we began wiring part of the central city almost from the start, so that nobody could say we were discriminating." He went on to say, "But I didn't feel we had done enough. Father had encouraged me to take an interest in the electronic side of the business, and I remember talking to John Karl (then president of Buckeye Cablevision), this must have been 1980 or 1981, and

---

6. The Block family shared ownership of WIIC-TV from 1955 – two years before it came on the air – until September 1964, when it was sold to Cox for $20.5 million ($168 million in 2020 dollars), which at that time was the largest amount ever paid for a TV station. The station was supervised by a board in which a Block employee was chair and a member of the local family who owned the other half was president. Both families agreed to hire a professional from New York (Robert Mortensen) to run the station. See *Broadcasting,* November 23, 1964, 64-65 for details about the sale.

asking when we were going to finish wiring it. I asked him more than once. This was at a time when nobody had ever heard of Central City Cablevision. There was no Central City then. He told me that there was a plan in place. I didn't think we were going fast enough." The reason, however, had nothing to do with race. "What happened was that my father was always reluctant to take on debt," Block said. "He didn't understand that sometimes debt makes sense, and so they expanded Buckeye's service area gradually, when they could afford to do so."

Naturally, the company had largely wired areas first where they calculated it could get the most subscribers, attract advertisers, and make as much money as possible, especially since they needed to generate revenue to finance further expansion.

Central City Cable was headed by Sylvester Gould, Jr., who had a background in labor relations and human resources; at the time he was the head of the Economic Opportunity Planning Association of Greater Toledo. He was joined by three men who had similar or market research backgrounds – but no apparent capital.[7]

Gould went before Toledo City Council's service committee, accused Buckeye Cablevision of "electronic redlining," and said his company could provide service to the approximately 70,000 residents in the underserved area.[8]

When asked Gould admitted he had no solid commitments for financing, but claimed Central City would have money if a franchise was granted.[9] Central City – and some members of Toledo City Council – expected Buckeye Cablevision to oppose giving the new company a permit. But at that point Buckeye made a very shrewd move.

Buckeye president John Karl sent a letter to the city council saying it should be "clearly understood" that Buckeye had no objections to their granting Central City a permit. A presumably relieved council, not wanting to get caught in a battle between the company that owned the newspaper and a minority group, then did so.[10]

Legally the permit was essentially the same as the one given Buckeye years earlier, giving Central City the right to compete fully with Buckeye.

7. Dawson, *Building Blocks: Buckeye CableSystem's Communications Revolution*, 28-29. His partners were Calvin Lawshe, Wayman Palmer (then head of Toledo's Economic Development Department), and Waymon Usher.

8. "Firm Gains Committee OK," *Toledo Blade,* March 5, 1982.

9. Dawson, 29.

10. "Central City Cablevision Franchise Is Awarded," *Toledo Blade,* March 17, 1982.

But they never did. There were, in fact, absolutely no grounds for Buckeye to oppose the permit, for at least three reasons. Most significantly, what was granted Central City did not prevent Buckeye from wiring the area in question; Karl's letter made it clear Buckeye remained committed to expanding its service to all areas of the city.

Buckeye was an established firm with capital and access to the tools and technology needed to wire the underserved area quickly. Central City Cablevision's principals had no expertise and little to no significant capital.

Finally, it was hard for anyone with a realistic grasp of economic reality to imagine that a cable company could be financially successful wiring and serving only the poorest areas of Toledo – which is what Central City claimed it intended to do – especially when it needed to raise huge sums for start-up costs.

At that point, however, Central City Cable became an unwitting pawn in another man's game. Don Barden, a former city councilman and TV personality in Lorain, Ohio, swept into town, joined Central City as majority partner, and pledged to invest big money and offer better programming at a lower price than Buckeye.

Barden, a wheeler-dealer who did have a tiny cable operation in the small Detroit suburb of Inkster, wowed Gould and his partners, who believed him.

Not, however, for long. Soon it became clear to everyone, including Sylvester Gould, that Barden was only interested in using Central City to beef up his resume to win a much bigger prize – winning the right to build a cable system in Detroit.

That worked – brilliantly. In July 1983 Barden, who billed himself as "the Black King of Cable TV," was awarded the right to build a cable system in the Motor City, which then did not have one. It later became clear that some members of the Detroit City Council thought he was running an existing successful cable operation in Toledo.[11]

For many months wire service stories referred to Barden as operating a cable system in Toledo.[12] Once he had the Detroit franchise, however, he gave up any pretense of wanting to build anything in Toledo and pulled out of Central City.

"Mr. Barden used Toledo as leverage for Detroit," a rueful Sylvester

---

11. Based on conversations I had in later years with Detroit City Council members.

12. See, for example, an Associated Press story from January 6, 1985, "Detroit CATV Firm's Proposal Criticized."

Gould, Jr., told the *Blade* in April 1984.[13] He said he had come to realize that Barden never intended to build anything in Toledo. Meanwhile, Buckeye had been busily finishing wiring the city; by July 1983 Cablevision president Karl said the task was 95 percent complete. "I don't dispute that," Sylvester Gould told me at the time.[14]

That was the end of Toledo Central City Cable Television's dreams of building an alternative cable system.[15] Don Barden had a rocky tenure in Detroit and ended up operating casinos in Gary, Indiana, and Las Vegas before dying of lung cancer in 2011.

Today Buckeye has thousands of customers, the majority of them subscribers to the high-speed, broadband internet connection provided by the company.

Kayla French, Buckeye's director of marketing operations and creative services, came to Buckeye in 2017; an African-American and native Detroiter, she had been performing a similar role for Comcast in West Palm Beach, Florida.

"I had a great job, but I was recruited to join the company" by a Buckeye executive with whom she had worked at Comcast. "People [in the business] thought very highly of the Block family. I've never heard anything bad."

She seemed unaware of the long-ago charges of "electronic redlining." Asked if she had ever heard of any complaints that would indicate problems minorities had, either with getting service or other forms of discrimination, she said,

"Not that I am aware of – and I think I would have, given my responsibilities here." Nor had she heard of "any kind of discrimination in the employment process."

Interestingly the job she now holds was once held by Allan Block himself, who took it on in 1985, three years after the Central City Cable controversy. He was eventually succeeded by Florence Buchanan, who went on to a long career with Buckeye before retiring in 2016 as vice president of sales and marketing.

---

13. Sarah Snyder, "Lack of Inner-City Cable TV Blamed on Chief Backer," *Toledo Blade,* May 1, 1984.

14. Jack Lessenberry, "Central City Cable TV Has Yet to Fulfill Commitment," *Toledo Blade*, July 9, 1983. I covered part of the Central City controversy until July 1983, when I took another job.

15. Central City encouraged potential subscribers to put a $25 down payment on future service, for which they got a sign that said "No thanks, Buckeye. I'm waiting for Toledo Central City Cable Television." They were later given their deposits back if they asked for them.

Buchanan, who is also African-American, additionally served a stint as vice-president and general manager of Monroe Cablevision, Inc., in Monroe, Michigan.

"I was interested in helping Florence Buchanan develop her career, but she wasn't given any job because she was African-American. She moved up in the company when I went downtown because she impressed me and worked her way up. I've never given special treatment to anybody. We don't care what you are, but what you do – I would be racist if I gave you special treatment based on race."

As for the company's over-the-air stations it is first important to understand that different legal standards apply to print and broadcast media.

Print publications can cover the news in any way they wish and take whatever positions they please – even racist ones – a right guaranteed them by the First Amendment to the Constitution of the United States.

True, when it comes to hiring, open discrimination on the basis of race, color, or gender was outlawed nationally by federal civil rights legislation in the 1960s and the U.S. Equal Employment Opportunity Commission, usually known as the EEOC, has the power to take action against any business that does so.

Those laws technically apply to newspapers – but in journalism there are often a lot of subjective factors that go into deciding which candidate may be better qualified. Proving discrimination can be difficult. While the *Toledo Blade* and the *Pittsburgh Post-Gazette* were among the first big-city papers to diversify their staffs there are still newspapers today with few or even no African-American editorial employees.

Broadcast television and radio are, however, much more regulated. The legal reason for that goes back to a concept called "spectrum scarcity" – there are only a limited amount of frequencies on broadcast airwaves. While everyone could theoretically own their own newspaper that's not true for over-the-air broadcast media.[16] There are, as they used to say, only so many spots on the dial.

During the early days of radio competing stations would sometimes broadcast on the same frequency and drown each other out. Eventually Congress stepped in (partly at the request of the companies trying to

---

16. Cable television properties do not operate under the same content and diversity requirements as broadcast media. They are subscription services which someone has to choose to pay to view and since they come in via "cable" and not over the public airwaves, the U.S. Supreme Court has ruled that "spectrum scarcity" arguments are irrelevant to cable.

broadcast) and passed a series of laws[17] that gave the government the right to regulate the airwaves, assign frequencies, and decide who could have a license to broadcast.

The airwaves were also declared to be public property. KDKA, an AM station in Pittsburgh, is commonly held to have been the first station continually on the air.[18]

But while KDKA broadcasts on 1020 AM, it doesn't "own" that frequency, any more than Block Communications "owns" the frequencies on which its television channels broadcast. Legally the nation owns the airwaves and the FCC has the power to issue station owners a license for exclusive use of that frequency in that particular geographic area. Those licenses must periodically be renewed – and there are strings attached.[19]

Any over-the-air station has to abide by rules and standards set by the federal government. Once that included strict censorship of profanity, for example.

Stations were also once required to provide programing "in the public interest," which mostly meant news and public service announcements. Broadcast stations these days are also expected to follow diversity standards in hiring and for years had to file reports indicating to what extent they had achieved those goals.

Barry Fulmer is the vice-president and director of news for WDRB-TV in Louisville, Kentucky, probably the most important of the Block broadcast properties.[20]

His newsroom had ninety-one employees in early 2020, making it the largest editorial operation in the state and eclipsing the once-dominant but dwindling newspaper, the Louisville *Courier-Journal.* Fulmer originally joined WDRB in 1991, eight years after it was acquired by Block Communications.

Though he left the station to briefly work elsewhere he has been back

---

17. Beginning with the Radio Act of 1912. the Federal Radio Commission was established in 1927 and became the Federal Communications Commission (FCC) in 1934.

18. WWJ-AM in Detroit disputes this, and the record is unclear. Both went on the air in 1920.

19. The U.S. Supreme Court has repeatedly ruled that the federal government has the right to impose content restrictions on broadcast properties and that it does not have the right to restrict for newspapers or other printed entities. See *National Broadcasting Co. v. United States,* 319 U.S. 190 (1943) and *Red Lion Broadcasting v. Federal Communications Commission,* 395 U.S. 367 (1969).

20. As of May 2020 these also included WBKI-TV, a CW affiliate which is housed with the Louisville station but licensed on the Indiana side of the border; the lower-powered WMYO, an NBC affiliate; WAND-TV in Decatur, Illinois; and WLIO-TV, their first station, a FOX affiliate in Lima, Ohio.

with the station since 1998, first as a reporter who won multiple Emmy and other awards, and the then the executive leading the newsroom for more than the past decade.

When it comes to hiring, he said "diversity is something I work on all the time. I've always worked to increase diversity, and I feel like I have corporate support [from the Block family]. That's a given."

The station's staff, both on-air and otherwise, is highly diverse, he said, noting that the station has both African-American and Asian anchors.[21] He has had some frustrations: "When you are looking to hire people – I think there have been times when I would have liked to have hired (minorities) but couldn't find the right candidate."

Like other managers in middle-market stations nationwide, he has also had the experience of recruiting talented minority journalists, only to have them soon go on to larger markets. "I had a very talented business reporter [who was African-American]" he said. "But within a few years she was in Dallas, and is now in Chicago," he added with a chuckle, noting that this is the nature of the business.

As for serious complaints about coverage of the community, "Nothing specific comes to mind," he said, though of course there are always people unhappy with some stories. He noted that in Louisville, as in many cities, there were always racial tensions to some extent, notably between the police and residents in some lower-income areas in the city, which tend to have high minority populations. When events there become newsworthy, he added "we try to do it right the first time."

---

21. U.S. Census bureau estimates in 2007 were that 22.2 percent of Louisville's 620,000 residents were Black, 2 percent were Asian, and 2.9 percent identified as Hispanic.

17

Reason as
Racism Revisited

Over the years the *Pittsburgh Post-Gazette* and the *Toledo Blade* were often criticized on various issues from downtown development to political endorsements.

Never, however, had either paper been systematically called racist – meaning that they were unfair to minorities, especially African-Americans. The opposite was more often true. In fact, they had been attacked for being too sympathetic to minorities.[1]

As ombudsman for the *Blade* during the entire Obama presidency, I dealt with a never-ending list of complaints from a small but noisy group of readers who demanded the newspaper accept that his birth certificate was phony and who called the president racist names. ("Communist Muslim" was one of the few printable ones.)

They sometimes called the editors equally bad names for supporting him.

A white caller in 2012 demanded, "Why doesn't your paper care about white people? Why do you only care about minorities? A lot of us sometimes really think you hate white people, you know?" before promising to cancel his subscription.

---

1. Local African-Americans did sometimes complain about coverage, but the local news editors generally were happy to work with me to get those complaints resolved.

No one, except perhaps white supremacists, was openly calling the Block newspapers racist when they were enthusiastically endorsing Barack Obama.

But the way the newspapers were portrayed changed dramatically in January 2018 when both newspapers published an editorial that would set off a firestorm of controversy, titled: "Reason as Racism: An Immigration Debate Gets Derailed."

The newspapers and their editors and owners were promptly denounced as essentially racist – often by other journalists, especially in Pittsburgh.

"This piece is so extraordinary in its mindless, sycophantic embrace of racist values and outright bigotry espoused by this country's president that we would be morally, journalistically and humanly remiss not to speak out against it," said a letter from the executive committee of Pittsburgh's Newspaper Guild.[2]

The editorial drew notice from national journalistic publications, including the respected *Columbia Journalism Review*, which, in a somewhat organizationally jumbled piece by a former *Post-Gazette* staffer,[3] criticized the editorial, but mainly used it to question other staff changes made at the paper. Though passages of the "Reason as Racism" editorial have been widely quoted, any proper assessment requires that it be reprinted in full:

> Calling someone a racist is the new McCarthyism. The charge is pernicious. The accuser doesn't need to prove it. It simply hangs over the accused like a great human stain.

> It has become not a descriptive term for a person who believes in the superiority of one race over another, but a term of malice and libel – almost beyond refutation, as the words "communist" or "communist sympathizer" were in the 1950s.

> Moreover, the accuser somehow covers himself in an immunity of superiority. If I call you a racist, I probably will not be called one. And, finally, having chosen the ultimate epithet, I have dodged the obligation to converse or build.

> If Donald Trump is called a racist for saying some nations are

---

2. Relations between the Newspaper Guild and the ownership had already been acrimonious for months over negotiations and contract issues.

3. Kim Lyons, "The *Pittsburgh Post-Gazette*'s Baffling Editorial Decision," *Columbia Journalism Review,* March 22, 2018.

"shithole countries," does that help pass a "Dreamers" bill to keep gifted young people in this nation – people who have something to give the United States and are undocumented only because they were brought here by their parents illegally?

That's the goal, is it not? To save the Dreamers? That's what the White House meeting last week was about. It's what the whole week was about, until we went down the "racist" rabbit hole.

We were having an immigration debate. To the president, it is a reasonable goal, and one that most Americans would agree upon, to want to naturalize more people based on "merit." We want more people who can contribute to our culture and economy, and they tend to come from stable nations.

If the president had used the world "hellhole" instead, would that have been racist?

If he had used the word "failed states," would that have been racist?

But there *are* nations that *are* hellholes in this world. And there are failed states. It is not racist to say that this country cannot take only the worst people from the worst places and that we want some of the best people from the best places, many of which are inhabited by people of color. That's not racism, it is reason.

Yes, we should take in unskilled refugees. We also want more Indian Ph.Ds. and engineers.

If Sen. Dick Durbin wants to disagree about placing merit at the center of our immigration policies, if he wants to take an unlimited number of unemployed and unemployable people because, after all, that's what most Poles and Irish were called in the 1900s, let him say that. And let Mr. Durbin and the president debate two concepts of American immigration policy honorably and finally find a middle ground where there is agreement and common purpose.

But, when we have a chance to reform the immigration system, and save the Dreamers, and find common ground, let us not get distracted by another cudgel to use against the president. Calling the president a racist helps no one –it is simply another way (the Russia and instability cards having been played unsuccessfully) to attempt to delegitimize a legitimately elected president.

Did the president use a crudity in a private meeting? He says he did not. No one who was there has said he did on the record. But if he did, so what? So what? America today is a sadly crass place where many of us use vulgar, corrosive language we ought not use in private and work conversations. How many of us would like to see and share a transcript of everything we have said in private conversations or at work?

And how many presidents have said crass things in the Oval Office in private meetings? Think of Kennedy, Clinton and Nixon, to name three.

If the president is wrong on immigration –on merit, on finding a balance between skilled and unskilled immigrants, on chain migration, on the lottery – let his opponents defeat him on these points, and not by calling him a racist. If he is to be removed from office, let the voters do it based on his total performance – temperament as well as accomplishment – in 2020. Simply calling him an agent of the Russians, a nutcase or a racist is a cowardly way to fight.

We need to confine the word "racist" to people like Bull Connor and Dylann Roof. For if every person who speaks inelegantly, or from a position of privilege, or ignorance, or expresses an idea we dislike, or happens to be a white male, is a racist, the term is devoid of meaning.

We have to stop calling each other names in this country and battle each other with ideas and issues, not slanders.[4]

"Reason as Racism: An Immigration Debate Gets Derailed" did not

---

4. The editorial ran in the *Toledo Blade* on January 12, 2018, and in the *Post-Gazette* on January 15, 2018, which happened to be Martin Luther King, Jr.'s. actual birthday and the federal King holiday that year, respectively.

please some members of the descendants of William Block, Sr., the longtime publisher of the *Post-Gazette,* who had died in 2005. Sixteen family members signed a letter denouncing it that the newspaper printed three days later under the headline, "This PG editorial did not reflect values we share with William Block Sr."

They invoked the elder Block's legacy as a champion of civil rights and said the editorial "goes against everything he worked for and valued," and accused it of violating his legacy by "attempting to justify blatant racism."

"We are so grateful that Bill never had to read it," they added.[5]

The respected Poynter Institute for Media Studies was more nuanced in its criticism. In an article on the ethics and trust section of its website, the author called it a "poorly reasoned, ill-timed and offensive-to-many-editorial on race."[6]

But it also quoted past and former employees as saying that while John Robinson Block "doesn't shy away from using his pulpit of the editorial page" for sometimes controversial views, "he rarely weighs in on the content of the news pages, and when he does, it is mostly in a benign way," like suggesting an interesting feature story.

While Tony Norman, the longtime *Post-Gazette* columnist, called the editorial "racist and indifferent to the newspaper's progressive legacy," he told Poynter, "it would be a mistake to lump Block in with those who are racist to the core of their being. He's genuinely interested in black history. That's why this editorial running on MLK Day in Pittsburgh is so inexplicably bad and morally indefensible. He knows better."

Interestingly, the reaction in Pittsburgh may have been much more intense among the journalistic community than in the community at large .

True, as the *Colombia Journalism Review* story reported, Maxwell King, the president of the Pittsburgh Foundation and a former editor of the *Philadelphia Inquirer,* and Grant Oliphant, president of the Heinz Endowments, both denounced the editorial – in a letter that the *Post-Gazette* promptly ran in full.[7]

---

5. "This PG editorial did not reflect values we share with William Block Sr.," *Pittsburgh Post-Gazette,* January 18, 2018.

6. Indira A.R. Lakshmanan, "Abomination: Pittsburgh publisher's editorial inflames newsroom, readers," Poynter Institute, https://www.poynter.org, (accessed January 19, 2018). The Poynter Institute is a non-profit journalism research organization that runs seminars and classes for journalists.

7. Grant Oliphant and Maxwell King, "We must face the realities of racism. President Trump's description of other countries was simply and frankly racist. The PG should have said so," *Pittsburgh Post-Gazette,* January 18, 2018.

However, none of the Black leaders I interviewed two years later brought it up; when I specifically asked Esther Bush, the head of Pittsburgh's Urban League about it, she could not remember the "Reason as Racism" editorial.

In Toledo, where the Black population is somewhat larger than in Pittsburgh,[8] the reaction was much more muted – perhaps because it did not run on the Martin Luther King, Jr., national holiday. Laneta Goings had missed the editorial when it appeared, and had never heard about it until I sent it to her.[9] The Rev. Robert Culp said that after it appeared he didn't call to complain – but that John Robinson Block called him.

"He's always asking, 'what does your community think about this or that,' and I tell him . He asked me, 'was it really that offensive?' and I told him, 'yes, it was.' We didn't agree on that. But he took my concerns seriously – he talked to me for about 30 minutes, and said we would talk more about it when he came to town."

Culp added, "You know, I would like it if the *Blade's* editorial page was more consistent. But I keep reading them because I never know what they are going to say. You have to recognize this about John. His philosophy is that he will always be independent. He doesn't dance with the Democrats; he doesn't dance with the Republicans. He is going to be independent, and that doesn't change."

But sometimes, he noted, he thought the issue that wasn't clear enough to those writing the editorials was "how do you distinguish between issues and personalities?"

Culp wasn't speaking specifically about the "Reason as Racism" editorial when he said those words; in fact, he was talking about an old controversy over a municipal judge.

But those words – *issues* and *personalities* – may be a key to understanding the controversy here. What follows is purely my analysis of the "Reason as Racism" editorial and the reaction to it, based on my conversations with John Robinson Block, his brother Allan, and Keith Burris, the vice-president and editorial director of both newspapers.

It is also based on a lifetime spent in journalism and more than a year of reading literally hundreds of editorials in the *Toledo Blade, Pittsburgh Post-*

---

8. According the U.S. Census Bureau's American Community Survey in 2019, the Black population of Toledo was 27 percent compared to 23.1 percent in Pittsburgh. The cities were of comparable size; Pittsburgh had an estimated population of 301,040 and Toledo, 274,975.

9. Goings declined to comment after she read it.

Gazette, and other papers owned by this family for this project:[10]

The bottom line:

I am convinced the editorial was *not* meant as racist. Nor was its main premise wrongheaded. Frankly, it is hard to sensibly disagree with the premise that it is wrong to smear anyone by calling her or him a "racist."

Racism is a complex issue, and intelligent people can disagree on what exactly it consists of and what it means. But again, there is a difference between issues and personalities. Though I am well educated, I was born in the early 1950s. Try though I might, I cannot be sure that I don't have some lurking subconscious racist attitudes.

Many of us do – not just older white males. Once, in Charleston, South Carolina, a Black cab driver who was a member of the Nation of Islam told me he knew that no whites really had to be homeless, that all of them could get money if they wanted to.

That was, obviously, an untrue racial stereotype.

But I would argue it would be wrong to label either of us as a racist. That driver and I ended up talking for nearly an hour; he was a decent man with an open mind, and hopefully we both learned something.

There are clearly those who do attempt to illegitimately use the race card. Kwame Kilpatrick, the thoroughly corrupt former mayor of Detroit, attempted to whimper that he was a victim of racism when he saw indictments coming. Kym Worthy, the county prosecutor and a proud Black woman, wasn't swayed, nor were the mainly Black jurors who eventually convicted Kilpatrick on both state and federal charges.[11]

But why was the reaction so furiously negative to this editorial?

The answer, I think, lies in what Bishop Culp said.

The root of the reaction in that this editorial seemed to conflate both an *issue* – the totally wrong-headed tendency to call anyone a 'racist' who someone wants to discredit – and a *personality* – President Donald Trump.

Additionally it combined two separate issues – the misuse of the term racism with the appropriateness of Donald Trump's language, tone, and immigration policies.

It is easy to imagine some readers agreeing that the term racist is overused,

---

10. My guess is that I have read more issues of newspapers owned by Paul Block and his descendants than anyone.

11. "I've been called a nigger more times than any time in my adult life," he said in a televised address in March 2008, adding that he was a victim of a "lynch mob mentality." Kilpatrick is currently serving a sentence in federal prison in New Jersey; he will be there until at least August 2037.

while firmly being repelled by President Trump's language on immigration.

The problem was further compounded in Pittsburgh by running the editorial on the Martin Luther King, Jr., federal holiday, a day many African-Americans hold as sacred to their traditions as Christians do Christmas.[12]

That made it appear to some, as Maxwell King and Grant Oliphant argued in their letter, that the editorial "provide(d) cover for racist rhetoric while masquerading as a sense of decency."

They meant, specifically, the language of the president. Race aside, whatever anyone thinks of the immigration policies of Donald Trump, he may be the most polarizing president the nation has had in modern times.

No other president has ever behaved as he has, in the sense of leveling personal attacks at his opponents and the press, sometimes even attacking their appearance.

All these things were likely factors in how this editorial was received.

There's nothing easier than being a "Monday morning quarterback," and saying how something could and should have been done better – whether it is analyzing a forward pass or a newspaper editorial or column. However, consider this:

What if the *Pittsburgh Post-Gazette* and the *Toledo Blade* had broken this topic into two separate editorials? There is certainly a legitimate argument that the term "racist" is overused. (Here's a personal example: Recently when I wrote something about wondering what Thomas Jefferson might have thought of America today, I was attacked by readers who said that nothing he wrote or said mattered because he owned slaves and had one, Sally Hemings, as his mistress. I was even called a racist for daring to suggest that we pay any attention to the ideas of the author of the Declaration of Independence.)

Such an editorial, on the wrongheadedness of being too quick to call people racists, had it been carefully crafted, might have even run on the Martin Luther King, Jr., federal holiday without provoking a firestorm.

Nor would there have been the same kind of reaction if the paper had published an editorial noting that regardless of Donald Trump's language he had some legitimate points when it came to immigration and

---

12. During an interview Allan Block agreed the timing was a mistake, though accounts differ about why the editorial ran in Pittsburgh on the Martin Luther King, Jr., holiday.

the wretchedness of some other countries,[13] and that calling the president a "racist" obscured the issue. Had such an editorial run on an ordinary day, it might have provoked grumbling at most.

That's not what happened.

There is no denying that many people felt that "Reason as Racism" was offensive. However, there's also no denying that it *was* widely read.

"It is our mission to make people think, and sometimes you have to risk offending people to make them think," Keith Burris, the main author of the editorial, told the *Yale Daily News* in an interview after "Reason as Racism" was published.[14]

What's not clear, however, is whether it actually made people think or just made them shut down in anger. In the same article John Robinson Block noted, "controversy goes right along with being an independent newspaper, and being an independent newspaper of course means that people on both sides are surprised when you take a position that they don't think is consistent with other positions you've taken."

That's certainly true.

"We've always taken a strong stance" when it comes to editorials, he noted, something that has often been true on both local and national issues.[15]

The controversy over one editorial aside, the *Toledo Blade* and the *Pittsburgh Post-Gazette* have proud records of being ahead of their time on issues from hiring minorities to supporting open housing legislation and the Civil Rights Movement.

The papers owned by the company's founder, the first Paul Block, won a Pulitzer Prize for exposing that a U.S. Supreme Court justice was a member of the Ku Klux Klan.

They were unfairly denied another for risking a reporter's life to expose what conditions were like for Blacks in the Jim Crow South more than a decade before *Black Like Me,* another author's attempt to do so, became a nationwide sensation.

---

13. Interestingly, while the times were very different, the first Paul Block was a strong supporter of immigrants and sometimes campaigned for those without proper documents to be allowed to stay in this country. Also, in a 1921 editorial, "The 'Speak English' campaign," his *Duluth Herald* argued that while it was a good idea for immigrants to learn English, "there is no thought of compulsion ... and no hint of resentment of anybody's previous failure to speak the language of the land habitually."

14. "Block '77 Blasted for Inflammatory Editorial," *Yale Daily News,* January 26, 2018

15. In 1979, when I was a reporter for the *Toledo Blade,* many in the community reacted angrily to the *Blade*'s editorial stance criticizing the police for going on strike. "This ain't nothing," a longtime reporter told me. "You should have seen how crazy they went when we endorsed Adlai Stevenson."

And when it comes to assessing where the family's heart really lies today it is important to look at another event that happened the same year as the controversial editorial. On October 27, 2018, an antisemitic white supremacist shot and killed eleven people at Pittsburgh's Tree of Life Synagogue and wounded seven more.

The *Pittsburgh Post-Gazette's* coverage was complete, thorough, and so comprehensive it ended up winning the Pulitzer Prize the next year.

The prize included a $15,000 cash award – and John Robinson Block instantly suggested that it be given to the synagogue to help with the costs of repair.

Additionally, at its own expense, the newspaper agreed to sponsor a yearly symposium named for Dina Wallach Block, John and Allan's grandmother.

"It will be in honor of the victims of the Tree of Life shootings, and devoted to an exploration of how free speech and free thought can be used to confront hate speech and violence and overcome both with decency and love," Keith Burris said when the award was presented to the congregation on September 4, 2019.[16]

When it comes to covering diversity and hiring minorities, the papers owned by Block Communications, Inc., have not always been perfect, but they were far better than many others, and their full record needs and deserves to be better known.[17]

---

16. "*Post-Gazette* Newsroom Donates Pulitzer Monetary Award to Tree of Life Congregation," *Pittsburgh Post-Gazette,* September 4, 2019.

17. As this book was nearing completion a new controversy erupted over whether the *Pittsburgh Post-Gazette* was preventing some reporters from covering the protests following the police slaying of George Floyd in Minneapolis on May 26, 2020, because they were Black, something the newspaper's top editors vigorously denied. See Miriam Berger, "Pittsburgh paper accused of barring black reporters from covering protests, censoring stories," *Washington Post,* June 6, 2020, and Keith C. Burris, "An Open Letter from the *Pittsburgh Post-Gazette,*" *Pittsburgh Post-Gazette,* June 10, 2020. These events are a still-developing story and I feel that they are still too new to properly assess here.

Acknowledgements

I am indebted to many people who have helped me with this book, and the research into this fascinating and complex subject. First of all, Allan Block, the chairman and president of Block Communications Inc. (BCI), whose idea this was.

His twin brother, John Robinson Block, now editor-in-chief and publisher of both the *Pittsburgh Post-Gazette* and the *Toledo Blade*, was very generous with his time and made me welcome in both his office and his home. He is a lover of books and history, including his own family history, and has a fine collection of knowledge, volumes, and other material relating to journalism and the African-American press.

The late Clyde Scoles, a man who devoted most of his life to building the Toledo-Lucas County Library system into one of the finest in the country, generously put the library's local history resources at my disposal.

His untimely death from a heart attack as he left the office on February 15, 2019, was a terrible loss. As of this writing the library is now in the capable hands of his successor, Jason Kucsma, who was also very supportive of this project.

Perhaps the best thing Clyde did to help this book was to introduce me to Jill Gregg Clever, the manager of the local history and genealogy department; she worked tirelessly to find where materials were located and to get one library in California to send the microfilm of a newspaper to Toledo to save me a trip. Somehow they managed to twice send microfilm of the wrong newspaper, but Jill didn't give up until they had it right. I also spent so much time reading microfilm in her collection that she and her excellent staff may have been tempted to charge me rent.

Also invaluable to me was Jordie Henry, the longtime librarian at the *Toledo Blade*. Jordie has an extremely demanding job – she does work that was once done by three full-time librarians – but was never too busy to track down information or a particular story or editorial that I needed and had trouble finding on my own.

Librarians are some of this nation's most valuable and underappreciated workers, and I was helped greatly by them in every city I visited. Katy Basile at the public library in Lancaster, Pennsylvania, was especially helpful, even tracking down key census data for her city from an era long before she was born.

Bill Steigerwald, a former *Pittsburgh Post-Gazette* reporter and the author of *30 Days a Black Man,* an excellent biography of Ray Sprigle, was beyond generous. Not only did he make time for a long interview, he drove me around Pittsburgh, showing me areas that were directly relevant to the coverage of race in that city.

He also presented me with a rare and invaluable item – the booklet issued by the *Post-Gazette* in 1949 that reprinted both Sprigle's series and Hodding Carter's rebuttal.

Laneta Goings, who is always well-connected, savvy, and charming, helped connect me with contemporary Toledo sources. Tom Walton, the former editor of the *Blade,* was generous with his time and memories as was Tom Gearhart, who covered race relations for the newspaper in the era of the Civil Rights Movement.

Mary Kay Filter Dietrich, vice-president for external relations and development for the Urban League of Greater Pittsburgh, went beyond the call of duty to suggest people for me to contact in Pittsburgh. Sheena Smith and Wendy Assally, Allan Block's capable assistants, assisted with logistics. Debra Sacco, John Robinson Block's longtime chief assistant, went out of her way to help me with arrangements in Pittsburgh.

Finally, this book is far better than it otherwise would have been because it was shepherded through to publication by Bill Haney, an author himself who has had a hand in the publication of more than 400 books, and who was the de facto publisher of this one. He knows more about books than anyone I know, and it has been a delight to learn from him and benefit from his guidance. Anne Zimanski, who is a professional illustrator, did a superb job of both interior and exterior design.

I was helped most of all by my favorite librarian, archivist, and intellectual and emotional soul mate, Elizabeth Zerwekh, with whom I share my life. Her skills and knowledge were invaluable not least because she, unlike the technologically challenged me, is much more easily able to save images to a portable thumb drive.

They were all extremely helpful. I have painstakingly tried to make this book a full, accurate, readable, comprehensive, and fair account of the events it covers.

Any errors of fact or interpretation are mine and mine alone.

Bibliography

This is not meant to be a comprehensive or academic biography but rather mainly a list of sources and material that may be interest to those who want to know more about these newspapers, race, and the role these papers filled in America during these times.

Most of what is reflected in this book comes from the actual newspapers, now preserved on microfilm, which the Block family owns or has owned over the years.

While a few are at least partly available on the very valuable subscription service *newspapers.com*, my archivist partner in life, Elizabeth Zerwekh, and I traveled to libraries in most of the cities in which these papers were originally published.

Those include the Toledo-Lucas County Public Library as well as public libraries in Milwaukee, Pittsburgh, Brooklyn, Newark, Duluth, and Detroit and the Tennessee State Library in Nashville, which has preserved the *Memphis News-Scimitar.*

The California State Library was gracious enough to send their microfilm of the relevant months of the *Los Angeles Express*, as well as Hearst's *Evening Herald,* which later absorbed the Express, to the library in Toledo.

Various other sources I have used – articles, interviews, U.S. Census reports, and other sources, are fully documented in the footnotes.

Books:

Brady, Frank, *The Publisher. Paul Block: A Life of Friendship, Power & Politics,* Lanham, MD, University Press of America, Inc., 2001.

Block, William, *Memoirs of William Block*, Toledo: Blade Communications, 1990.

Brooks, Michael, *The Ku Klux Klan in Wood County, Ohio*, Mount Pleasant, SC: The History Press, 2014.

Dawson, Tom, *Building Blocks: Buckeye CableSystem's Communications Revolution,* Lanham, MD: Hamilton Books, 2015.

Gibson, Campbell, and Kay Jung, *Historical Census Statistics on Population Totals by Race, 1790 to 1990 ... For Large Cities and Other Urban Cities in the United States,* Suitland-Silver Hill, MD: U.S. Census Bureau, February 2005.

Gregory, James, *The Southern Diaspora: How the Great Migrations of Black and White Southerners Transformed America,* Chapel Hill: University of North Carolina Press, 2007.

Griffin, John Howard, *Black Like Me,* New York: Houghton Mifflin, 1961.

Harrison, John, *The Blade of Toledo: The First 150 Years,* Toledo: The Toledo Blade Co., 1985.

Hatley, Elizabeth Dorsey, *The Ku Klux Klan in Minnesota,* Mount Pleasant, SC: The History Press, 2013.

Lewis, Tom, *Empire of the Air: The Men Who Made Radio*, New York: Harper Collins, 1991.

Michaeli, Ethan, *The Defender: How the Legendary Black Newspaper Changed America from the Age of the Pullman Porters to the Age of Obama,* New York: Houghton Mifflin Harcourt, 2016.

Newman, Roger, *Hugo Black: A Biography*, New York: Pantheon Books, 1994.

Ottley, Roi, *The Lonely Warrior: The Life and Times of Robert S. Abbott,* Washington, D.C.: Henry Regnery Co., 1955.

Patterson, Grove, *I Like People,* New York: Random House, 1954.

Roberts, Gene, and Hank Klibanoff, *The Race Beat: The Press, The Civil Rights Struggle, and The Awakening of a Nation*, New York: Alfred A. Knopf, 2006.

Sprigle, Ray, "I Was A Negro in the South for 30 Days," and Carter, Hodding, "The Other Side of Jim Crow," booklet reprinted by the *Pittsburgh Post-Gazette*, 1949.

Sprigle, Ray, *In the Land of Jim Crow,* New York: Simon & Schuster, 1949.

Steigerwald, Bill, *30 Days a Black Man: The Forgotten Story That Exposed the Jim Crow South*, Guilford, CT: Lyons Press/Globe Pequot, 2017.

Seldes, George, *Lords of the Press,* New York: Blue Ribbon Books, 1938.

Thomas, Clarke M., *Front-Page Pittsburgh: Two Hundred Years of the Post-Gazette*, Pittsburgh: University of Pittsburgh Press, 2005.

Thornton, J. Mills, *Dividing Lines: Municipal Politics and the Struggle for Civil Rights in Montgomery, Birmingham and Selma*, Tuscaloosa: University of Alabama Press, 2006.

Tifft, Susan, and Alex Jones, *The Trust: The Private and Powerful Family Behind the New York Times,* New York: Little, Brown and Co., 1999.

Tyson, Timothy, *The Blood of Emmett Till,* New York: Simon & Schuster, 2017.

Washburn, Patrick, *The African-American Newspaper: Voice of Freedom,* Evanston, IL: Northwestern University Press, 2006.

Films:

Burns, Ken, dir., *Empire of the Air: The Men Who Made Radio,* 1992; Florentine Films and WETA Washington, D.C.

Nelson, Stanley, dir., *Soldiers Without Swords,* 1999; Half Nelson Productions.

Index

Index note: italic page numbers indicate images on the page. Additionally, indexed footnotes will appear in italics.

K

About the Author

Jack Lessenberry has been a writer for many national and regional publications, including *Vanity Fair, Esquire,* the *New York Times,* the *Washington Post,* and the *Boston Globe.* Currently, he is a contributing editor and columnist for *Dome Magazine,* the *Toledo Blade,* and occasionally other newspapers, and is the co-author of the book, *"The People's Lawyer, The Life and Times of Frank J. Kelley, the Nation's Longest-Serving Attorney General,"* published by Wayne State University Press.

He is a former head of journalism at Wayne State University, a past president of the Historical Society of Michigan, and has been a longtime news analyst on Michigan Public Radio and on other radio and TV stations.

Lessenberry lives in Huntington Woods and Charlevoix, Michigan, with his partner in life, Elizabeth, their dogs Ashley and Chet, and entirely too many and not nearly enough books.

You can see much more of his work and hear his podcasts on his website, *Lessenberryink.com*